AF790861

Constitutional Reform in Britain and France

Constitutional Reform in Britain and France

From Human Rights to Brexit

Elizabeth Gibson-Morgan

University of Wales Press
2017

© Elizabeth Gibson-Morgan, 2017

All rights reserved. No part of this book may be reproduced in any material form (including photocopying or storing it in any medium by electronic means and whether or not transiently or incidentally to some other use of this publication) without the written permission of the copyright owner. Applications for the copyright owner's written permission to reproduce any part of this publication should be addressed to the University of Wales Press, 10 Columbus Walk, Brigantine Place, Cardiff CF10 4UP.

www.uwp.co.uk

British Library CIP Data
A catalogue record for this book is available from the British Library

ISBN 978-1-78683-122-4
eISBN 978-1-78683-123-1

The right of Elizabeth Gibson-Morgan to be identified as author of this work has been asserted in accordance with sections 77 and 79 of the Copyright, Designs and Patents Act 1988.

Typeset by Marie Doherty
Printed by CPI Antony Rowe, Melksham

FSC www.fsc.org MIX Paper from responsible sources FSC® C013604

To Kenbach

Contents

List of Abbreviations

AV	Alternative Vote
CC	*Conseil Constitutionnel*/French Constitutional Council)
CE	*Conseil d'Etat*/French Council of State
CPCR	Commons Political and Constitutional Reform Committee
CRA 2005	Constitutional Reform Act 2005
CSM	*Conseil Supérieur de la Magistrature*/French High Council of the Magistracy)
EAW	European Arrest Warrant
EC	European Commission
ECHR	European Convention on Human Rights
EJN	European Judicial Network
ENM	*Ecole Nationale de la Magistrature*/French Judicial Training College
EP	European Parliament
EU	European Union
FN	*Front National*/French National Front
FPTP	First-Past-the-Post
GWA	Government of Wales Act
HC	House of Commons
HL	House of Lords
HRA 1998	Human Rights Act 1998
JAC	Judicial Appointments Commission
JPCHR	Joint Parliamentary Committee on Human Rights
LCO	Legislative Competence order
MP	Member of Parliament
PR	Proportional Representation
RPR	Rassemblement pour la République/literally the 'Rally for the Republic', a neo-Gaullist conservative party
QC	Queen's Counsel
QPC	*Question Prioritaire de Constitutionnalité*/preliminary ruling on constitutionality
SNP	Scottish National Party
TEU	Treaty on the European Union
UK	United Kingdom

UKIP	United Kingdom Independence Party
UKSC	United Kingdom Supreme Court
UMP	Union pour le Mouvement Populaire/French Union for a Popular Movement

Foreword

In this book, I examine the course of constitutional change in the United Kingdom and France in the past few years. The sweeping transformation of British constitutional systems and institutions since the advent of the Blair government in 1997 has been analysed by many scholars and commentators. Those in the French Republic since the turn of the century have been far less widely noted, yet here too there have been fundamental reforms both at national and regional level. The novelty in this work is that, instead of examining each country on an individual basis, I have deliberately opted for a comparative approach. I have realised this offers new insights into the pattern of institutional development in the two countries. It also chimes in with my own deep attachment to both as a Franco-British person with dual nationality, committed to the vision of an *entente cordiale.* I was able to complete my work after the historic referendum on membership of the European Union in June 2016 and the important High Court of Justice judgment on it later in November, which bore directly on many key aspects of my work.

I have found research on either country deeply fascinating over the past few years, and in each case I have much cause for gratitude to those whose learning and personal guidance have helped me along the way. In France my understanding was much assisted by the wise advice of Professor Jean Gicquel of the Sorbonne, along with Professor Mélin-Soucramanien – now the Ethics Officer of the French National Assembly – and the Dean of the Bordeaux Law School, Professor Jean-Christophe Saint-Pau. In the United Kingdom I received many stimulating ideas from my colleagues at King's College London, Professor Robert Blackburn (Hon. QC), Professor Vernon Bogdanor and Dr Andrew Blick. I also benefited from the legal wisdom of Matt Kelly QC and of the members of the Franco-British Lawyers Society. Simon Blundell was immensely helpful in allowing me access to the library at my Club, the Reform; the Law Library at the Bodleian in Oxford was a treasure-house, while my son-in-law, Tim Spillane, kindly assisted me with current legal literature. Dr Alexis Chommeloux offered much professional and personal support at the University of Tours, while to Professor Geoffrey Thomas, former President of Kellogg College, Oxford, I can only say – *diolch!* In the University of Wales Press I received constant encouragement and assistance from Helgard Krause and Sarah Lewis. Finally, my greatest debts of all are to my parents in Bordeaux (Marie-Magdelaine and Derek Gibson) and to my husband Ken (Lord Morgan of Aberdyfi) for making the writing of this book personally enjoyable as well as intellectually stimulating.

Elizabeth Gibson-Morgan
Long Hanborough, Oxon, 3 November 2016

Introduction

'A revolution narrowly averted ... a moment of extreme crisis and haste'.[1] This is how the historian David Starkey described the Magna Carta of 1215. In fact, the defining constitutional moment for both England and France was to come later with the 1225 Magna Carta which, unlike the 1215 one, turned out to be a lasting settlement of fundamental liberties and rights such as access to justice. In the thirteenth century, England and France were not the two clearly distinct countries with their own identity and territory as we know them today, but were very much entangled. The barons who imposed the 1215 Great Charter on King John[2] were of Norman origin while the reigning English king, though he had lost Normandy as well as his family's other ancestral lands in France, still held Aquitaine. The latter was not any ordinary French territory, but one particularly dear to him, as it originally belonged to his mother, Eleanor, Duchess of Aquitaine.[3] When she married King Henry II, after having been married to the French King Louis VII, she was also Duchess of Normandy, Countess of Poitou and Anjou, half of what is now modern France. As Helena Kennedy, pointed out, 'As we hear proud claims about Magna Carta being an English invention, let us remember that it came into being a hundred and fifty years after the Norman Conquest and was probably greatly influenced by the French.'[4] It presupposed a form of legal cross-border collaboration between the two countries which has now become essential.

The two constitutions – whatever their key differences – are part of a long legal story which started with written documents considered as the founding acts of their respective legal order: Magna Carta (1215)[5] and the *Déclaration des Droits de l'Homme et du Citoyen* (1789). The French text appears as a symbol of permanence and continuity in the otherwise broken constitutional history of France. It has survived to this day without ever having been modified, unlike Magna Carta which was reissued thirty times. The 1789 Declaration, though referred to in the preamble of the 1958 Constitution, has now acquired the same constitutional status as the main body of the Constitution of the Fifth Republic. Even if Lord Sumption described Magna Carta as a very English document – 'as a document for Englishmen'– it is in fact as much French as English. As for the 1789 Declaration, it partly found its inspiration in the English Magna Carta as well as in the American Declaration of Independence of 1776. In any case they form a bond between the two countries that has endured up to this day and they are part of a common history.

If the two founding documents are at first sight similar in form, since both were fully written documents[6] – the founding document of the British mainly unwritten constitution was fully written down – they differ significantly in tone and substance. Magna Carta was in fact a feudal, highly technical, lengthy charter dealing with feudal obligations linked to the possession of the land as the main source of wealth and power. The rebellious barons who had imposed the charter on the king sought to protect property right from the arbitrary power and interference of the king. Through this charter, the English king granted new rights to his barons. Two in particular were to outlive the charter and still form the main pillars of the British constitution. One was the right to be represented and not have taxation imposed without representation; thus article 36 of the original charter stated: 'Neither scutage nor aide shall be imposed on our kingdom, unless by common counsel of our kingdom', although no Parliament as such existed at that time.[7] The other was to have an even more important impact, as the charter asserted that the king himself is subject to law, thus laying the foundation of what came to be known as the rule of law.

Unlike Magna Carta, which was very pragmatic, providing remedies for specific grievances, the French 1789 Declaration was – and still is – a very abstract document, restating pre-existing rights described as natural rights. It was thus different from positive law, starting with the principle of equality before the law. As its very name suggests, it was a statement of principles binding the state in the very specific context of the Revolution. It was to form the preamble of the very first French constitution – the constitution of 1791, a brief French attempt at constitutional monarchy. So it had in a way an ideological and political dimension that the English Magna Carta did not. It was fiercely criticised in his *Reflections on the Revolution in France* (1790) by Edmund Burke on these grounds.[8]

Yet, it would be unfair to Magna Carta to consider it as 'just a local bargain'. This is the judgement of Robert Tombs, in explaining that 'not only did it cover the whole Kingdom and concerned everyone, but it did take on an extended meaning.'[9] Both documents have remained of crucial importance to this day since they shaped the relationship between those who govern and those who are governed, identifying very early on the need to constrain sovereign power – to set limits to the arbitrary power of rulers. 'They remain an aspiration to people and a warning to rulers.'[10]

Eight hundred years later, England and France have become very different countries, though they still have much in common. They are both proud of their legal culture and tradition. They have a high sense of being unique as well as of their own national genius. Lord Sumption referred to the 'English instinct' or 'English exceptionalism',[11] but the French claim it for themselves also. Both define their respective country as the cradle of human rights and civil liberties, and both claim the legacy of the eighteenth-century Enlightenment – with philosophers like John Locke for the United Kingdom, and Jean-Jacques Rousseau for France.

At first sight they offer many contrasts. France is very attached to its fully written codified constitution as the fundamental rule and legal standard to which all other texts, including the already enacted laws passed by parliament, must abide alongside a precise hierarchy of norms based on the supremacy of the constitution in the national legal order.[12] In the same way, the United Kingdom is committed to its non-codified, only partly written, informal, flexible constitution. Though trying to define the British constitution is not an easy task as it is not contained in a clearly identifiable single document, the Constitution Committee of the House of Lords in its very first report in 2001 identified five fundamental principles or 'basic tenets',

> The sovereignty of the Crown in Parliament, the rule of law – encompassing the rights of the individual, the Union State, Representative Government and finally membership of the Commonwealth, the European Union as well as other international organisations.[13]

While French legal experts do not question the very existence of this very rare type of constitution – as only Israel and New Zealand's constitutional arrangements fall into the same category of 'unwritten constitutions' – they look upon it with a certain disdain, even contempt. But British judges themselves take pride in their 'unwritten' constitution. Lady Arden asserted, 'it is part of our national character',[14] adding, 'and I hope it will survive' – not so much an act of history as an act of faith.

However, there are strong historic, cultural, legal, commercial and military ties between the two countries. France and the United Kingdom have more that unites than divides them. After World War II, both chose freely to yield part of their sovereignty as nation-states, respectively in 1958 and 1973, to embark on a common European path which entailed significant constitutional changes, even if a growing minority in the United Kingdom wanted it to leave the European Union and reject the principle of a union contained in the founding Treaty of Rome of 1957. In the momentous referendum of 23 June 2016, by 52 per cent to 48 per cent, England and Wales (though not Scotland or Northern Ireland) ensured that this negative view prevailed, and a new, more difficult, chapter in Anglo-French relations thus began, with incalculable consequences.

The commemorations of Magna Carta and the birth of the first British Parliament – where the Frenchman Simon de Montfort played a key role – could provide a rare opportunity to revive the links between the two countries and thus to build a new *entente cordiale*,[15] more than ever necessary as France and the United Kingdom have reached a critical point from political, social and economic viewpoints. They are both faced with political fragmentation. In Britain there is an aggressive nationalism with the rise of the separatist Scottish National Party (SNP) and an essentially English form of nationalism with the Eurosceptic United Kingdom Independence Party (UKIP), alongside the rapid progress of the xenophobic anti-European far-right Front National in France. There has also been an economic and financial crisis in both countries followed by austerity programmes of fiscal rigidity that have exacerbated social division and inequalities. The Front National is progressively and steadily making its way towards power after a series of successful elections – in the May 2014 European elections, the March 2015 French departmental elections, a historic breakthrough in the French Senate – its ultimate goal being the 2017 presidential election. Though the official motto of the French Republic enshrined in the constitution, carved in the stone of French town-halls is 'Liberty, Equality, Fraternity', it sounds today more like wishful thinking, an ideal beyond reach in contemporary France.

The United Kingdom for its part is not being spared, since its territorial and political integrity is at stake with a possible new referendum on the independence of Scotland in the wake of the referendum on the European Union in June 2016. On 18 September 2014, the United Kingdom experienced a critical moment with the referendum which could have led to the break-up of the United Kingdom. Although those in favour of remaining within the Union officially won with a clear margin (55 per cent against 45 per cent), the Scottish question has certainly not been settled, as was confirmed by the outcome of the United Kingdom 2015 General Election – and to a certain extent the May 2016 Elections in Scotland. The European referendum of June 2016 gave the issue a profound and dangerous twist. This has revived the English or West Lothian Question and thrown the whole country into great turmoil, including over its long-established constitution.

Every aspect of the British constitutional settlement is now subject to intense debate. It could provide a new momentum for constitutional reform and a rare opportunity to examine constitutional arrangements, their purpose, their efficiency and finally their adequacy with people's expectations. No one, including constitutional experts, seems to agree on whether there is a need for a special constitutional moment to codify the British constitution or for that matter to change the French constitutional settlement. But the 2016 referendum on the United Kingdom's membership of the European Union can be considered as a pivotal moment of constitutional change with the success of 'Brexit' having profound implications for Scotland's place in the United Kingdom. A vital key to almost every issue is the rise of nationalism in Scotland, and to a much lesser extent Wales: as British commentators have observed, 'in parts of Britain, nationalist and religious identities are threatening older solidarities',[16] and raising the possibility of the United Kingdom ceasing to be a unified state.

Constitutional revolution sounds at first like an oxymoron as it is difficult to imagine a revolution within the boundaries of the law. But the term 'revolution' suggests a fundamental, perhaps irrevocable, change or break with the past. Jacob John and Gary Jeffrey defined the notion as 'change that entails significant breaks or departures in the workings of the constitutional order'.[17] The concept of revolution is fundamentally enshrined in French history and the French psyche. The 1789 Revolution is where the idea of a French written constitution started. The irony is that French law, especially French constitutional law, was born out of this revolution. It was built on key principles set forth by French Revolutionaries – the sovereignty of the people, equality before the law, the principle of separation of powers. Members of the 1789 Constituent Assembly that emerged from the Third Estate were aware of the need to put together the laws, conventions and constitutional practices in a single written constitution. For them, the constitution-building process began with the drafting of a text that was intended to serve as the preamble of the new constitution, that of 1791, which is now referred to in the preamble of the constitution of the Fifth Republic: the (1789) Declaration of the Rights of Man and the Citizen, a symbol of permanence in French law rather than constitutional change. In its famous 1971 decision, the French Constitutional Council, which has constitutional review powers, gave the 1789 Declaration of the Rights of Man constitutional validity, thus recognising it as a full part of the 1958 Constitution. Today, in countries like France, drafting a new constitution without providing for a Declaration of Rights would be unthinkable. A constitution is not just a technical document setting clear rules, defining the relations between the various institutions and powers, but also aims at protecting the fundamental rights and liberties of the people while being at the same time a powerful symbol. The only time the United Kingdom for its part had a fully written constitution was under the Commonwealth of Oliver Cromwell with his Instrument of Government (1653) concentrating power in the hands of one individual under a so-called 'Republic' or 'Protectorate'.

In both countries, there is now an urgent need to improve the understanding of fundamental rights, to clarify the constitution and adapt it to a changing society and to people's aspirations. Yet it does not mean that France has to move to a Sixth Republic or that the United Kingdom has to abolish its monarchy. There is a firm constitutional substructure. They can build on existing institutions, reform them rather than break away from them and start all over again in a revolution of the type experienced by France in 1789. As the Fabian Society wisely observed, 'neither Britain's history nor its constitution is a clean sheet.'[18]

In this work, important legal and political issues on both sides of the Channel – the nature of sovereignty, the status of the Head of State and Head of Government, the use of war powers, the French and British Upper Houses as 'constitutional anomalies', the next steps of devolution in the United Kingdom and decentralisation in France, the protection of human rights with the possible repeal of the Human Rights Act 1998 and its replacement by a British Bill of Rights in the United Kingdom, the question of legal aid and, more generally speaking, access to justice, and finally the European building process – will be examined from a comparative Franco-British perspective. Although the European Community – later, the Union – has helped to secure peace, stability and security in Europe for well over half a century and has contributed to strengthening democracy, notably in Greece, Spain and Portugal (now threatened by the Eurozone and its policies), the British Prime Minister David Cameron, having secured a majority for his Conservative party in the 2015 General Election, was determined to renegotiate Britain's relationship with the European Union for party reasons. He then proposed holding an in/out referendum on Britain's membership by 2017. As promised first in his 2013 Bloomberg speech, then in the 2015 Conservative manifesto, Cameron sought to devolve power away from Brussels and especially to opt out from the theory of 'ever closer union' enshrined in very general terms in the 1957 Treaty of Rome. He was also prepared to challenge another key principle at the basis of the European

Union, the principle of the free circulation of people, by introducing curbs on immigration and the social benefits attached to it, while the European Commission for its part tries to impose minimum immigration quotas on each member state to deal with the influx of non-European migrants. The United Kingdom's late entry into the EEC in January 1973 proved to be detrimental to its own interests. Its premature withdrawal[19] from the European Union after the 2016 referendum could be even more damaging and destructive of the whole European building process.

In both France and the United Kingdom, there is a need to provide a stable, balanced, workable, lasting settlement. Now is the right moment as 'the United Kingdom has reached a constitutional crossroads.'[20] To be effective, a constitution must be endorsed by the people, and it must inspire them so that they can identify with it more easily. This is very much the case in the United States of America, where, apart from the Bible and the English Magna Carta, no text has a higher value. French and British people should also be proud of their constitutions. As the British constitutionalists of King's College (London) put it, 'a constitution must sing'– or at least must speak to the people.

In the last few years, both the French and British constitutional frameworks have undergone deep changes. This book aims at analysing them in a comparative approach. Chapter 1 deals with the amending process of the French and British constitutions in an attempt to respectively rewrite and codify them. The second chapter for its part focuses on the Head of State in France and the United Kingdom as well as on their subtle relationships with their Prime Ministers. Chapter 3 is devoted to parliamentary reform and the revival of bicameralism in both countries. As for Chapter 4, it concentrates on the need for a more independent judiciary and a better protection of human rights, now seriously challenged by the fight against terrorism. In Chapter 5, priority is given to the subnational level, with a brief retrospect of devolution in the United Kingdom and decentralisation in France followed by different options for the future. Finally, Chapter 6 introduces a European dimension retracing the French and British membership of the European integration process before focusing on the impact of the 2016 United Kingdom's European Union membership referendum on the two countries and on Europe.

This book has two underlying purposes. One is to explore recent constitutional changes in France and the United Kingdom in a clear, accessible way. The more personal aim is to use my own Franco-British background to give French and British readers a better understanding of the two countries and thus fight prejudices born out of misunderstanding of who the French and the British are. Far from denying their difference, what is important is to understand in which precise ways they are different and what their difference conveys to each other. They can do better together than each one acting unilaterally. Even after the outcome of the 2016 European referendum in the United Kingdom, they have so much in common and so much to hope for as partners and allies.

Notes

1. David Starkey 'The Magna Carta of 1215 was designed to create a revolutionary regime', *BBC History Magazine* (May 2015), 63–5.
2. His brother Richard, more commonly known as Richard the Lionheart, had died from wounds after besieging a French castle.
3. In 2015 following the restructuring of French regions as part of the third stage of the French decentralisation process, the New Aquitaine region was born out of the fusion of Aquitaine, Poitou-Charentes and Limousin, thus restoring the medieval contours of this part of France, the biggest region in France with 5.8 million inhabitants and 84,100 square miles.
4. Helena Kennedy, 'French Kissing', *New Statesman* (5–11 June 2015), 24 – in its cover story 'The glory and the myths of Magna Carta'.
5. In the case of Magna Carta it only became the founding document of the British constitution when it was rescued from obscurity and revamped by the eminent lawyer Coke.
6. Though the French 1789 Declaration has not always been written.
7. The very first one was to be summoned by the Frenchman Simon de Montfort in 1265.
8. L.G. Mitchell, *Edmund Burke: Reflections on the Revolution in France* (Oxford: Oxford University Press, 1993).
9. Lancaster House, London, 11 June 2015, conference on 'Magna Carta and the *Déclaration des Droits de l'Homme et du Citoyen*', organised by the French Embassy and the British Foreign Office.
10. Lancaster House, London, 11 June 2015.
11. Speaking at the conference at Lancaster House, London, 11 June 2015.
12. Though some French constitutional lawyers like Patrick Fraisseix denounce the current diversified content of the constitution of the Fifth Republic, which has made it 'more and more difficult to read', in Jean-Pierre Camby, Patrick Fraisseix and Jean Gicquel, *La révision de 2008: Une Nouvelle Constitution* (Paris: L.G.D.J., Lextenso, 2011), p. 8.
13. House of Lords, Constitution Committee, 'Reviewing the Constitution: Terms of Reference and Method of Working', First Report Session 2000–2001, HL 11 (London: The Stationery Office, 11 July 2001).

14. House of Lords Constitution Committee, HL11, July 2001, p. 2.
15. The original *Entente Cordiale* was a flexible diplomatic accord, primarily over colonial issues, dating back to 1904.
16. 'Britain confronts a profound choice. Labour offers the best chance of a new direction', editorial, *The Guardian*, Saturday 2 May 2015, p. 38.
17. 'Theorizing the Constitutional Revolution', *Journal of Law and Courts*, 2/1 (March 2014), 1–32.
18. Report of the Fabian Commission, 'The Future of the Monarchy' (London: Fabian Society, July 2003), p. 5.
19. Though the UK has much criticised it, the Lisbon Treaty is the first ever European treaty containing an exit clause.
20. 'A Constitutional Crossroads: Ways Forward for the United Kingdom' (London: Bingham Centre for the Rule of Law/British Institute of International and Comparative Law, May 2015), p. ix.

Chapter One

Constitutional Change: Codifying the British Constitution, Rewriting the French

The commonly held view is that constitutions originally set up to fight arbitrary power and protect citizens' rights were carefully drafted in order to last for as long as possible, even for ever. Yet constitutions are living instruments; as the French constitutional law Professor Mélin-Soucramanien wrote: 'Constitutions are living organisms; they were born, they live, suffer the distortions of political life, experience more or less significant changes and may even die.'[1] They are not isolated texts based on the eternal verities, but were conceived at particular times in history and in specific legal and political contexts. Judge Stephen Sedley, for his part, underlines the importance of 'the balance of power at the moment of enactment of constitutions'.[2] In the same line of argument, Professor Robert Blackburn explains that

> the key question of balance lies at the heart of any constitutional settlement, which is to be understood not only as 'the balance of power, between the various branches of government but also between flexibility and rigidity – between making a constitution too easy to change and almost impossible to alter it.[3]

In France the unity of the Republic is a fundamental principle – almost sacred – and thus cannot be affected by constitutional change.[4]

Nothing is immutable, including constitutions themselves. Sometimes changing a constitution may be the only way of saving it. Besides, most constitutions include provisions, generally a formal process, for their own amendment – thus amending the American, Italian or German constitutions is strictly regulated. For though they are rooted in the past, one of the main purposes of constitutions is to 'give guidance for the future'.[5] Revising a constitution generally means 'modifying a specific set of legal norms following the rules included in the constitution for that purpose'.[6] It is all the more necessary since 'no documentary constitution can hope to embrace absolutely every aspect of its politics and government.'[7] Indeed, beyond the objective of defining collective norms, constitution-makers themselves sometimes deliberately leave gaps or choose a very vague wording to enable the constitution to evolve – and to avoid making it too rigid a text, as was done by the founding fathers of the American Constitution. Thus, for example, many constitutions hardly contain any provisions on the status of political parties or the political process itself, which is the case of the constitution of the Fifth Republic. The practice of power – or the real political life – therefore is not to be found in the text of the constitution but in what Samuel E. Finer and Vernon Bogdanor describe as the 'working constitution'.[8] They further explain that 'each text operates within a matrix of customs, conventions, case law and cautious compromise.'[9] This is particularly the case in common law countries where, unlike France, case law is an official source of the law.

Several attempts have been made to introduce constitutional change in the United Kingdom and France, yet constitutional debates about constitutional reform have been fragmented, lacking coherence and vision in both countries.[10] France has had a fractured constitutional history: 'it is probably the country which, since the Revolution has experienced the highest number of constitutions, one constitution every fourteen years on average.'[11] French constitutions have always been a permanent work in progress, motivated by the search for the perfect model. Those drafting the 1791 constitution that provided for a constitutional monarchy thought they had written the perfect document and had not included any amendment process, thinking their constitutional arrangements would last for ever.[12] In both countries, constitutional change has very much remained the preserve of experts,[13] yet in the words of Hywel Williams this 'is surely too important a matter to be left to constitutionalists alone'.[14] The problem until now – perhaps even more in the United Kingdom than in France – is that constitutional change has not involved civil society and the wider public, whereas it is essential to allow citizens themselves to take part in the process.

Two main questions immediately come to mind: why are constitutions amended and how? Changing constitutions may serve a wide range of purposes, starting with trying to fill in a gap left by the original drafters – by adding provisions or details initially neglected or forgotten. Thus, four years after the adoption of the American constitution, a Bill of Rights was added in 1791. Revising a constitution can stem from a very pragmatic approach aiming at improving mechanisms that did not prove to be workable in practice or not very effective after some years of political and institutional practice – or from trying to make constitutional arrangements more coherent. New political and or legal developments, not to speak of a regime change in a country, such as the accession to independence of Canada (a former dominion), or the fall of communism, which paved the way for the reunification of Germany in 1990, can also generate change. It is significant that all the new states that have won their independence since 1945 have had as a priority to endow themselves with a written constitution. Constitutional change in modern times can also be brought about by the European Union building process. Thus, the successive limits and/or transfers of sovereignty that being a Member State engendered led to significant amendments to make them compatible with existing constitutional arrangements. The Maastricht Treaty very well illustrates the legal and political problems raised in the United Kingdom by (willingly) surrendering some state powers in 1992, but some twenty years earlier the country experienced what can be considered as a legal watershed, introducing for the first time a hierarchy of norms as it is understood in France. The Communities Act 1972 enabled the United Kingdom to join the European Economic Community (EEC) in January 1973. As is stated in the standard work of Erskine May, 'accession of the United Kingdom to membership of the EEC – now the European Union – on 1st January 1973 qualified the exclusive legislative authority of the United Kingdom Parliament.'[15]

Whatever the purpose, changing constitutions should be for the benefit of the people. In the words of Professor Jeffrey Jowell QC,[16] constitutional reform is 'an intention of moving towards some higher plane or better world'. Yet sometimes constitutional change may be more questionable and its deep motivations mainly partisan – this is what Philippe Ardant, the editor of the journal *Pouvoirs*,[17] describes as 'pretext changes'.[18] Some changes can, indeed, be introduced for political reasons in haste and without consultation. The United Kingdom itself has experienced this recently – all the more as the British constitution can be altered at any moment without a formal process, as there are no settled procedures for dealing with constitutional reform in the country. Questionable practices have recently revived the need for rethinking constitutional change in the United Kingdom, not only to make it more efficient but also more transparent as well as more democratic.

To change constitutions, not only is there a need for clear, workable legal mechanisms, but also a political context without which constitutional change cannot be effective. Such a context emerged in France, Italy and many other European countries at the end of the trauma of the Second

World War with its urge for a new beginning. Indeed, constitutional change may significantly alter the existing balance of power: hence the need for wide political support. Besides, there is no necessary link between the scope of constitutional change and the political obstacles and reluctance it can encounter. So constitutional change does not only raise complex legal issues but also political ones. Beyond the formal and informal methods of constitutional amendment, what is at stake is the democratic aspect of constitutional change and its legitimacy. We will examine here how well the French and British constitutions are able to accommodate major changes within established structures.

All countries except the United Kingdom have formal processes of constitutional amendment. As there are many different types of constitutions, there is not just one single way of changing constitutions. Besides, all countries have also developed informal methods of constitutional amendment through constitutional conventions and practice. Written constitutions like the French include revising procedures laid down by the original constitution-makers. Thus a comparative approach will be developed between the United Kingdom and France, bearing in mind that there is no perfect constitutional amending process and that constitutions are more than just sets of procedural rules, but are also important political symbols.

The French constitution as a living organism and the British constitution in flux

In most countries, like France, a distinction is made between the constitution as the fundamental rule at the apex of the hierarchy of legal norms endowed with some superior or special status, and ordinary legislation passed by the legislature. Such a distinction becomes particularly meaningful in the constitution-amending process. Yet, other countries like the United Kingdom do not make any distinction between constitutional and legislative bills. Their constitutions are described as flexible constitutions, as opposed to rigid constitutions where some special formal process is needed to change the constitution, such as a two-thirds majority required from parliaments and a ratifying process via a referendum as well as specific bodies in charge of constitutional change. These could be parliaments sitting not as separate chambers but united to form a Congress such as in France. Upper Houses tend to have particular powers and play a more important role than in the ordinary legislative process such as in France where the Senate is much more powerful when dealing with constitutional change.

Thus rigid constitutions include what was described by Samuel E. Finer and Vernon Bogdanor as 'a more arduous procedure for the abrogation or alteration of a constitutional provision than that established for ordinary laws'.[19] In fact, the level of rigidity might vary according to the procedural differences between the ordinary law-making process and amending the constitution. Far from being a simple technicality or a procedural difference, such a formal amending process – usually more complex and longer than the ordinary law- making process – provides 'an added protection for citizens' rights and an aid to political stability'.[20]

In the constitution-amending process in every democracy, ideally the constituent power should belong to the people, the *demos*. However, in most modern constitutions the *demos* is mainly invited to take part in ratifying the revising process only after parliaments have voted constitutional change. So the people may be directly involved in constitutional change via a referendum. Whereas in France national sovereignty belongs to the people[21] (under article 3 of the constitution of the Fifth Republic[22]), in the United Kingdom, Parliament is sovereign.[23] In both countries, in practice, however, the people exercises its sovereignty through elected representatives, in the British House of Commons and the French National Assembly, but also by way of referendum. In the French Republic, which is the archetype of the unitary state, the expression 'the people' might be misleading for a British observer since, far from representing the French population in its ethnic, cultural and religious diversity, it is an abstract universal notion standing for French citizens. As Félicien Lemaire explained in his comparative approach between France and Britain,'unlike the Anglo-Saxon integrating model which is much more receptive and welcoming to minorities, France does not recognise the minority principle.'[24]

In the same way, the French Constitutional Council denied the inhabitants of the island of Corsica the status of 'people'[25] – distinct from the French people – as for the French constitutional judge there can only be one people and there can only be one official language. Indeed, under article 2 of the Constitution, 'the language of the Republic is French.'[26] This was not part of the original text of 1958 but was introduced in 1992 following a highly controversial constitutional change, the official aims of which were to protect the French language from the growing influence of English, and to protect France from autonomist aspirations, especially from the Basque Country, though this was not officially asserted. In fact, it proved to be mainly detrimental to regional and minority languages[27] and prevented France originally from ratifying the European

Charter of Regional and Minority Languages.[28] Some limited progress was made in the wake of the Balladur Report of 2008, yet not without a fierce parliamentary debate which set the National Assembly against the more conservative Senate, dominated by the right until the brief Socialist breakthrough with Jean-Pierre Bel[29] as Speaker in 2011[30] – as well as making for hostility between individual members of the two Houses themselves. A new provision was added to the constitution – under Title XII devoted to Territorial Communities: article 75-1, which reads 'Regional languages are part of France's heritage.' Unlike the constitution of the Fifth Republic, which still does not mirror the multicultural, multilingual forum French society has become, the multinational British Union state has given official status to a language other than English (Welsh) in one of its four component nations, namely Wales, a process extended under Welsh devolution since 1999.

Constitutions should be modified along the lines provided by the original drafters. But it is different with the customary arrangements of the United Kingdom, where there are no such guidelines provided by the constitution itself. Unlike France, there are no settled procedures for dealing with constitutional reform. In this chapter, the emphasis will not so much be on the substance of change but rather on the processes – to try to find what would be the best solution for the United Kingdom at a time when there are many uncertainties regarding the future of its current constitutional arrangements – notably with the country leaving the EU in the wake of the 2016 referendum.

Amending the British constitution

'Looking back over the past ten years or so, process has been a constant problem in constitutional reform', as Professor Robert Blackburn of King's College London pointed out in 2011, while giving evidence before the Lords Constitution Committee in charge of scrutinising the process of constitutional change. The problem alluded to here is not so much linked to any particular government, but is a more structural one linked to the very nature of the British constitution as its inherent flexibility has enabled reformers to introduce major changes without having to think of their impact on existing constitutional arrangements. Its flexibility has often been praised but is not without its dangers, as it can lead to unnecessary or ill-thought-out changes introduced for the wrong reasons – that is to say, not for improving the general constitutional framework and not for benefiting the people. We may wonder, therefore, how far constitutional changes should go without a codified constitution.

What is at stake here is not so much the government's right to initiate constitutional change but the vital need to hold it to account, especially to make sure that the whole process is both democratic and transparent as well as respectful of parliamentary scrutiny. This does not appear to have been the case, for example, with the 2011 measure for revising constituency boundaries and for calling a referendum on the voting system for the UK Parliament, since scrutiny by the House of Commons was very restricted, and extensive debate in the Lords did not really redress the balance. Since New Labour, headed by Tony Blair, in the late 1990s introduced changes that were to have a long-lasting impact on Britain's constitutional arrangements, such as the incorporation of the European Convention on Human Rights via the Human Rights Act 1998 providing a legislative source of basic rights across the United Kingdom, proposals for further significant changes have been on the agenda, notably after the 2010 General Election that led to a hung Parliament.

The British constitution, being uncodified and flexible, can theoretically be amended at any time without any specific amendment procedure. François Venter, an Advocate of the High Court of South Africa and Professor of Law, wrote as an external observer of the British Constitution: 'There is irony in the fact that one of the longest surviving systems which has influenced, inspired and sometimes spawned the current systems of constitutionalism, remains the prime example of a system without a written constitution.'[31]

The inherent qualities in the United Kingdom's partly unwritten constitution, such as its flexibility and longevity, arise from its ancient history and its many centuries of broadly stable internal development, which enabled the country to cope with world wars and accommodate so formidable a challenge as the growth of working-class power in the wake of the industrial revolution. It is a product of the modern concept of democratic representation. A constitution as such does not exist in the United Kingdom in the sense of a pre-eminent document providing checks and balances or addressing the rights of the individual. The British constitution is seldom understood as embodying any kind of normative or legal standard. In the so-called 'traditional' British constitution, changes have been for the most part piecemeal, ad hoc changes: that is to say, the evolution and development of the constitution have been made organically as in those aspects that affect the machinery of government, such as changes in the civil service since 1871, when it was thrown open to public competition. But most changes amending the relationships between the Crown, Parliament and the people were effected through Parliament, such as the three Reform Acts of 1832, 1867 and 1884 in the nineteenth century, and later that of 1918, which gave votes to women over thirty. Again, most significant changes to the constitution in the twentieth century were introduced through major statutes – the Parliament Act 1911, the Representation of the People Act 1918, the European Communities Act 1972, the Human Rights Act 1998, the Scotland Act 1998 and the House of Lords Act 1999.

But, the 1997 landslide victory of New Labour, elected on a broad manifesto including an ambitious programme of constitutional reform, led to a significantly different approach to constitutional change. Before 1997 individual constitutional amendments emerged in reaction to particular political problems or pressures. Rodney Brazier argued that 'Changes to the British Constitution have, in the past, tended to have been undertaken in response to events.'[32] After 1997, however, under the new Prime Minister Tony Blair, not himself a man notably interested in the minutiae of constitutional issues, a wide-ranging programme of constitutional reforms was introduced, including, as it happened, a referendum on electoral reform that was destined never to be actually held. As Lord Morgan, a member of the House of Lords constitution committee, interviewed in *The Government Gazette*[33] argued, 'New Labour was the first Labour government to take constitutional reform seriously. There was reform of the House of Lords, devolution, the Human Rights Act, elected mayors, the Freedom of Information Act, and a Supreme Court.'

Gordon Brown took a much more serious intellectual interest in constitutional reform, including the idea of a codified constitution, although he did not advance the agenda as much as he could. Indeed, it is under the Labour government of Tony Blair that devolution in its modern form was introduced, giving Scotland, Wales and Northern Ireland their own devolved governments and parliamentary assemblies, albeit on an individual and asymmetrical basis, as will be seen in Chapter 5. Although England was left out of the devolution process, London gained a directly elected Mayor. Forms of proportional representation were introduced for elections to the European Parliament, the new devolved assemblies, the Greater London Assembly and the direct election of the London Mayor.

If political parties, whether in office or opposition, do take the initiative of constitutional amendments, other independent bodies can contribute and share the initiative. Parliament itself can take the lead through its select committees, especially the House of Lords Constitution Committee, the

Commons Political and Constitutional Reform Committee (abolished in 2015)[34] and the Joint Parliamentary Committee on Human Rights. The remit of the House of Lords Constitution Committee, amended early in its existence in 2002, is to examine the constitutional implications of all public Bills coming before the House. More generally, it acts as a watchdog over the operation of the constitution. Yet Rodney Brazier, lamenting the absence of a permanent body fully independent of the government, has taken a negative view: 'the Constitution Committee of the House of Lords has an apparently general remit allowing it to keep the whole of the British constitution under review but peers are mostly part-time legislators with limited resources.'[35]

This somewhat oblique point (which has been rebutted by other academics such as Dawn Oliver) could be countered by reference to the greater legal or academic expertise to be found amongst peers, compared with the necessarily more miscellaneous character of the membership of the Commons. Nor are peers distracted by having constituencies to attend to. It is significant that several Attorneys-General, such as the late Lord Williams of Mostyn or Baroness Scotland, have commonly come in recent years from within the Lords because of the fairly limited number of distinguished lawyers amongst MPs, whereas in the nineteenth century QCs and even judges were relatively commonplace in the House of Commons.

For significant amendment, the executive holds the initiative. Even if it is possible for members of Parliament to introduce Private Members' Bills, they are less likely to be successful, especially those which arouse any substantial degree of opposition. Difficult issues such as ones dealing with parliamentary representation and parliamentary election law can be referred to a conference chaired by the Speaker of the House of Commons, making recommendations or calling the government for action. Well-known historical examples are the Speaker's conference of 1917 to consider electoral reform, including possible proportional representation (PR), and that of 1944 to discuss the revision of post-war parliamentary constituency boundaries. The latter achieved its objectives, the former failed to do so. There have also been ad hoc Speaker's conferences at times of political crisis, such as that set up to consider the desperate issue of Irish Home Rule in the summer of 1914 just before the outbreak of the First World War. A Speaker's conference,[36] set up at the initiative of the Prime Minister (as they always are), was also convened for the highly sensitive issue of reform of the House of Lords before the introduction of the eventually unsuccessful Parliament (No. 2) Bill in 1968.

Therefore, legal changes to even the most basic aspects of the political and constitutional system can be made through the same process as an ordinary Act of Parliament. The passage of 'constitutional' statute law operates in the same manner, broadly speaking, as the passage of any other legislation. Most bills are tabled in the House of Commons for a first reading, then a second reading and committee stage after second reading conducted in the House of Commons by a Public Bill Committee. In the House of Lords they are considered by the whole House or, for less important or controversial measures, in a Grand Committee, a committee of unlimited membership which all members may attend. As is explained in Erskine May, 'the Grand Committee gives the Lords an opportunity to engage in general debate on a particular issue, or to interrogate ministers, in a relatively informal setting and without the need to reach a decision.'[37]

Then, there is the report stage and a final third reading, followed by the Royal Assent. In the legislative process, the House of Lords has limited legislative powers – it acts mainly as a revising chamber and cannot vote many bills. Conventions govern the exchange of amendments between the two Houses.

In the constitutional amendment process, some variations on normal legislative processes are applicable to bills dealing with major constitutional issues. Thus bills are presented initially in the form of a draft bill allowing pre-legislative scrutiny by one or more select committees. As stated in Erskine May, 'it should lead to better legislation and less likelihood of subsequent amending legislation.'[38] This is what happened with the House of Lords draft bill (2010–12) – which was accompanied by a White Paper under the same name. Then, in the Commons, it is customary for the bill to go to a Committee of the whole House rather than a much smaller Public Bill Committee – as, for instance, with the EU Act 2011 and the Fixed-Term Parliament Act 2011.[39] In the Lords, a practice of referring first-class constitutional bills to a committee of the whole House, presided over by a chairman instead of the Lord Chancellor (or later the Lord Speaker), evolved after the Second World War even if no clear definition of such bills has ever been provided. But a committee of the whole House can only consider the matters referred to it. A simple majority is all that is required in the voting on the various stages in a bill, however fundamental in nature. However, in the constitutional amendment process, the House of Lords has tended since the reform of 1999 to be more assertive on issues dealing with the constitution or civil liberties.

An additional point is that referendums are not a general requirement for constitutional amendment in the UK. Prior to 1970 they were unknown and popularly associated, both by Clement Attlee and Margaret Thatcher, with totalitarian or authoritarian regimes overseas. Only three national UK-wide referendums have been held so far, one on Europe in 1975, one on the Alternative Vote in 2011 and the latest one on the United Kingdom's membership of the European Union, even if the devolution process in Scotland and Wales has led to a number of consultative referendums there – the latest one in Wales in 2011 being about granting the Welsh Assembly primary legislative power. In addition, the EU Act 2011 now requires an Act of Parliament and a referendum – a 'block' referendum – to be held before the UK government may agree to any treaty changes that represent an extension of the powers or competence of the EU or its institutions.

One of the main criticisms of the current practice of constitutional amendment in the United Kingdom is the lack of a rigorous process of consultation regarding the traditional pre-legislative stages – that is, a Green Paper followed by a White Paper, a draft bill presented to Parliament for pre-legislative scrutiny by each House and its committees – to secure genuine parliamentary debate and scrutiny of legislative proposals. Major constitutional changes should not be the result of rushed deliberations in the days after a general election (as they were in 2010), but rather of mature reflection. They should not be motivated by partisan politics but by a will to strengthen British democracy for the general benefit. Unlike the French one, the British constitution does not derive its authority from the people.

Revising the constitution of the 'one and indivisible' Republic

France initially changed constitutions rather than revising them. In the 200 years after 1789, the country experienced no less than eleven codified constitutions. One thread of constitutional continuity was the Council of State – the Conseil d'Etat – created by Napoleon I and the consequent development of administrative law. French people initially were very suspicious about amending the 1958 constitution as they did not want to disturb a balance of powers achieved at long last after decades of constitutional instability dating back to the revolution of 1789.[40] In Title XVI on amendments to the constitution, the beginning of article 89 reads: 'The President of the Republic, on the recommendation of the Prime Minister, and members of parliament alike shall have the right to initiate amendments to the constitution.'

So constitutional amendments may be introduced both by the President of the Republic on the proposals of the Prime Minister, and by any member of parliament. Thus, officially the National Assembly and the Senate both have the constitution-making authority (*le pouvoir constituant*) as they have the power to propose, amend and oppose the revision of the constitution. But if officially the initiative of revising the constitution belongs concurrently to the President of the Republic and to members of parliament *de facto*, the initiative for any revision stems from the executive. Indeed, any attempt to change the constitution requires the agreement of the government. In addition, the formal amendment process is based on a perfectly balanced bicameralism as amendments proposed must be passed by both Houses of Parliament in identical terms. No qualified majority is required for constitutional amendment. In due course, the amendment becomes final on its approval by referendum. However, there is an important difference from the ordinary legislative process since, unlike what happens with ordinary legislation, under article 89, the government cannot leave the last word to the National Assembly. The French Senate can block an amendment as it has a veto power. As Meg Russell has explained, 'The Senate has more power in this area [of constitutional reform] than over ordinary bills – whilst the lower House may have the last word, after mediation, on ordinary bills, the Senate has an absolute veto over constitutional bills', adding that 'the Upper Chamber can act as a real block to constitutional change.'[41] In fact, any proposed revision can be hindered by the opposition of one of the two chambers – not only the Senate. The opposition of one House is enough to stop the revising process.

Amendments normally require the consent of the two chambers of the legislature, and, as the provisions of the constitution envisage no method which does not involve the legislature, the President has a certain freedom of action. If the amendment bill is passed by both Houses, the President may then put it to the people or resubmit the bill to both Houses convened into one body – called the Congress – with three-fifths of the vote required. In that case, the government amendment is not put to referendum. The President of the Republic also has another powerful device that he can use, if necessary, to bypass the legislature, and thus potential opposition from Parliament, which is to use article 11. But this is highly unpopular.

Indeed, another way of amending the French constitution is to invoke article 11, which is part of Title II of the 1958 text devoted to the French President of the Republic. Article 11 reads:

> The President of the Republic, may ... submit to a referendum any government bill which deals with the organisation of the public

> authorities, or with reforms relating to the economic or social policy of the nation, and to the public services contributing thereto, or which provides for authorisation to ratify a treaty, which, although not contrary to the constitution, would affect the functioning of the institutions.

Although the text itself does not say so, it has sometimes been misinterpreted as allowing the President to submit the constitutional amendment directly to the people and without the intervention of the legislature. Thus, in agreement with the Prime Minister, the President has used article 11 to revise the constitution instead of article 89. This is what happened in 1962, when President de Gaulle was successful, and 1969 when he failed.

Whatever means exist to amend the French constitution, there is a prohibition – or rather an immutable provision – referred to at the end of article 89, which is that the Republican form of government cannot be altered. This can be partly explained by the political circumstances of the drafting of the 1958 constitution, notably the threat of the use of force by the army engendered by the Algerian conflict, though of course it also reflects the dominant French political tradition since the successive ending of Bourbon, Orleanist and Bonapartist regimes. Such a threat of force proved to be a real one as in 1962, a few years after the establishment of the new constitution, when de Gaulle used the President's exceptional powers provided for in article 16 (on 23 April) following the failed military coup by a group of French rebel generals in Algiers. During the subsequent events in France, de Gaulle himself came close to being assassinated by OAS terrorists, which illustrated the dangers attached to his approach.

Thus, there are two main limits to the formal process for amending the French constitution. First, there cannot be any popular initiative, and therefore the people cannot initiate a revision. Secondly, it is possible for either the National Assembly or the Senate to block, or at least delay, constitutional changes, until the President decides to use article 11 for the revision of the constitution. The use of article 11 to revise the constitution enables the President of the Republic to hold a referendum, and it is a way of putting pressure on members of parliament by brandishing the threat of the use of a referendum to bypass any opposition from parliament. In 1962 the National Assembly called on the government to resign via a motion of no confidence following the use of article 11 by de Gaulle. Yet, it is more difficult to put pressure on the Senate, since the Upper House, unlike the National Assembly, cannot be dissolved. Using article 11, instead of the formal parliamentary process, for amending the constitution under article 89 is a way of abolishing the veto that the Senate has over constitutional change. Thus the French constitution of 1958 has evolved mostly through amendments by Congress and through popular referendums. It has also evolved by means of the jurisprudence of the Constitutional Council and the practice of governmental institutions. In the light of France's varied historical experiences in the two centuries prior to 1958 that must surely be considered a highly beneficial outcome.

Unprecedented constitutional change: towards a constitutional revolution?

Two men – one British, Tony Blair, the leader of New Labour which won the 1997 General Election, the other, French, Nicolas Sarkozy, the leader of the Conservative Union for a Popular Movement (UMP) and winner of the 2007 French presidential election, initiated unprecedented constitutional change that went far beyond their expectations.

The 2007 presidential election campaign confirmed the move in France towards multi-party politics as the result of the French first-past-the-post system based on two rounds, instead of one as in the UK.[42] There were no less than twelve contenders from the far left to the far right of the political spectrum. In spite of their variety of opinions and political leanings the great majority was convinced that the 1958 constitution was no longer adapted to the evolution of French society, and that major constitutional change was therefore needed. They almost unanimously denounced a two-headed executive characterised by the supremacy of the President of the Republic and the excessive personalisation of the presidential office. Some went so far as to suggest a regime change, pleading for a Sixth Republic based on a modern parliamentary regime in France. Some favoured an assembly regime where power resides in the popularly elected legislative chamber to which the government is responsible – oblivious of the fact that it led to constant instability under the Fourth Republic. Others advocated a British type of parliamentary regime based on the supremacy of the Prime Minister. Long before that, in the early 1960s, leading figures of the left, both anti-Gaullist, like Pierre Mendès-France and François Mitterrand, in their respective books, *A Modern French Republic* (1962) and *The Permanent Coup d'Etat* (1964), denounced 'a regime of personal power', the concentration of power in the hands of a judicially and politically unaccountable President and thus the presidential drift of the Fifth Republic. This was echoed by the winner of the 2007 presidential election, the UMP's[43] Nicolas Sarkozy saying that 'it is unsound for the President of the Republic to control in fact and in law the whole institutional framework.'[44] The constitutional change initiated by Sarkozy altered thirty-five articles of the 1958 constitution, completely redrafted three and added nine new articles, which means that around half of the constitution was amended in one single constitutional reform.

In the United Kingdom Tony Blair remained in power for ten years from May 1997 to June 2007 – the first Labour Prime Minister to win three General Elections in a row – Nicolas Sarkozy served only one term in office under the five-year presidential mandate introduced in 2000. But, whatever the time they spent in office, both men initiated constitutional reforms which were to change significantly the constitutional narrative of their own country. Tony Blair and Nicolas Sarkozy were an odd political couple, yet they had much in common. Though politicians are often denounced as people without a proper professional career, both men read law and practised as lawyers before entering politics. Both were very much pro-Europe and tried to place their own country 'at the heart of Europe'. Thus the 1997 Labour manifesto contained the following commitment: 'We will give Britain the leadership in Europe which Britain and Europe need.'[45]

Nicolas Sarkozy became President of the French Republic just as Tony Blair was about to resign as both British Prime Minister and Leader of the Labour party in the wake of the unpopular 2003 war in Iraq. The man, described as the most pro-European British Prime Minister, and his doctrine, more commonly known as 'the Third Way',[46] had inspired continental European politicians, notably French ones like Jacques Delors, for a decade. Both Tony Blair and Nicolas Sarkozy adopted the same style of public-relations leadership, which in turn influenced the evolution of national institutions. While French commentators described Nicolas Sarkozy's leadership as a form of 'hyper-presidency', Tony Blair's style was more correctly described as presidential than prime ministerial. His large array of 'special advisers' confirmed this tendency, which Gordon Brown continued.

However, what really matters for our purpose is the long-lasting impact of the constitutional change they initiated, in the United Kingdom after 1997 and in France after 2007. As stated by the Fabian Society, 'Since 1997, Britain has undergone the single most significant period of constitutional reform in over a century … from Scottish and Welsh devolution through the Human Rights Act to the proposed abolition of the Lord Chancellor's Office.'[47]

The constitutional reforms initiated by Tony Blair in the United Kingdom, and some ten years afterwards in France by Nicolas Sarkozy, partly under the need to better comply with the European Convention on Human Rights, aimed mainly at rebalancing and renewing institutions. Apart from the general objective of introducing more transparency, accountability[48] – and therefore trust in politics and national institutions – that pervaded both Sarkozy's and Blair's programmes of institutional renewal, they contained many specific proposals.

The 1997 New Labour Manifesto entitled 'New Labour because Britain deserves better' focused on the need for 'national renewal' based on 'a contract or covenant' with the British people in order not only 'to rebuild and renew the country' but also 'to renew faith in politics'.[49] In the same way as New Labour had rewritten its own constitution redrafting in 1995 its controversial socialist Clause IV which allegedly frightened part of the electorate, it wanted to revisit the UK constitutional settlement in order to modernise it. It contained 'ten specific commitments' – reminiscent of the Ten Commandments – to transform a changing society, though constitutional change only ranked ninth and did not appear as an urgent priority. The ninth commitment, towards the bottom of the list reads: 'We will clean up politics, decentralise political power throughout the United Kingdom and put the funding of political parties on a proper and accountable basis', a particularly ambitious objective, and probably unattainable.

New Labour's proposals included the reform of Parliament, starting with the composition of both Houses of Parliament. It tried to make the House of Lords 'more democratic and effective' by abolishing the hereditary principle by statute,[50] while securing a 'more effective' House of Commons by modernising its procedures, improving Prime Minister's Questions and replacing the first-past-the-post (FPTP) voting system by proportional representation (PR). The former was more successful than the latter during Labour's years in government.

Some ten years afterwards in France, the decree of 18 July 2007 setting up the committee in charge of working on the modernisation and rebalancing of the institutions of the Fifth Republic included the assignment letter of President Sarkozy where he presented his views regarding constitutional reform. Like les Compagnons du Devoir in their own field of expertise, every President of the French Republic is eager to achieve his masterpiece – his *chef d'oeuvre* – as his institutional and political legacy. General de Gaulle,[51] one of the founding fathers of the constitution of the Fifth Republic, did so in 1958, with Michel Debré as the main drafter of the constitution. Along with the major role he played during World War II as the leader of Free France, organising the French Resistance from London, de Gaulle's main contribution to his country, is indeed the constitution of the Fifth Republic. This was very much influenced by his own vision of France as a strong nation-state. Even today the country has a Gaullist inspiration.

Fifty years later in 2008, the sixth president of the Fifth Republic, Nicolas Sarkozy[52] – whose party, the Union for a Popular Movement (UMP), now renamed Les Républicains (the Republicans) – is a neo-Gaullist party, tried to make history in his own way by modernising and democratising the 1958 constitution. He had been elected the previous year on a programme promoting constitutional change while claiming his attachment to the Fifth Republic, and promised to set up a special commission for that purpose. At a press conference at the Elysée on 8 January 2008, Sarkozy spoke of 'the need to take into account the fundamental changes that have taken place in the world and in French society in the last fifty years', 'to modernise and rebalance French institutions' and, last but not least, 'to reassert fundamental values at the basis of the French Republican identity'.

The institutional and political choices of the founding fathers of the 1958 constitution established a constitutional settlement which was unbalanced from the start. Hence the setting up by Sarkozy of a committee of experts chaired by a former Prime Minister, Edouard Balladur, with the task of making proposals to 'modernise and rebalance the institutions of the Fifth Republic'. It became more commonly known as the Balladur Committee. Its seventy-seven proposals paved the way for one of the most fundamental changes to the constitution of the Fifth Republic. Sarkozy had asked the Balladur Committee to focus on the executive and, within the executive, on the division of powers between the President of the Republic and the Prime Minister in order to clarify them. It was also asked to examine the relationship between the executive and parliament in trying to strengthen the latter.[53] Finally, part of the remit of the Balladur Committee was to concentrate on the constitutional status of the judiciary with a view to better protecting fundamental rights, for 'the institutions of the Fifth Republic do not give citizens enough rights and do not protect them sufficiently.'[54]

Sarkozy's programme of reform also aimed at strengthening parliament and making it more representative. Yet rather than focusing on the composition and procedures of the French parliament – though Sarkozy asked the Balladur Committee to consider some measure of proportional representation in the French National Assembly as well as changes to electoral boundaries – it gave priority to making parliamentary control over the executive more effective, by enabling parliament to take part in determining its own agenda, increasing the number of permanent parliamentary committees[55] and giving a proper status to the French Opposition. The Balladur Committee was to conclude in its report that 'strengthening Parliament is the main way of rebalancing French institutions.'

Ten years earlier in the United Kingdom, Tony Blair had been aware of the need to strengthen the Westminster Parliament. He was perhaps even more concerned with the urgency of 'strengthening the Union itself'. On the one hand, the idea was to devolve powers to Scotland and Wales without challenging the sovereignty of the national Parliament as a way of preventing separatism. On the other hand, the cause of decentralisation would be forwarded through elected Mayors for London and other cities as well as possible regional assemblies in England. The 1997 Labour manifesto included the following provision: 'The Union will be strengthened and the threat of separatism removed.'[56] As far as decentralisation is concerned, the objective was not only to give Mayors more legitimacy, but the means that go with effective power, as is the case for French Mayors, rather than a merely ceremonial role like, for example, that of the Lord Mayor of Bristol.[57] Although in France Mayors, who are the chief executives of the *communes*, are not directly elected by the people but by the municipal councils, they have significant administrative and policing powers for which they are accountable to French civil and criminal courts. It is most notably the case when they act as state representatives under the supervision of French prefects in administrative matters or under the control of public prosecutors in judicial matters. Their great responsibility for security and public health matters has led to a substantial increase of legal actions against them before French courts, in an increasingly litigious society where citizens are more and more aware of their rights.

In the UK, the 2015 Queen's Speech[58] which unveiled the list of bills of the second Cameron government included a Cities and Devolution Bill to decentralise more powers to city regions, starting with Greater Manchester, and to transfer more economic and policing powers to elected Mayors in a combined authority of councils – not only in Greater Manchester but also in other major English cities. There was, however, initially no great enthusiasm in the country for directly elected Mayors, as the 2012 English mayoral referendums showed.[59] Out of the twelve largest cities outside London which were invited to elect their own Mayors, Leicester and Liverpool agreed to do so following resolutions by their respective city councils, while Bristol was the only one out of the ten remaining cities to vote 'Yes' to an elected mayor in its referendum held in May 2012.

Constitutional reformers in 1997 in the UK and in 2008 in France were themselves eager to better protect existing civil liberties and fundamental rights while securing new rights for citizens at the local and national level. The 1997 New Labour manifesto devoted a whole section to 'real rights for citizens', to be achieved by the incorporation of the European Convention on Human Rights (ECHR) that French and British lawyers like Professor Pierre-Henri Teitgen and Sir David Maxwell-Fyfe had either inspired or helped draft and that the country had ratified as early as 1951. New Labour promised, 'to incorporate the ECHR into UK law by statute to bring those rights home and allow our people access to them in their national courts', adding that 'Parliament will remain free to enhance these rights, for example by a Freedom of Information Act.'[60]

In France, where the ECHR had long been incorporated into domestic law, the idea was to allow French citizens themselves to have access to French constitutional judges by directly referring cases to the Constitutional Council in the course of legal proceedings when they seriously believed that a law already enacted or some of its provisions violated their constitutional rights[61] via the 'preliminary ruling on constitutionality' – *Question prioritaire de constitutionnalité* (QPC). French citizens were also granted the equivalent of an ombudsman, the so-called 'Human Rights defender' – *le défenseur des droits*, nominated by the President of the Republic to hear claims lodged by ordinary people against any public services dysfunction.[62] Those new measures amounted to a revolution in French and English law in the field of human rights as they strengthened citizens' rights with a force and precision not previously known.

In Britain, the Human Rights Act of 1998 can without doubt be considered as the most important statute, and therefore constitutional legacy, of the Blair years, along with devolution. As for the French, the Constitutional Law of 23 July 2008 is the most important revision that the constitution of the Fifth Republic has experienced, and the priority preliminary rulings on the issue of constitutionality, which it introduced in the new article 61.1, are what it will be remembered for, even if it proved disappointing on many other aspects, including a more participatory type of democracy. Citizens too often have been the great absentees in debates on constitutional reform in the United Kingdom and in France, as constitutional issues tend to be discussed behind closed doors by legal and academic experts and political analysts, even if people can be invited to endorse them afterwards in a referendum. Bertrand Mathieu, the chairman of the French Association of Constitutional Law and a member of the Balladur Committee,[63] concluded that, to be effective, the 2008 constitutional reform would have needed to 'reinvigorate democracy and especially to develop citizens' participation at every possible level'.[64] The Political and Constitutional Reform Committee of the House of Commons, appointed for the lifetime of the 2010–15 legislature and chaired by the Labour MP Graham Allen, also came to the same conclusion. It launched a vast consultation process on options for constitutional reform, including a British codified constitution[65] to engage fully with members of the public and allow them to have their say in constitutional matters.[66]

While Tony Blair's and Nicolas Sarkozy's programmes of constitutional reform had in common the same formal objective of democratising and modernising institutions, there were also significant differences. Whereas the next step of the French decentralisation process was deliberately kept out of the remit of the Balladur Committee as it had been dealt with already by a significant constitutional reform five years before in 2003 and was to be further examined separately by a different committee, devolution was at the heart of the constitutional agenda of Tony Blair and the Cabinet's Constitutional Committee chaired by Lord Irvine, a very powerful one. The next phase of the decentralisation process in France, known as the third stage, which aimed at reorganising French territory into thirteen big regions instead of the existing twenty-two, in order to enable them to compete with their European neighbours, was to be launched later, under the presidency of Nicolas Sarkozy's Socialist successor, François Hollande.[67]

Conclusion

There was one notable absentee in this busy period of reform – the Queen. Whereas the 2008 constitutional change in France very much focused on the status of the Head of State, the British 1997 programme deliberately left out the monarch and the future of the monarchy. This seems surprising at first sight as it is a dominant institution and would particularly need to be clarified, since it is very much based on custom and practice instead of being legally defined and codified, unlike in other European constitutional monarchies. But tampering with the Crown was seen as a distraction and a danger. The 1997 Labour party manifesto laconically stated, 'We have no plans to replace the Monarchy'.[68] In the next eighteen years under successive British governments – Labour under Gordon Brown, Conservative-Liberal

Democrat under David Cameron (and Nick Clegg) or Conservative (David Cameron serving a second term in office prematurely ended in 2016) – no significant constitutional change affecting the British monarchy was introduced other than some limited reform[69] to the Act of Settlement of 1700 altering succession rules by putting an end to male primogeniture and therefore gender discrimination.

Yet, the Conservative manifesto – then the Queen's Speeches of 2015 and 2016 – of David Cameron, whose party won a small majority in the Commons in the 2015 General Election, clearly wanted to break with Blair's constitutional legacy. This was most notable in the field of Human Rights. Two provisions of the 2015 Conservative manifesto, the in/out referendum on Britain's EU membership by 2017 and the proposal to repeal the Human Rights Act 1998 and replace it by a so-called British Bill of Rights as a first step towards the UK's withdrawal from the European Convention on Human Rights could lead to the break-up of the United Kingdom. The vulnerability of this fundamental Act of Parliament to the political ambitions of the government of the day, along with the easy constitutional change mechanisms that characterise the flexible British constitution, are thus an explosive combination. The only way to entrench both human rights and devolution as a permanent settlement is to incorporate them into a codified French type of constitution to replace the 'make-it-up-as-you-go-along Britain's unwritten constitution'.[70] In fact, a year and a half after it first appeared in the Queen's Speech, a British Bill of Rights languished under benign neglect. The rare and refreshing fruit of Human Rights reform withered on the vine.

Notes

1. Pierre Pactet and Ferdinand Mélin-Soucramanien, *Droit Constitutionnel* (Paris: Dalloz, 2012), p. 57.
2. Dobner and Loughlin, *The Twilight of Constitutionalism* (Oxford: Oxford University Press, 2010), p. 88.
3. Robert Blackburn, *Engineering Constitutional Change: A Comparative Perspective* (London: Routledge, 2012), p. 32.
4. It is interesting to bear in mind that constitution-makers often included immutable provisions – prohibitions and limits. If they are breached nothing really can be done as no sanctions, no legal remedies are generally provided against constitutional bills.
5. Martin Loughlin, 'What is constitutionalism?', in Peter Dobner and Martin Loughlin (eds), *The Twilight of Constitutionalism* (Oxford: Oxford University Press, 2010), p. 52.

6. Otto Pfersmann, 'La révision constitutionnelle en Autriche et en Allemagne fédérale. Théorie, pratique, limites', in Louis Favoreu, *La Révision de la Constitution* (Aix–Marseille: Presses Universitaires d'Aix-Marseille, 1993), p. 10.
7. Blackburn, *Engineering Constitutional Change: A Comparative Perspective*, p. 32.
8. Samuel Finer and Vernon Bogdanor, *Comparing Constitutions* (Oxford: Clarendon Press, 1995), p. 1.
9. Finer and Bogdanor, *Comparing Constitutions*, p. 39.
10. Wales especially has experienced constant constitutional changes in the last fifteen years or so.
11. 'Redécouvrir le préambule de la Constitution', Report of the Committee presided over by Simone Veil (Paris: La Documentation française, 2008), p. 11.
12. What has lasted until this day in France is the preamble of the 1791 constitution which was no less than the famous Declaration of the Rights of Man and of the Citizen (1789).
13. 'a Westminster Village debate', as Philip Norton describes it.
14. 'The Future of the Union' (Legatum Institute, November 2014), p. 2.
15. Erskine May's *Treatise on the Law, Privileges, Proceedings and Usage of Parliament*, 24th edn (London: LexisNexis, 2011), p. 184.
16. House of Lords, Constitution Committee, 'The Process of Constitutional Change', oral evidence (23 March 2011), Jeffrey Jowell, p. 32.
17. See Philippe Ardant, 'La révision constitutionnelle en France; problématique générale', in Favoreu (ed.), *La révision de la Constitution*, p. 79.
18. Favoreu , *La révision de la Constitution*, p. 82.
19. Finer and Bogdanor, *Comparing Constitutions*, p. 40.
20. Peter Wales, *Elements of Comparative Government* (London: Butterworths, 1967), p. 43.
21. Significantly, the preamble of the constitution of the Fifth Republic starts with 'The French people'. The notion of 'the people' finds its origin in the 1789 Revolution, yet it was originally conceived as a fairly abstract notion with no clear legal value.
22. 'and the principle of the French Republic is "government of the people, by the people, and for the people"' (art.2).
23. The Cabinet Manual, 'A guide to laws, conventions and rules on the operation of government' (October 2011), p. 2.
24. Félicien Lemaire, 'The notion of the people in the 1958 Constitution', in Dominique Chagnollaud (ed.), *Les cinquante ans de la Constitution* (Paris: LexisNexis, 2008), p. 43.
25. For further information see the ruling of the French Constitutional Council on Corsica (91-290 DC, 9 May 1992).
26. It was not in the original constitution of 1958 but was introduced by the constitutional law of 25 June 1992.

27. Regional languages can be used within the privacy of the home and can be taught in French schools yet cannot be part of the compulsory (national) curriculum. This is in stark contrast to the support for the Welsh language, both as a subject and a medium of instruction provided in Welsh schools and universities.
28. For further information see the ruling of the French Constitutional Council on minority and regional languages, 99-412 DC, 15 June 1999.
29. He remained Speaker or President of the Senate from 2011 to 2014.
30. In 2011, for the first time in more than fifty years the Socialists won a majority in the Senate.
31. François Venter, *Constitutional Comparison* (Cambridge, MA: Kluwer Law International, 2000), p. 21.
32. Venter, *Constitutional Comparison*, p. 8.
33. *The Government Gazette* (July 2010), 8.
34. It was succeeded by the Public Administration and Constitutional Affairs Committee chaired by Bernard Jenkin.
35. For more information see Rodney Brazier, *Constitutional Reform: Reshaping the British Political System*, 3rd edn (Oxford: Oxford University Press, 2008).
36. The conference consists of Members of Parliament from all sides of the House of Commons, nominated by the parties themselves and formally appointed by the Speaker, who chairs the conference.
37. May, *Treatise on the Law, Privileges, Proceedings and Usage of Parliament*, p. 510.
38. May, *Treatise on the Law, Privileges, Proceedings and Usage of Parliament*, p. 533.
39. The Parliament 2015–20 has a fixed term of five years, putting an end to the privilege enjoyed by the British Prime Minister of choosing the date – within five years – to call a general election. The Fixed-Term Parliament Act 2011, another part of the package of proposed constitutional reforms of the coalition government, provides for fixed days for polling for parliamentary General Elections.
40. For more information see Favoreu, *La révision de la Constitution.*
41. Meg Russell, *Reforming the House of Lords: Lessons from Overseas* (Oxford: Oxford University Press, 2000), p. 182.
42. The first round leading to a multiplicity of presidential contenders.
43. On 5 May 2015, the political office of the UMP approved the reform of the statutes of the party initiated by Nicolas Sarkozy by 50 votes out of 51.
44. Bastien François, *La VIe République: Pourquoi, Comment* (Paris: Les Petits Matins, 2015), p. 21.
45. 'New Labour because Britain deserves better', Labour party manifesto, 1997, p. 4 (number 10 in the list of 10 commitments).
46. For more information see Anthony Giddens and Tony Blair, *La Troisième Voie. Le renouveau de la social-démocratie*, with foreword by Jacques Delors (Paris: Seuil, 2002).

47. 'The Future of the Monarchy', The Report of the Fabian Commission (London: Fabian Society, July 2003), p. 4.
48. 'New Labour because Britain deserves better', Labour Party Manifesto, 1997, p. 1.
49. Labour Party Manifesto, 1997, p. 1.
50. It became the1999 House of Lords Act.
51. He served a first full term (of seven years) in office as President of the Republic but put a premature end to his second term in office after the failure of his 1969 referendum on the reform of French regions and the reform of the Senate. He died only one year later, in 1970.
52. He only served one term in office, from 16 May 2007 to 15 May 2012.
53. The Balladur Report went as far as saying that the objective was to 'emancipate Parliament' which included moving away from French rationalised parliamentarianism.
54. 'Une Cinquième République plus démocratique', Comité de réflexion et de proposition sur la modernisation et le rééquilibrage des institutions de la Cinquième République (Paris: La Documentation française, 2008), p. 4.
55. From six to eight today.
56. Labour party manifesto, 1997, p. 23.
57. Among the ten mayoral referendums held in England's largest cities on 3 May 2012 (Birmingham, Bradford, Bristol, Coventry, Leeds, Manchester, Newcastle, Nottingham, Sheffield and Wakefield), Bristol was the only city where a majority (53 per cent of the electorate) voted in favour of a directly elected Mayor.
58. 'Her Majesty's most gracious speech to both Houses of Parliament', delivered on Wednesday, 27 May 2015 (London: Her Majesty's Stationery Office).
59. The people of Manchester themselves voted against a directly elected Mayor in 2012.
60. The Westminster Parliament did pass the Information Act in 2000.
61. This was included in the constitution as a new article 61-1.
62. The late Dominique Baudis, former Mayor of Toulouse was the first to be appointed to this position. He was succeeded by Jacques Toubon in July 2014.
63. In his assignment letter to the Balladur Committee, President Nicolas Sarkozy wrote that in the course of the run-up to the 2007 presidential election he had been struck by French citizens' aspiration for more open politics, closer to their own preoccupations. As a reaction, he thought that some measure of direct democracy needed to be introduced; hence the proposal of the so-called right of popular initiative/*droit d'initiative populaire*, taking the form of a referendum initiated by one-fifth of members of parliament and one-tenth of registered voters under the new article 11 of the constitution. It was in fact based on a shared initiative between parliamentarians and citizens as a kind of compromise between 'developing a more participatory form of democracy while

emancipating parliament' as it was encapsulated by the Balladur Committee. It remained very much a dead letter as it proved to be almost impossible to implement.

64. Bertrand Mathieu, *Constitution: Rien ne bouge et tout change* (Paris: Lextenso, 2013), p. 179.
65. Drafted by Professor Robert Blackburn and his team (including the present writer) at King's College London.
66. At the end of the consultation process in March 2015, some 3,000 people had sent in their own proposals and comments.
67. Hollande won the 2012 presidential election.
68. Labour party manifesto, 1997, p. 22.
69. See the Succession to the Crown Act 2013.
70. Christopher G. A. Bryant, 'Reconfiguring Britain: The 2010 O'Donnell Lecture', *Contemporary Wales* (2011).

Chapter Two

The French Presidency and the British Monarchy: Changed and yet Unchanging Institutions

Constitutional reformers in the United Kingdom and France have been driven by the quest to have more efficient and legitimate institutions at the same time, though the two do not always go together.

In the French credo inherited from the eighteenth-century Enlightenment and especially Rousseau's *Social Contract*,[1] legitimacy can only derive from the will and consent of the people. A government can be efficient but still lack legitimacy if it does not have the approval of the people. Democratic legitimacy can only be based on universal suffrage in France. In the French context, a constitution is not only the search for constitutional perfection and the source of all expectations; it is also a project. It is not, or not only, the result of specific circumstances, but it is also the outcome of a carefully conceived scheme. Both the British constitutional settlement and the French constitutions have been a permanent work in progress or in 'flux', as Philip Norton[2] described the British constitution in the early 1960s.

This chapter will examine the key question of who runs the country in the United Kingdom and France or, in the words of Walter Bagehot, 'the secret machinery of decision-making'. The question is even more accurate in France because of the complexity of its executive divided between the President of the Republic as Head of State and the Prime Minister as the official Head of Government.

An unbalanced executive–legislative relationship: a common area of concern

Institutions unbalanced in favour of the executive and to the detriment of Parliament characterise the British and the French regimes today. Yet, it would be excessive to describe the legislative as being subordinate to the executive, as they very much interact and depend on each other. The whole system operates on a form of collaboration, not to say interdependence of the two. In the case of the United Kingdom, Walter Bagehot went so far as to speak of 'a fusion of the two'.[3]

Adhémar Esmein (1835–1922), one of the founding fathers of French constitutional and comparative law, who fought hard for the recognition of French constitutional law as an autonomous branch of the law, was suspicious of the executive. He thought it could easily become uncontrolled and uncontrollable. He was an Anglophile who particularly admired the British constitution, unlike so many French constitutionalists today who still deny its very existence. He believed in a necessary hierarchy of the executive and the legislative supporting the supremacy of the law and thus Parliament, praising the English 'for having invented representative and parliamentary government'.[4] Not only was he greatly influenced by the transformation of the nineteenth-century monarchies into parliamentary regimes, but he also developed a keen interest in the writings of his British contemporaries, particularly Albert Venn Dicey and Walter Bagehot, though he sometimes strongly disagreed with them. His writings were based on a mix of admiration for and scepticism towards orthodox British parliamentary government, and they may well reflect the ambivalence of the Anglo-French relationship. Yet, when Walter Bagehot published his landmark book *The English Constitution* in 1867, Britain was in fact moving away from a classical parliamentary regime under the influence of the extension of the franchise – (male) universal suffrage – and the rise of political parties.

Following on from the line of thought of Adhémar Esmein, the late French constitutional lawyer Guy Carcassonne in his 2013 analysis of the constitution of the Fifth Republic expressed his own concerns about the 'omnipotence and omnipresence of the executive',[5] a comment that could very well apply to the British executive. The imbalance between the executive and the legislative to the detriment of the latter can be observed not only at the level of the British union state but also within each of its four nations – that is between the devolved executives and legislatures. This can be highly paradoxical both in a traditional parliamentary regime based on parliamentary sovereignty like the British and in a regime like the French, which is formally a parliamentary regime but which is *de facto* tilted in favour of the President of the Republic as a result of the constitutional practice of de Gaulle and his successors.

Whereas France in its constitutional history experienced regimes characterised by strong executives – like the Consulate and the Empire under Napoleon Bonaparte – followed by regimes dominated by powerful assemblies and/or collegial executives such as the Directory in an attempt to break away from the flaws of previous regimes, the United Kingdom is firmly rooted in a parliamentary constitutional settlement with a sovereign Parliament which, as a central British institution, has traditionally acted as an element of continuity and stability like the British monarchy. In their quest for the most efficient and balanced constitution for France, the drafters of the constitution of the Fifth Republic hesitated between the British model of parliamentary regime or more presidential constitutional arrangements like the American.

The search for the perfect constitution: French hesitations between a presidential regime and a British type of parliamentary regime

Though the 1958 constitution was part of the rebuilding process in the wake of the Second World War and followed a failed military coup by the supporters of those who wanted Algeria to remain French, it was not merely dictated by national circumstances, but was based 'on a genuine project fit to its time'[6] while being very pragmatic. The drafters of the 1958 constitution wanted to give France the best of presidential regimes – a president as a highly commanding figure – and the best of a parliamentary regime, with a stable government accountable to parliament. They were trying to give France its own specific regime adapted to its own legal and political culture. The difficulty the founding fathers of the Fifth Republic faced in choosing the right type of regime for France was well encapsulated by Michel Debré himself when he wondered whether it was possible to move away from the Assembly regime, where parliament is all-powerful, towards rationalised parliamentarianism, where parliament is carefully kept within its own legislative boundaries. He was also eager to give the President effective powers without introducing a presidential regime in France.

The new constitution was driven by an aspiration for change, but also by a man who proved providential, Charles de Gaulle. Michel Debré developed his views in his book *Refaire la France: L'effort d'une génération*, a blueprint for the future constitution, echoed the following year by de Gaulle in his famous Bayeux speech of 16 June 1946. The two maybe most influential men in the drafting of the 1958 constitution did not share the same view of French institutions, however. Debré was very much attached to parliamentarianism whereas de Gaulle promoted a more presidential approach while being extremely suspicious of the American presidential regime. Michel Debré admired the British parliamentary regime and would have liked to introduce it in France. In the speech he delivered before the Council of State, Michel Debré set out his views regarding the future constitution of the Fifth Republic: first that the existing institutions 'were no longer suitable', then presenting the draft constitutional project 'to redesign the parliamentary regime of the Republic'.[7]

The 1958 constitution was determined by the desire to break away from a remote and more recent past – the Third and Fourth Republics, especially the trauma of 10 May 1940 and the French debacle in the Second World War. The drafters of the 1958 constitution wanted to avoid the parliamentary instability which had plagued previous Republics by moving the political centre of gravity from parliament to the government via rationalised parliamentarianism. They provided for the creation of a new body, the Constitutional Council which was to help in checking that parliament remained within its legislative remit without encroaching upon the government. The 1958 constitutional project was conceived to reduce the role of a structurally unstable undisciplined parliament to the advantage of a stronger government, though accountable to parliament, with a President of the Republic acting as an arbitrator or legal safeguard. The drafters of the constitution of the Fifth Republic established what was and still remains in essence a parliamentary regime with a government politically accountable to parliament and the right of the executive to dissolve the National Assembly. The President can decide on this after consulting the Prime Minister and the Presidents of the two Houses of parliament, while not being himself accountable to parliament.

While the drafters of the 1958 constitution were very much attached to the Republican tradition and to the parliamentary regime, they were aware of the need to avoid the flaws of the Third and Fourth Republics. Those Republics had in common the principle of parliamentary sovereignty – more specifically the sovereignty of the only institution directly elected by the people, the Chamber of Deputies – yet unlike Britain, where parliamentary sovereignty did not hinder the emergence of a strong executive, the French executive was very weak. Governments were at the mercy of parliament, which voted censure motions on very slight grounds. They were under constant threat of being overthrown, including by the Senate, which under the Third Republic had almost the same powers as the Assembly. Even a Premier as powerful as Clemenceau, *père de la victoire*, was soon dispatched in 1920.The drafters of the 1958 text opted for a strong stable executive, with governments difficult to overthrow, and at the top of the executive a strong president.

Both de Gaulle and Michel Debré thought highly of the presidential office and of the President as a dominant figure, unlike the Presidents of the Third and Fourth Republics, who were fairly weak and could not act on their own, and whose office did not enjoy much prestige. Under the Constitutional Laws of 1875 the President of the Republic hardly had any autonomy as all his acts had to be countersigned by the 'President of the Council' – the name given to the Head of the Government who was the leading figure of the executive, today the Prime Minister. By contrast, de Gaulle was determined to establish a real Head of State endowed with effective powers. De Gaulle and Michel Debré wanted the President no longer to be a weak character restricted to a ceremonial role, but a 'working President'. He was to share some characteristics with the British constitutional monarch who, though she 'reigns but does not rule the country',[8] enjoys high moral authority – especially Elizabeth II, who has a profound sense of duty and is universally respected, even by people who claim they are republicans. Like the British monarch, the President of the French Republic was to embody the unity of the nation. This is more important than ever in both countries, as their respective civil societies need strong benchmarks at a time of many uncertainties – of identity and institutional crisis including political leadership – when Parliament itself now much discredited following a succession of financial and political scandals can no longer fulfil this role. The President of the Fifth Republic was to be a democratically elected Head of State, though not by direct universal suffrage initially, above the machinery of political parties – de Gaulle was indeed fiercely opposed to what he called the 'exclusive regime of parties' – politically unaccountable to parliament, immune from suit, able to grant mercy (a huge responsibility until the abolition of the death penalty under President Mitterrand in 1981) to the extent that he was sometimes compared with a constitutional monarch. Under the Fifth Republic, the President was to be the guardian of the constitution and of the independence of the judiciary – a role performed in the UK by the Lord Chancellor and Secretary of State for Justice. One of the constitutional provisions most influenced by de Gaulle was – and still is – article 5 of the 1958 constitution. Under article 5 the President is described as the 'custodian of the constitution' and as the 'arbitrator'. If both words are devoid of any legal dimension and any clear meaning altogether, they are more to be understood as a kind of moral duty for the one who embodies France and its Republican values.

Even if the 1958 French constitution was built on a specific project it led to unexpected and unpredictable developments. Thus de Gaulle almost immediately departed from the very letter of the 1958 constitution that he had helped to draft. His time in power from 21 December 1958 to 1969 was to have long-lasting political and institutional consequences. His strong personality, associated with his aura, tilted the institutions towards the supremacy of the President to the detriment of the Prime Minister.

Blurred lines between the Head of State and the Head of Government

Born out of constitutional practice, then established as a constitutional convention, the British prime ministerial office was never officially set up and thus never clearly defined. Today, as it is stated in the Cabinet Manual,[9] 'the role of the Prime Minister and Cabinet are governed largely by convention', and he has 'few statutory functions'; hence the difficulty of clearly identifying his role and fixing boundaries to his powers. In both the United Kingdom and France the function of the Prime Minister emerged at a fairly late stage in the history of the country. It only started to be identified as such in the early eighteenth century in the United Kingdom as the executive role of the Crown declined under George I, Sir Robert Walpole being considered as the first to officially hold this office (1721–42). Whereas the title Prime Minister was traditionally given to the British Head of Government, in France it is a fairly recent title: from 1815 to 1958 the name used was 'President of the Council of Ministers'. Today, the French Council of Ministers, where strategic decisions are taken, is not chaired by the Prime Minister but by the President of the Republic himself. Thus the confusion in the very name of the office was symptomatic of deeper ambiguities and uncertainties regarding the constitutional status and role of the prime ministerial office holder, which to some degree continues.

The nomination of French and British Prime Ministers

The main drafter of the 1958 Constitution and first Prime Minister of the Fifth Republic was the first victim of the presidential drift of the regime. It set up a precedent contrary to the very letter of the article 8 of the constitution which, though it gave the President of the Republic a discretionary power to appoint the Prime Minister, did not gave him the power to dismiss him at will. Under article 8 of the constitution, the President of the Republic appoints the Prime Minister.[10] In fact, this appointment process is very much at the discretion of the President of the Republic as he is under no constitutional obligation to choose someone following precise legal requirements. He must however make sure that he will be able to command the support of the parliamentary majority.

Under the 1958 Constitution the Prime Minister tenders his resignation to the President, but this is supposed to be a voluntary move, certainly not dictated or initiated by the President. It made the Prime Minister not only officially accountable to parliament – as it is the rule in a parliamentary regime, but also *de facto* accountable to the President himself.

To be able to stay in office, the French Prime Minister needs not only to hold the confidence of parliament but also the confidence of the President of the Republic. The political discretion of the President concerning both the nomination and the dismissal of the Prime Minister is an anomaly which has not been removed by the 2008 constitutional change. The recommendations of the Balladur Committee regarding the Prime Minister were not followed, and the constitutional provisions regarding the latter, unlike the rest of the constitution, have remained largely unchanged. So, unlike most European parliamentary regimes where the political centre of gravity has shifted to the benefit of the Prime Minister as the leader of the parliamentary majority, the constitutional reform initiated by President Sarkozy has weakened the French Prime Minister. In a highly critical article, the law academic Dominique Rousseau concluded that 'all the proposed reforms have had one and the same victim: the Prime Minister.'[11]

In France today, there is an executive presidency where the President *de facto* defines national policy and the Prime Minister conducts it, whereas in the United Kingdom the monarch is separated from the actual business of government and thus is only the ceremonial head of the executive. The British monarch has been superseded by the Prime Minister, politically accountable to Parliament in the exercise of the prerogative power of the Crown. While the French parliamentary regime has evolved towards a more presidential regime via the direct election of its president by the people and presidential practice as well as the personality of the successive presidents, the British prime ministerial office has become more and more presidential in style and practice irrespective of the individual Prime Minister.

Although both the British and the French Prime Ministers under their respective constitutional settlements are in a unique position of authority, neither of them is directly elected by the people. As we have seen, under article 8 of the French constitution, the French Prime Minister is appointed by the President of the Republic *de facto* on political and sometimes also personal grounds. Unlike his British counterpart, the French Prime Minister is not chosen from among members of Parliament. Whereas the British Prime Minister must by convention be a member of the House of Commons, in France, under article 23 of the 1958 constitution, the functions of members of the government are incompatible with the exercise of any parliamentary mandate. In France a fundamental incompatibility between being a member of government and belonging to parliament, in the name of the strict separation of powers, remains a key principle at the basis of the French constitution inherited from Montesquieu.[12] Unlike Britain, where the Prime Minister will normally be the accepted leader of a political party that commands the majority of the House of Commons, in France the head of the parliamentary majority does not become the Prime Minister. It is the person who has been appointed by the President of the Republic as the Prime Minister who becomes the head of the parliamentary majority. The legitimacy of the French Prime Minister is based on the confidence he retains – and must command – from the members of the National Assembly elected by direct universal suffrage and from the President of the Republic, who is also elected directly by the people. Under article 20, the French Prime Minister as the official Head of the Government is accountable to parliament. In fact, he is responsible before the only fully democratic chamber, officially called the National Assembly.[13] It is also the only Chamber which can overthrow the government through a successful censure motion; thus it can withdraw its confidence from the Prime Minister and the government even if this power is rarely used today with that purpose.

The lack of a clear mandate for the French and British Prime Ministers

In France, being elected is considered as the ultimate form of legitimacy and of the very essence of democracy,[14] which might explain why some eminent French legal experts like Maurice Duverger advocated direct universal suffrage for the French Prime Minister.[15] It is still a topical issue in both countries. Adhémar Esmein criticised Walter Bagehot for arguing that the British Prime Minister was elected. The British constitutionalist wrote that 'he [the Prime Minister] is not elected directly by the people; he is elected by the representatives of the people', describing the House of Commons as 'an electoral college' and 'a reservoir of ministers',[16] and adding that 'after he has been elected, the British First Magistrate remains responsible to Parliament.'

In fact, under the British constitution, the Prime Minister is formally appointed by the monarch, which is one of her few royal prerogatives. It is only by convention that the leader of the party which has won a majority in the last general election is designated Prime Minister by the monarch, and this convention has been challenged in wartime or when there is a hung Parliament, as happened in the 2010 general election. It could well happen again.

In the United Kingdom, the question whether the British Prime Minister ought to be directly elected by the British people was raised in a parliamentary survey launched by the political and constitutional reform committee of the 2010–15 UK Parliament. Paul Webb, Professor of Politics at the University of Sussex, giving evidence on this issue concluded that 'if directly elected Prime Ministers were to be introduced, I would recommend combining this with separation of powers and the continuing right of the power to dissolve Parliament', adding that 'there was no compelling case for changing from the more orthodox form of parliamentary government that the UK operates.'[17]

If doubts remain on both sides of the Channel about how the holder of that office should be appointed – in other words the lack of clear democratic mandate of the Prime Minister, especially at a time when it is more difficult for political parties to win a clear majority in the House of Commons – a solution could be the one recommended by Professor Robert Blackburn. He argued that 'the Prime Minister should be elected by the House of Commons from among its members by way of motions presented to the House and supported by a majority.'[18] In any case, in both countries the objective is to build strong stable governments to rule the country as long as they enjoy the confidence of their parliamentary majority. Governments are accountable to Parliament and through Parliament to the people. In both countries it is more and more difficult to overthrow a government by means of a censure motion. The Fixed-Term Parliament Act 2011 in the United Kingdom has reinforced this trend, allowing weak governments to stay in power. It removed a key strategic power which belonged to the Prime Minister, which consisted in deciding when to hold the next General Election within the five-year legal maximum duration of a Parliament.

Although under the original 1958 constitution the President as Head of State and the Prime Minister as Head of the Government were to fulfil complementary functions, very early on, under the constitutional practice of the successive Presidents of the Fifth Republic, the Prime Minister became the junior partner in the executive couple except in periods of *cohabitation*.

The French Fifth Republic experienced periods, known as *cohabitation*, when the President of the Republic and the Prime Minister, supported by different political majorities (drawn from opposite parties), ruled the country together. It happened twice under the presidency of the first Socialist President, François Mitterrand, who shared power with the Gaullist and politically conservative (RPR) Prime Minister Jacques Chirac, from 1986 to 1988, then with RPR Prime Minister Edouard Balladur from 1993 to 1995. Jacques Chirac, in turn, when he became president, went through the same experience with Socialist Lionel Jospin from 1997 to 2002. *Cohabitation* can only be effective if both the President and the Prime Minister, in spite of their different political leanings, accept working together and reaching permanent compromises for the benefit of the country. Paradoxically, although *cohabitation* was the exception to the rule during the Fifth Republic, it provided a more faithful reading of the constitution by enabling the Prime Minister to exercise his powers to the full along the lines of article 20 – that is to say 'determining' and 'conducting' the policy of the nation. Under the constitution, the French Prime Minister is very powerful as he has the use of the administrative machinery and the armed forces; yet in practice, he is in a subordinate position within the executive.

The presidential drift of the French system and the all-powerful British Prime Minister

In France, in spite of a deeply rooted codified constitution, the constitutional settlement of the Fifth Republic remains surprisingly vague regarding the status and functions of the French Prime Minister. This is all the more surprising since the drafters of the 1958 constitution were determined to strengthen the executive to secure a strong, efficient government. In the original 1958 constitution only a few articles were officially devoted to the government and the Prime Minister. Under Title III, only three articles discuss the accountability of government before parliament, though they are fundamental ones – from articles 20 to 23, completed by articles 49 and 50 further down. On the other hand, there are fourteen articles devoted to the President of the Republic, from article 5 to article 19 under Title II of the constitution. It shows formal imbalance between the Head of State and the Head of the Government. Yet the French Prime Minister permeates many other parts of the constitution since hardly anything can be done without him. If one sticks to the letter of the constitution, the Prime Minister is in a strong position. Under the 1958 constitution, the role of the French

Prime Minister is twofold. He plays a key role in the everyday functioning of the government, coordinating governmental work, and is in charge of liaising with parliament. Thus, he is also a key intermediary between the government and parliament. Under articles 20 and 21, the French Prime Minister directs the activities of the government, which decides on and conducts national policy. Article 21 also states that the Prime Minister is responsible for national defence, perhaps one of the most controversial provisions of Title III of the constitution, since it overlaps with the powers granted to the President of the Republic as commander-in-chief of the armed forces under article 15 of the constitution, which is devoted to the President himself.

In the United Kingdom, the status of the Prime Minister and the limits of his powers are also not clearly defined. In spite of various recent attempts at introducing a legal framework to better delineate the position and functions of the British Prime Minister, such as the Cabinet Manual in 2011, there still has not been a codification of the prime ministerial office as such, clearly defining his powers and competences. The Cabinet Manual however provides the following definition of the Prime Minister's function: 'the Prime Minister is the Sovereign's principal adviser, chairs Cabinet and has overall responsibility for the organisation of government.'[19]

It does not provide many more details as it only states that the British Prime Minister, just like his French counterpart, 'is responsible for the overall organisation of the executive and the allocation of functions between ministers in charge of departments'.[20] As Walter Bagehot[21] explained, the Prime Minister plays a strategic role, the 'hyphen joining the legislative to the executive'. The same kind of analysis is to be found in the writings of French contemporary constitutional analysts who when commenting upon the key role of the French Prime Minister describe him as 'the buffer between the Majority, which he needs to conduct the national policy, and the Opposition, which sees him as a target'.[22]

In both countries, it is also the personality of the Prime Minister of the day and his ability as a leader which *de facto* make the prime ministerial office what it is. To take but one example, President François Hollande[23] chose at first in 2012 a former academic, a politician almost unknown to French people, Jean-Marc Ayrault, who kept a very low profile throughout his premiership.[24] Then, following major setbacks for his Socialist party in the March 2014 mayoral elections to the benefit of the main right-wing opposition party, but also to the far right of Marine Le Pen, Hollande decided to reshuffle his Cabinet. He replaced his Prime Minister by his former Interior Minister, Manuel Valls,[25] closer to the right and to the business world, but also much more popular and forceful than his predecessor.

Yet, the 2008 constitutional reform in the wake of the Balladur Report missed the opportunity to reform and improve the prime ministerial office. This is universally described as one of the great gaps of the 2008 redrafting of the constitution of the Fifth Republic. The 2008 constitutional change aimed primarily at clarifying the constitutional position of the executive, and within the latter the division of competences between the Head of State and the Head of the Government, respectively the President of the Republic and the Prime Minister. But successive constitutional and political changes have in fact made things worse in the sense that they have reinforced the presidential drift of the regime to the detriment of the Prime Minister. Some legal commentators even wonder whether there is still a Prime Minister or whether the office of the Prime Minister should not be abolished. However, the decline of the prime ministerial office should not be overestimated since *de facto* neither the President of the Republic nor parliament can do anything without him.

In France, the President of the Republic has superseded the Prime Minister as the leader of the parliamentary majority, acting more as a Prime Minister rather than what is expected from him as the President of the Republic. He is the one who really governs the country. By contrast, in the United Kingdom, the all-powerful Prime Minister who is the leader of the parliamentary majority rules the country more like a president rather than a Prime Minister in other European democracies like France. Not only have British Prime Ministers adopted a more presidential style of leadership with a small team of close counsellors and a larger group of special advisers and press officers, as under Blair and Cameron, but they also try to be more visible via the growing use of presidential type televised debates and the news media more generally. The archetype of a British Prime Minister behaving like a president is Tony Blair. He went on acting like a Head of State in international affairs after his resignation in 2007, touring the planet, meeting Heads of States and ambassadors in the Middle East and elsewhere.

Not only had France been dominated by the same political leader, de Gaulle, for a decade from 1959 to 1969, but the Fifth Republic, unlike the British parliamentary system, did not experience any alternation of political parties in power until 1981 with the landslide victory of the first Socialist President of the Fifth Republic, François Mitterrand. This followed the disintegration of the once powerful Communists. Ironically, as France was hit by a Socialist wave which generated many expectations, the

UK alongside the United States with Ronald Reagan was to know its own 'political revolution' – a Conservative one – with the triumphant victory of Margaret Thatcher in 1979.

The presidential drift of the regime in France was further aggravated with the reduction of the presidential term in office from seven to five years following a referendum held in 2000, and also by the inversion of the electoral calendar in 2001: the presidential election from then on taking place ahead of the legislative parliamentary elections. Until 1962, the President of the Republic had been appointed by an electoral college of some 80,000 people who were members of Parliament, representatives of general and municipal councils – the latter forming the great bulk of the electoral panel.[26] Though the 1962 constitutional reform did not provide for additional powers for the President, his enhanced legitimacy[27] gave him *de facto* a new status. His role has become highly politicised as the President could from then on rely on a parliamentary majority of his own political leanings. The shortening of the presidential term in office from seven to five years, aligning it with the mandate of members of the National Assembly, has led the President to perform both his own role as Head of State but also *de facto* as Head of Government. It is the relationship between the two heads of the executive which has been fundamentally altered by such a reform to the disadvantage of the Prime Minister. It was against the letter of the 1958 constitution and imposed in practice a single-headed executive. This presidential drift has led to a major anomaly and has been a source of many criticisms in what is still fundamentally a parliamentary regime, which are that the 'real' Head of the Government today, the President of the Republic, is not accountable to parliament, while the Prime Minister, who no longer determines the policy of the nation, is. It challenged an essential principle which emerged with the English Magna Carta – 'with power must come accountability' – which is essential in the British and French democracies alike. Indeed, one of the main flaws of the French Fifth Republic is 'to have introduced unaccountability where power lies'.[28]

The non-accountability of the French President and the British monarch

In the French case, the evolution of the President's role towards more governmental functions would not matter so much were he accountable to parliament. As regards the British Prime Minister and the French President, the former is accountable to Parliament and the latter is not. The

British Prime Minister can be dismissed by his party while in office, which cannot be the case for the French President, as he is directly elected by the people. The main way to sanction a French President is not to re-elect him at the next presidential election – at least if he is in his first term. Tony Blair, who had become highly unpopular following his 2003 decision to wage war in Iraq, anticipated a public disavowal by his own party by standing down on 27 June 2007 after ten years as Prime Minister and thirteen as party leader. Yet, to this day he remains the only Labour Prime Minister to have served three terms in office in a row. He was succeeded as party leader of the Labour party and Prime Minister by Gordon Brown, who decided not to hold a snap election and suffered politically for it.

The immunity from suit of the French and British Heads of State

The French President, like the British Monarch, is Head of State, guardian of the independence of justice though not fount of justice, commander-in-chief of the armed forces, guardian of the indivisible, secular,[29] democratic and social French Republic. The British monarch since 1534 is the Supreme Governor of the Church of England. The French Head of State is not hereditary but directly elected by the people. Unlike the British monarch, who has to swear the Coronation Oath,[30] and unlike other presidents like the US President, the French President does not have to swear an oath on taking office. His acts cannot be reviewed by the courts, at least not while in office, as is also the case for the British monarch. Like the Queen, he is immune from suit[31] and legal process, though not from criminal proceedings. It is now clearly enshrined in the constitution under article 67 that the President is not accountable for the acts committed as President of the Republic, which can be perfectly understandable as the President embodies the French nation.

Yet, were the President to commit crimes against humanity or war crimes, he would not be immune from suit and could even be tried by the International Criminal Court, as is stated under article 53-2 of the constitution of the Fifth Republic. His status as Head of State would not protect him, and this is very much the result of the progress made in international law thanks to the original 1998 landmark decision of the Law Lords of the Appellate Committee of the House of Lords in the Pinochet case.[32] Their initial ruling lifted his immunity as Head of State, which made Pinochet liable for crimes against humanity. The Law Lords ruled by a majority of three to two that immunity applied only to acts which international law recognised as being among the functions of a Head of State. Through their ruling, they contributed to the development of international justice and showed the importance of judicial cooperation between countries. Thus French and British judges exchange legal knowledge and work together effectively. Save under exceptional circumstances like High Treason in the past, while in office, the French President is not treated like any other citizen. It means that the key constitutional principle of equality before the law does not apply to the President of the French Republic. But when no longer in office, he reverts to his status as ordinary citizen – or almost, as he still benefits from a number of security privileges linked to his former status, including bodyguards – and thus can be prosecuted. Thus former President Jacques Chirac was given a suspended sentence in 2011 of two years for embezzlement and breach of trust. More recently, in July 2014, for the first time ever, a former French President, Nicolas Sarkozy, was held in custody for questioning over alleged unlawful financing of his 2007 presidential campaign.

Political circumstances may lead, and already have led, the Head of State to perform functions that go beyond his or her powers allocated by the constitution or by convention. The Head of State is supposed to be above party politics both in France – as was seen previously – and even more in the United Kingdom, where he/she is not elected but hereditary.

The French President's political interference and the lobbying practices of the monarch-in-waiting

In France the President tends to behave more and more like a party leader. The British monarch for her part unusually indicated her satisfaction at the survival of the United Kingdom as a union of four nations in the wake of the 2014 referendum on the independence of Scotland. What is more, in case of a new hung Parliament, the British monarch may be invited to play a more active role in the appointment of a new Prime Minister. It is not so much that she would go beyond her powers, but she would simply use her prerogative powers of consultation to the full. In fact, the current monarch, Queen Elizabeth II, has always made a point of fulfilling her duties and of being irreproachable in her private and public behaviour. The one who is more likely to cause problems once on the throne is the heir to the current monarch. Indeed, Prince Charles's active lobbying on such issues as alternative medicine and traditional architecture has raised the question of a future monarch refusing to abide by constitutional conventions.

Prince Charles lobbied the democratically elected government, including the Prime Minister himself, Tony Blair, in 2004 and 2005 to try to influence legislation via a series of personal letters on a wide range of issues such as health, education, the environment and defence. The question of lobbying itself is a serious matter that the Conservative/Liberal Democrat coalition of David Cameron tried to tackle in the 2010–15 Parliament. Even if the phenomenon of lobbying in the UK has not yet reached the scope of that in the United States, it has already put British legislators under huge pressure, giving access to Parliament to all kinds of groups that promote interests that do not always serve the general public interest. While it is important to protect the expression of the plurality of opinions and to enable the various sections of society to use Parliament as a forum to discuss important contemporary social issues, an Act was passed – the Transparency of Lobbying, Non-Party Campaigning and Trade Union Administration Act 2014 – to try to better regulate lobbying and make it compulsory for lobbies to register and declare their interests. In such a context, the persistent lobbying from the heir to the throne appeared as even more inappropriate.

Charles has in a way interfered with politics by putting pressure on ministers and Members of Parliament, and trying to influence legislation. The Conservative Attorney- General, Dominic Grieve, tried to put forward Prince Charles's right to privacy and the confidentiality of his correspondence with government ministers as a legal argument to plead the cause of the heir to the throne and therefore prevent the publication of his letters. However, such an argument was rejected by the courts after a legal battle that lasted ten years to allow a journalist of *The Guardian*, using the Information Act 2000, to obtain the release of the letters written by Prince Charles.

Apart from the need to comply with the enacted legislation, the Information Act 2000,[33] this legal case raises the question of the status and role of the heir to the throne. If the current constitutional settlement under the latest guidance of the Cabinet Manual defines the status and powers of the monarch, there is a gap in the law regarding the heir to the throne. He is only mentioned in the 1701 Act of Settlement, recently amended by the Succession to the Crown Act 2013. In the eighteenth century, the political relations of George I and II with their sons and heirs were highly contentious. As is stated in the Cabinet Manual, 'on the death of the previous Sovereign the heir succeeds without any further ceremony … and can reign without any further ceremony.' The only other provision is for the temporary absence of the Queen from the country or when she 'is temporarily incapacitated'.

In the latter case, 'his or her functions are delegated to Counsellors of State' who include the heir to the throne. Except for those few provisions, the heir to the throne has no legal existence before access to the throne, in the sense that he does not have constitutional rights, unlike the reigning monarch. Thus, the three main rights – to consult, to warn and to advise – identified by Walter Bagehot, while applying to the reigning monarch, do not apply to the heir to the throne. Yet, *de facto*, he cannot be considered as any other ordinary citizen for the monarch-in-waiting is already expected to behave as the monarch he is to become. The same self-restraint and political neutrality are constitutionally expected from him. The question which worries constitutional experts is whether Prince Charles would behave differently, that is to say with more self-restraint, once on the throne.

Among the prerogatives of the monarch is the Royal Assent to legislation, which has become a formality since Queen Anne famously refused to give it in 1708 on the advice of her ministers. A comparison has sometimes been made with the French President, who under article 10 of the 1958 constitution is in charge of promulgating laws finally adopted by parliament within fifteen days of their transmission to the government. He can also ask parliament to reconsider the whole text or some of its provisions within that lapse of time without any possible refusal on the part of parliament. Though at first sight it appears as a huge prerogative, possibly encroaching on the powers of parliament, it is mainly a way of making the laws final and enforceable.

In the UK, one might wonder what might happen if the current monarch or heir to the throne refused to give her/his Royal Assent. It would trigger a constitutional crisis, as a non-elected Head of State would be blocking the laws passed by the democratically elected Members of Parliament and thus opposing the will of the people or their representatives.

Highly unlikely as it is, this could lead one day to a constitutional crisis involving the monarchy. Until now the monarchy has been spared by constitutional reform, but this might change. A national constitutional convention about the future of the UK as a Union should include the monarchy, bearing in mind that the Scots themselves wanted an independent Scotland to be a constitutional monarchy and not a republic. While Scottish nationalists were determined to repeal the union of parliaments they expressed their will to keep the current Queen as their Head of State (which seems paradoxical at first sight, especially for an external observer coming from a republic). Besides, in the last few years, several constitutional monarchies of the European continent have experienced serious institutional crisis followed by a series of abdications,[34] the most serious one involving King Juan Carlos of Spain in 2014, a country which like the UK is faced with the rise of separatist movements.

What is really at stake is not so much the personal behaviour of the heir to the throne but the future of the monarchy, the impact it can have on the monarchy itself as an institution. Of all the British institutions, the monarchy was the one which seemed to have retained some of its prestige and popularity. It stayed on in London during the blitz, it spoke for its people on VE Day. Unlike other constitutional monarchies in Europe, the British monarchy seems stable. The current monarch, Queen Elizabeth II entering the sixty-fourth year of her reign, has become the longest-serving monarch in the United Kingdom and in Europe. She has survived the Second World War, the fall of the Empire, the crisis surrounding the death of Lady Diana, the near-dismemberment of her kingdom by the 2014 referendum on the independence of Scotland. The line of succession is secured, the Duke and Duchess of Cambridge having produced a future heir to the throne, Prince George in 2013; he now has a sister Princess Charlotte born in 2015. The French by contrast, who beheaded their own monarch, Louis XVI, in 1793 after a brief attempt at a constitutional monarchy and never really recovered from it, have built their Republic on monarchical traditions and are fascinated by the British monarchy.[35] So one might wonder, together with Walter Bagehot, what the secret of the longevity of the British monarchy is, and beyond that of the British constitution itself. It is rooted not just at the centre of the constitution but in the national psyche.

Yet, the 26 March 2015 ruling of the UK Supreme Court[36] clearing the way for the publication of Prince Charles's secret letters to ministers might serve the cause of constitutional reform involving the monarchy this time. The changes introduced in other European constitutional monarchies in the last few years might also further the cause of a constitutional debate over the British monarchy before waiting for an open constitutional crisis. However, in codified constitutions, there are provisions which cannot in any way be affected by constitutional change as they deal with and protect the fundamental nature of the regime, as is the case for the French Republic (under article 89 of the constitution)[37] or the federal state in Germany. France for its part has enshrined in its constitution the main characteristics of its Republic and they cannot in any way be amended.

The drafters of constitutions knew that trying to alter them might affect the whole balance and thus trigger a chain reaction. In the case of the United Kingdom, trying to alter the nature of the regime, or at least the constitutional status of the monarch, might be a kind of Pandora's Box, raising other serious questions such as the disestablishment of the Church of England. Unlike France, where a clear separation between Church and State was officially introduced by a law back in 1905, the Anglican Church is still the official established Church, for all its dwindling numbers. If prayers have been abolished in British schools, they are still present in Parliament, before each sitting day of the House of Lords. It is also the case at the opening of the official legal year, as there are also prayers for Her Majesty's judges. Wales disestablished the Church in 1920 and Scotland has its own Presbyterian independent Church, but it would be more difficult to disestablish the Church of England. It would mean abolishing the spiritual Lords in the Upper House of Parliament, and also further altering the Succession to the Throne Act 2013, which has already abolished discrimination based on gender but not religious discrimination against non-Protestants. As such a constitutional change involving the British monarchy would be a fundamental one, it would have to be put to the people themselves by referendum, as France did in 1962 when French people were asked whether they wanted the President to be directly elected.

The case of Australia is also very informative as Australians were asked in a referendum in 1999 whether they wanted to keep the British monarch – who is neither Australian nor elected – as their Head of State or whether they would like a Head of State elected by Parliament. They decided to keep the British monarch. Indeed, to the question whether they wanted their constitution to be altered to establish the Commonwealth of Australia as a Republic with the Queen being replaced by a President appointed by a two-thirds majority of the national parliament, 45.13 per cent voted 'Yes' and 54.87 per cent 'No', so the proposal was not carried out. The Fabian Society in its report on the monarchy more than ten years ago concluded that the constitutional reform agenda of the Blair government had been 'facilitated by the reassuring presence of an unchanging monarchy'.[38] Thus the British monarchy has remained on the whole unchanged.

Conclusion

In both France and the United Kingdom, there is a need for the depoliticisation of the Head of State. If the current British monarch has a high sense of duty and has always been careful to act within the boundaries of her royal prerogatives, the heir to the throne is more prone to express his own political views. As explained by David Starkey,[39] even if the 1215

Magna Carta was to be short-lived and its legal impact far more limited than the 1225 drastically redrafted version, it succeeded in keeping under control an unpredictable monarch, King John, who ruled the country in a very arbitrary way, making his whim the law. Eight hundred years later, in 2015, in far less momentous circumstances, Prince Charles was defeated not by rebellious barons but by judges – of the Information Tribunal, Court of Appeal and UK Supreme Court – who ordered him to comply with the Information Act 2000 and disclose letters he had written as a means of lobbying ministerial departments. This raises the question of a non-elected, non-accountable Head of State too much involved in party politics and thus not sufficiently representative of the whole nation. In the same way, the French democratically elected yet non-accountable-to-parliament Head of State has become too politicised to represent the French nation as a whole. Besides, both the French and British Heads of State still have much political discretion, notably over the nomination of the Prime Minister, which is an anomaly in a democracy. Among the constitutional changes which could be introduced to curtail their political discretion, a constitutional or a statutory provision concerning the recruitment process of the Prime Minister could introduce more transparency and thereby reinforce the role of the Head of State as well.

Notes

1. Jean-Jacques Rousseau, *The Social Contract or Principles of Political Right* (1762), translated into English by G. D. H. Cole (Markham, ON: Fitzhenry and Whiteside, 1973).
2. Philip Norton, *The Constitution in Flux* (Oxford: Blackwell, 1982), p. 31.
3. Walter Bagehot, *The English Constitution* [1867] (introduction by Richard Crossman) (London: Fontana Press, 1963), p. 61.
4. Stéphane Pinon (ed.), *Le droit constitutionnel d'Adhémar Esmein* (Paris: Montchrestien, 2009), p. 33.
5. Guy Carcassonne, *La Constitution* (Paris: Seuil, 2013), p. 27.
6. Bastien François, *La VIe République: Pourquoi, Comment* (Paris: Les Petits Matins, 2015), p. 34.
7. Michel Debré's speech before the Council of State on 27 August 1958, in Didier Maus (ed.), *Les grands textes de la pratique constitutionnelle de la Ve République* (Paris: La Documentation française, 1998), pp.2–8.
8. Bagehot, *The English Constitution*, p. 61.
9. It is a statutory code of practice clarifying the constitutional position, role and responsibility of the Prime Minister.
10. This nomination takes the form of a decree signed by the President alone.

11. Dominique Rousseau, 'La Ve République dynamitée', *Le Monde* (13 June 2008).
12. Montesquieu, *De L'Esprit des Lois*, foreword by Victor Goldschmidt (Paris: Flammarion, 1979).
13. The French Upper House is also elected, but by direct universal suffrage, so it is considered as less democratic than the National Assembly.
14. Yet French judges are not elected, unlike American state judges, for example.
15. Maurice Duverger, 'A New Political System Model: Semi-Presidential Government', *European Journal of Political Research*, 8/2 (1980), 165–87.
16. Bagehot, *The English Constitution*, pp. 60–1.
17. February 2011, written evidence submitted by Paul Webb on 'Issues and Questions; Prime Minister, Prerogative and Power'.
18. *A New Magna Carta?*, House of Commons Political and Constitutional Reform Committee, Second Report of Session 2014–2015, HC463 (London: The Stationery Office, 10 July 2014), p. 290.
19. *The Cabinet Manual: A Guide to Laws, Conventions and Rules on the Operation of Government*, first edn (October 2011), pp. 21–2.
20. *The Cabinet Manual*, p. 22.
21. Bagehot, *The English Constitution*, p. 65.
22. Carcassonne, *La Constitution*, p. 24.
23. He was the second Socialist President in the history of the Fifth Republic, after François Mitterrand.
24. Following the departure of Laurent Fabius as Foreign Minister, President Hollande recalled his former Prime Minister Jean-Marc Ayrault, well known for his expertise in Franco-German diplomacy, on 26 April 2016.
25. He is a former rival of Hollande as he had fought the Socialist primaries in the run-up to the 2012 presidential election.
26. They are also the ones who elect French senators, as they are indirectly elected.
27. He is the only one to be elected by direct universal suffrage together with the 577 members of the National Assembly
28. See Jacques Julliard's article in *Le Monde* (5/6 October 2014), 'Vive le régime présidentiel'.
29. Secularism is a key characteristic of the French Republic and central to French identity, though not always well understood and accepted abroad.
30. As is stated in *The Cabinet Manual*, p. 8, 'Under the Coronation Oath (1689), the Sovereign swears by oath to govern the people of the UK and the Commonwealth realms.'
31. He cannot be put under investigation or asked to testify while in office.
32. *R v Bow Street Metropolitan Stipendiary Magistrate, ex parte Pinochet Ugarte* (N1), 25 November 1998.
33. It was introduced by the first Blair government as part of his constitutional reform agenda and since then amended by the 2010 Act.

34. Queen Beatrix of the Netherlands, King Albert of Belgium and King Juan Carlos of Spain in 2014.
35. See the article published by *The Economist* (14 June 2014), entitled 'Why the French love Britain's Queen'.
36. *R (on the application of Evans) and another (respondents) v Attorney General (appellant)*, 26 March 2015.
37. Article 89, in its paragraph 5, states that 'the Republican form of government shall not be the object of any amendment.'
38. The Report of the Fabian Commission, *The Future of the Monarchy*, first edn (London: Fabian Society, July 2003), p. 38.
39. See David Starkey's book entitled *Magna Carta: The True Story behind the Charter* (London: Hodder & Stoughton, 2015).

Chapter Three

Emancipating and Reforming Parliaments in France and the United Kingdom

This chapter focuses on what makes parliaments in the United Kingdom and France the way they are and how constitutional change has affected this central institution in both countries, where the regime is still officially defined as parliamentary. Though the drafters of the French 1958 constitution opted for a parliamentary regime, they introduced at the same time a series of constitutional instruments to limit drastically the role of parliament so as to avoid the misuse of their powers by the parliamentary assemblies which plagued the previous republics. They allowed members of parliament to fulfil their functions but only within a very rigid restrictive framework more commonly known in French law as rationalised parliamentarianism, defined by one scholar as 'constitutional provisions allowing the government to mastermind the work of the assemblies'.[1] Thus, to strengthen the executive branch and guarantee its stability, the parliamentary yearly session was divided into two fairly short periods of three months each, the parliamentary agenda and the legislative process itself were put under government control, the use of no-confidence motions was strictly regulated and the number of standing committees was limited to six. However, the Senate, which has always been attached to its specific rules of procedure and to its independence tried to bypass rationalised parliamentarianism by resorting to customary rules and conventions as often as it could.[2] Fifty years afterwards, such strict limitations imposed on the French parliament were to be seriously challenged by the Balladur Committee which denounced rationalised parliamentarianism as a way of straitjacketing parliament.

Rationalised parliamentarianism: its decline in France and its emergence in Britain

This attempt by the drafters of the 1958 Constitution at keeping parliament strictly under control can be contrasted with the long tradition of the uncontrolled Westminster Parliament. The two reflect a very different perception of parliament. In France, a certain suspicion towards parliament and parliamentarians, as well as the fear of the return of an Assembly regime, can explain such drastic rules imposed on the French legislature. Conversely, in the United Kingdom any attempt at controlling Parliament, especially when it comes from abroad, notably from the European Court of Human Rights, has always been highly resented as it is considered a challenge to national sovereignty itself. This reaction can be fairly easily understood given the nature of British sovereignty, as the latter lies in Parliament. Memories of the seventeenth-century civil wars between King and Parliament colour this view: King Charles's head casts a long shadow! So the French principle of rationalised parliamentarianism was – at least until the Fixed Term Parliament Act 2011 – alien to British parliamentary law.

Under the new drafting of article 24 of the 1958 constitution initiated by the 2008 constitutional change, the parliament of the French Republic is composed of two chambers, the National Assembly and the Senate, both elected by universal suffrage, directly for the former and indirectly for the latter, both representing the French nation. The constitutional statute of 23 July 2008, based on the main lines of the Balladur Report, secured the supremacy of the constitution itself, including over parliament, to the detriment of parliamentary sovereignty, as the French legislature cannot go beyond the powers and competences given by it to the constitution, and as the law is now considered as the expression of the will of the people provided that 'it respects the constitution.'[3] Thus, though the 2008 constitutional change officially aimed at strengthening the French parliament, in fact it contributed to putting an end to parliamentary sovereignty, understood in France as the absolute primacy of the law as the expression of the will of the people, derived from Jean-Jacques Rousseau's *The Social Contract* in 1762 and then enshrined in article 6 of the 1789 Declaration of the Right of Man and Citizen. The long-standing Republican tradition of self-regulated Houses of parliament had already been undermined by the original article 61, paragraph 1, of the 1958 constitution[4] according to which the standing orders of the two chambers cannot be implemented without the go-ahead of the Constitutional Council in charge of checking their compatibility with the constitution beforehand.

By contrast, in the United Kingdom, there is still no higher authority than Parliament other than European law. The United Kingdom Parliament, defined by the Cabinet Manual as 'a sovereign Parliament, supreme to all other government institutions'[5] consists not only of two Houses – the House of Commons, directly elected by the people, described by Walter Bagehot as 'the people's House' or the 'efficient part of the constitution', and the mainly nominated House of Lords or the 'dignified part' of the constitution – but also of the Sovereign, as the country is still a constitutional monarchy. All the laws are voted in the name of and with the official approval of the British monarch as it is encapsulated in the well-established notion of the Crown in Parliament.[6] If the British constitution has significantly changed since Bagehot's much celebrated but also much criticised analysis, it still rests on two core principles which are parliamentary sovereignty and the 'supremacy of the law of the land'[7] or rule of law rooted in the original 1215 Magna Carta.[8] The rebel barons who imposed 'the Charter of Runnymede' – as Magna Carta was originally called – on King John limiting royal authority by law acted as the representatives of the community of the realm. Thus, in the United Kingdom there has been a long tradition of self-government very early on as it can be traced back to the thirteenth century, whereas France has always been considered as a highly centralised country in the wake of Jacobinism.[9]

In 2015, declared 'the Year of Parliament', the United Kingdom celebrated not only the 800th anniversary of Magna Carta but also the 750th anniversary of its very first Parliament. Sir Robert Worcester, the chairman of the Magna Carta 800th Anniversary Commemoration Committee, wrote that 'as any parliamentarian will be aware, its acknowledgement of limits on the authority of the monarch allowed the establishment of the power of Parliament.'[10] The 2015 British Parliament for its part was faced with a variety of key constitutional issues including further devolution for Scotland, Wales and Northern Ireland, English Votes for English Laws and decentralisation in England as potential answers to the English or West Lothian Question, and the United Kingdom's membership of the European Union (and therefore indirectly its relationship with France), the protection of human rights with the proposal of a British Bill of Rights and ultimately, the future of the United Kingdom as a Union state. Ongoing constitutional change made all of them more complicated.

Reactivating conventions and constitutional practice in French and English parliamentary law

The English and the French parliaments did not originate as deliberative assemblies but rather as judicial courts,[11] delivering justice on behalf of the King. In France, in the *ancien régime*, *les parlements* were powerful lawcourts in which royal decrees were registered and which rendered justice according to rules, customs and practices that varied in the different parts of the kingdom. One of the most famous of those *parlements* apart from the one located in Paris was the *parlement* of Bordeaux[12]. Not only was it famous because of its distinguished presiding officer, Montesquieu – who was the fourth person in his family to hold such a high legal office – but as Alain Juppé,[13] the Mayor of Bordeaux explained, 'It was one of the most prestigious institutions of Guyenne',[14] being judicially powerful and politically very influential also. What Montesquieu did not like for his part was not so much the privileged social background of the members, who belonged to the gentry – as he was one of them – but more their obsession with procedural rules. In any case, the French revolutionaries were determined to abolish the *parlements* and did so with the law of 16–24 August 1790, which was to shape the French system of courts to this day.

In the United Kingdom, this judicial past of Parliament was deeply rooted in the House of Lords, the first of the two chambers from a historic viewpoint. What made it very much an exception among other Upper Houses is that until 2009 it had officially both a judicial and a legislative role – in total opposition to the views of Montesquieu, for whom legislators ought not to be judges at the same time. In 1876 professional judges joined the Appellate Committee of the House of Lords as Lords of Appeal in Ordinary – more commonly known as Law Lords – becoming life peers by convention to hear cases of general public interest in the last resort, as will be seen in the next chapter.

However, if the British and French parliaments were originally courts of justice, their functions have evolved considerably, and even more so in the last few years. Unlike the French constitution, which now clearly states that 'Parliament shall pass statutes. It shall monitor the acts of the government. It shall assess public policies',[15] the functions of the British Parliament – except for a few statutes like the 1911 and 1949 Parliament Acts – are still mainly defined by conventions and constitutional practice. For, as David Feldman wrote, 'Unlike the legislatures of almost all other democracies, the parliament of the United Kingdom does not derive its existence or its powers from a written constitution.'[16] However, one should not underestimate the importance of the fully written standing orders of both Houses of the British Parliament[17] – which are regularly updated – as well as the *Treatise* of Erskine May on parliamentary procedures, which is used as a fundamental parliamentary code, not to say a kind of Bible for Parliament's clerks and MPs, taking pride of place near the dispatch box in the chamber. In addition, the Cabinet Manual acting as an authoritative though not legally binding guide – already providing some form of codification to the British constitution – defines the main functions of the United Kingdom Parliament as, 'controlling national expenditure and taxation; making law; scrutinising executive action; being the source from which the Government is drawn; and debating the issues of the day'.[18]

In the case of France, the importance of unwritten rules and conventions should not be underestimated either in spite of the existence of a codified constitution, and they are in fact one of the main characteristics of French parliamentary law, as opposed to other branches of the law. The case law of the French Constitutional Council has even become one of the main sources of parliamentary law in France today.

As is well known, the founding father of parliamentary law in the United Kingdom, whose key writings contributed to the official recognition and prestige of this branch of the law, is Thomas Erskine May, a House of Commons clerk, whose landmark book *Treatise on the Law, Privileges, Procedures and Usage of Parliament*, published in 1844, provides an analysis of parliamentary practice, in a way making up for the absence of a codified constitution. His French counterpart Eugène Pierre, the secretary-general of the then House of Deputies, published his own parliament's guiding principles under the name *Traité de droit politique, électoral et parlementaire*, some years afterwards in 1893. In a country like France where much importance is given to the codification of the law, parliamentary law appears as an exception, given that it is mainly based on constitutional practice, conventions and precedent.[19] Thus, one of the most famous parliamentary conventions in France is the equivalent of the United Kingdom Question Time or 'Questions to the Government' – *questions au gouvernement* – informally introduced by President Giscard d'Estaing in 1974, then becoming a well-established convention before being enshrined in law and finally officially incorporated in the constitution in August 1995.[20]

Even if 'Parliament does not have a mission statement' but is 'a reactive, unpredictable organism rather than an organisation', in the words of Robert Rogers,[21] parliament in France and in the United Kingdom is first identified as the official law-making body. Though English common law is often described *de facto* as a judge-made law because of the importance of judicial decisions in the evolution of the law, Parliament, as in France, is still the primary source of legislative authority. Even in a country like France, which has a codified constitution setting the rules which govern the relationships between the institutions of the state, it is no longer clear where the competences of the executive and the legislative lie in the law-making process because of the growing importance of delegated legislation and the substantive government amendments to bills. In the United Kingdom, an interesting proposal officially called 'a concordat between Parliament and government' was put forward by the Hansard Society to try to clarify the relationships and responsibilities of the executive and the legislature, including the legislative process[22] in the absence of a codified constitution.

If voting laws is generally thought to be the main activity of parliaments, the other main function consists in checking and controlling the executive – the 'faculty of criticising the executive',[23] in the words of Walter Bagehot – as the accountability of the government before Parliament or at least before the democratically elected chamber is at the core of any parliamentary regime. As David Feldman explained, 'Perhaps the major function of Parliament, given the dominance of the executive in its legislative activity, is the scrutiny of government, its policy and its administration',[24] and it is now very much the role of the Opposition[25]. In the United Kingdom, there is undoubtedly a strong awareness of the key role of the Opposition, which benefits from a proper official status. This is still not the case in France in spite of the progress made in the wake of the Balladur Report.

Yet, one of the key functions of the British Parliament, unlike the French one, where holding a ministerial office is incompatible with being a member of parliament, is that it forms the government, since ministers, starting with the Prime Minister, come from within its ranks – today mainly the House of Commons. As Walter Bagehot wrote, 'The relation of Parliament, and especially of the House of Commons, to the executive government is the specific peculiarity of our constitution.'[26]

This also explains why the British Lower House is bigger than the French National Assembly whose size is now limited to 577 members. The British Boundary Commission in 2016 proposed reducing the Commons membership from 650 to 600. Walter Bagehot went so far as to describe the House of Commons as 'a reservoir of Cabinet ministers'.[27] The absence of a clear separation between the executive and the legislative, as well as the kinship between ministers and MPs, immediately raises the question of the independence and effectiveness of parliamentary control over the government in the United Kingdom as they are largely the same people.[28] If it means that ministers can sit and vote in the Commons, 'it also means that ministers remain subject to the rules of parliament', as experts of the all-party law reform and human rights organisation Justice observed.[29]

The French parliament for its part has its own specific duties, as in addition to 'voting the law and controlling governmental action' – under article 24 of the 1958 constitution – it is also expected 'to assess public policies'. As Sophie Boyron wrote, 'the latter function is not so much a new function as a different understanding of parliamentary control', less perceived as a way of sanctioning the government than introducing more transparency – a specific committee has been set up to that effect, the Committee of Public Evaluation. She described 'a new culture of control and assessment'.[30] Thus, since 1999, within the French Finance Committee, there has been an Assessment and Monitoring Committee modelled on the National Audit Office of the Westminster Parliament. Yet, the latter is closer to the French *Cour des Comptes*, which takes part in the evaluation of public policies, though its main task consists in auditing the use of public funds in France – acting entirely independently of the government and parliament. However, far from being a specifically French system, a fairly similar type of parliamentary assessment process has developed in the United Kingdom, even if it is not so much about government action but rather about government implementation of legislation once passed by Parliament. Indeed, under the Cabinet Manual, once legislation has been passed, ministers are expected to publish 'a post-legislative scrutiny memorandum' including a preliminary assessment of how the Act is working in practice relative to its original objectives.[31] Bertrand Mathieu, the President of the French Association of Constitutional Law, though acknowledging the improvement introduced by the 2008 constitutional change as far as strengthening parliamentary control over the French government and assessing public policies is concerned, nevertheless regrets the absence of post-legislative scrutiny in France.[32]

An original yet still strategic function that parliaments hold, whatever the nature of the regime, is to vote the budget or give its assent to the budget – 'the right of imposing taxes upon the people and of voting money'.[33] One of the key and very few surviving provisions of Magna Carta (1215) in English common law is no taxation without consent (at that time baronial consent) – 'the consent of the realm in return for certain taxation'.[34] The Bill of Rights of 1689 upheld the principle under which the Crown cannot levy taxes without parliamentary consent. This function rests in the Commons alone, which regards it as its 'financial privilege'.

Unlike the French Senate, the House of Lords has been deprived of this strategic power by the Act of Parliament of 1911 to prevent it from blocking government budgets as it did with David Lloyd George's 'People's Budget' of 30 November 1909.[35] The latter provided for an increase of taxes on alcohol and tobacco and also of inheritance tax. Graduated income tax went up shortly, while a higher 'supertax' was introduced. But the most controversial provision for the Lords was the introduction of land taxes, notably in the incremental value of urban land, as a great number of members of the House were landowners. The 1911 Parliament Act fundamentally altered the position of the House of Lords in the constitution, even if there were at the time debates among ministers over whether to turn the absolute veto of the House of Lords into a delaying power or to introduce a mechanism for resolving disputes between the two Houses, as is the case in France with the Joint Mediation Committee of the Senate and the National Assembly (*la commission mixte paritaire*). The second option was finally dropped. Since then, the power to vote money bills has become the 'financial privilege of the House of Commons'. As is stated in the first blueprint of the House of Commons select committee report on a *New Magna Carta*, 'The House of Commons alone may propose alterations in financial charges on public funds taxes or other charges.'[36]

Both the United Kingdom[37] and France share a well-established tradition of bicameralism, though both countries are still unitary – or union – states, as opposed to federal states where bicameralism finds its natural *raison d'être* with the second chamber representing federate states, as in the United States or *Länder* as in Germany.

Reviving bicameralism in the United Kingdom and France

Unlike in Britain, the constitutional history of bicameralism in France was not a smooth unbroken process, owing to the deeply ingrained perception of national sovereignty as one and indivisible. The very first constitution of 1791 – considered as one of the most perfect French constitutions[38] – only included a single-chamber parliament. Bicameralism in France was initially introduced not so much for positive reasons but rather as a tool to fight the excesses of single-chamber parliaments[39] and as a way to weaken the legislative branch by dividing it into two Houses. France had to wait until the constitutional laws of 1875 to experience permanent bicameralism, even if twice in more recent history, in the referendums of April 1946 and April 1969, the existence of the French Senate was jeopardised. In both cases French people, however, showed their attachment to a bicameral parliament. The Senate of the Fifth Republic[40] finds its origin in the Senate of the Third Republic,[41] a regime which lasted almost sixty-five years and led to the foundation of key fundamental rights and civil liberties. Just like the contemporary House of Lords, the Senate of the Fifth Republic – in line with the Upper House of the Third Republic – has focused on the defence of civil liberties and human rights. By contrast, bicameralism emerged very early on in the United Kingdom and, once established, was never really challenged, with the major exception of the 'English Republic' or Commonwealth and Protectorate under Oliver Cromwell and his successors from 1649 to 1660, which saw the temporary abolition of the monarchy and the House of Lords.

Undemocratically elected yet more legitimate second chambers

Both countries have an unequal or asymmetrical type of bicameralism, where the House elected by direct universal suffrage – elected by the people and representing the people – respectively the House of Commons and the French National Assembly – holds a dominant position except when constitutional change is at stake. There is a strong link between the representative function of a House and its legitimacy: the more representative of the people it is, the stronger its legitimacy. As Jean Mastias and Jean Grangé point out, 'today a parliamentary House is referred to as second for it is more remote from democratic legitimacy than the other House'[42] – they speak of 'the original sin of second chambers'[43] – but also because its ability to hold the government to account is more limited. Thus second chambers like the French Senate and the British House of Lords cannot overthrow the government, and as a counterpart they cannot be dissolved by the President of the French Republic or, in the United Kingdom, by the government.

They have to find a compromise between being representative and being efficient, but in any case there is no easy way for second chambers in unitary states. So they have to find a different type of representation or be different and forge their own identity and role in the national institutional framework. The Lords' virtues stem from the upper House being different in character from the Commons. It has certainly been the case for the French Senate, which has experienced a long quest searching for its own identity until fairly recently. One of the main specialists of the French Senate, Dr Verdier, describes the Senate as 'a House which alerts public opinion, its mission being to raise public awareness regarding gaps in the law, fundamental principles and key problems affecting society'.[44]

Not only can bicameralism work if the two chambers are in some way or other different, but each House must agree to fulfil its own competences without trying to encroach on the prerogatives of the other. This is particularly important for a country like the United Kingdom where there is no codified constitution clearly defining and regulating the relations between the two Houses of Parliament. A closer look at the British and French types of bicameralism shows significant differences as to its origin and nature. Under the classification established by Jean Grangé,[45] the British kind of bicameralism falls under the category of aristocratic bicameralism (at least it was originally), whereas France, for is part, has a form of bicameralism where the Upper House 'has a moderating role' – in line with the thinking of the French philosopher Montesquieu.

In the United Kingdom, though until then the two Houses had been formally co-equal, the 1911 Parliament Act entrenched an asymmetrical type of bicameralism which emerged with the extension of the franchise in the nineteenth and twentieth centuries. As stated in Erskine May, 'the House of Commons possesses the most important power vested in any branch of the legislature, the right of imposing taxes upon the people and of voting money for the public service',[46] whereas the House of Lords has been reduced to little more than a rubber-stamp chamber, at least in financial matters. As is written in the Cabinet Manual, 'The role of the House of Lords in relation to taxation and expenditure is to agree, not to initiate or amend.'[47] However today, the relations of Lords and Commons are in some flux regarding the interpretation of financial privilege, starting with the definition of money bills, which need to be certified as such by the Speaker of the House of Commons, all the more as almost every bill involves expenditure of some kind. Some commentators claim that the coalition government's definition of financial privilege in 2010–15 went far beyond what Asquith's Liberal government had intended in 1911.

In the same way, the constitution of the Fifth Republic includes a bicameral parliament which is also based on the ultimate supremacy of the National Assembly – the democratic legitimacy of which is stronger than that of the Senate. This is most certainly the case over financial and social security financing bills, as the National Assembly is given priority in the scrutiny of such bills[48] and is also allotted more time than the Senate over such bills in the legislative process, whereas the Upper House shares powers with the National Assembly over all other bills in equal terms.

As for the contemporary House of Lords, it has been a half-reformed chamber in a never-ending transitional phase since the House of Lords Act 1999. One of the first functions of the Senate of the Fifth Republic, by contrast, is to represent the grand electors – the 162,000 members of the senatorial Electoral College – who have themselves been elected at the local level. If the Senate, like the National Assembly, in fact represents the whole nation, it also embodies local interests at the national level in Paris, since the grand electors are people with a local mandate who work close to French citizens in the field. The other main mission of the Senate is to represent territories, as it is an institution deeply rooted in local territories, especially remote rural France (*la France profonde*).

In the wake of Bagehot's famous analysis, the House of Commons was traditionally considered as an 'efficient' part of the constitution in the British psyche before progressively losing its sense of prestige and credibility. This happened most notably with the MPs' expenses scandal in 2009, which tainted their reputation for a long time. Both the House of Commons, and the House of Lords to a certain extent, have thus become less and less dignified with the various revelations concerning the financial and sexual behaviour of some of their members – 'a few bad apples' in the words of Baroness Boothroyd. Parliament could end up being neither 'efficient' nor 'dignified'. So, together with Iain McLean, one might wonder 'what is wrong'[49] with the United Kingdom Parliament, though the latter used the expression to describe the British constitution rather than a specified institution.

The Labour Party in its 1997 manifesto identified a House of Commons in need of modernisation while arguing that the House of Lords could gain in efficiency, democracy and representativeness. Interestingly, priority was given to the reform of the House of Lords, and especially to the composition of the Upper Chamber. One of the shortcomings of the reform proposed by the Labour party in 1997 was to focus exclusively on the composition of the House of Lords without thinking of the potential impact it might have on its powers and constitutional position – a more democratic House logically would have been expected to claim more powers. Another flaw of the reform was to consider reforming the House of Lords and reforming the House of Commons as two separate measures without taking into account how each might affect the working of the other House and the relationship between the two. The only fundamental requirement that reformers had to respect was to maintain the supremacy of the House of Commons. The relations between the two Houses are essentially based on conventions, on subtle unwritten rules, the golden rule once again being that the supremacy of the democratically elected House representing the people be unaffected by constitutional change. Besides, unlike the French parliament, there is neither a joint mediation committee nor an official dispute resolution mechanism to settle serious disagreements over legislation between the two houses. The

1911 and 1949 Parliament Acts were rarely used to delay legislation for two years and one year respectively.

Unlike the French 2008 constitutional reform, the reform of the Westminster Parliament initiated by the Labour government in 1997 was not part of a wider reappraisal of the relations between the government and Parliament. It was just part of a series of self-contained reforms without any major guiding principle or vision, except the general attempt at democratising and modernising British institutions. By contrast, one of the main merits of the 2008 constitutional reform which followed the Balladur Report was to avoid the trap of piecemeal measures, considering the task as a coherent whole with one key objective: rebalancing French institutions starting with the relationships between the executive and parliament. Yet the 2008 constitutional change did not provide for a new composition of either the National Assembly or the Senate. As experts of the Balladur Committee argued, 'the main way of re-balancing French institutions is by strengthening parliament.'[50] They were highly critical of the restrictive measures imposed on parliament by the drafters of the 1958 constitution, which, though originally justified by the abuses of the previous Republics, were no longer adapted in 2008 with the all-powerful omnipresent executive. Members of the Balladur Committee went as far as writing in their report: 'The French parliament is locked in the straitjacket of the rationalised parliamentary system characterised by a quasi-subordination of the legislative to the executive', adding that 'it has to be loosened.'

To do so, they made a number of recommendations, starting with incorporating in the constitution a clear definition of the functions of the French parliament in a newly drafted article 24, as seen previously. But one of their main proposals was to alter the parliamentary agenda – too much dominated by the government – allowing parliament to control its own agenda and above all giving the Opposition a say, even if limited, over the latter. The French government appeared to follow the recommendation of the Balladur Report as a new article 48 was incorporated in the constitution clearly stating: 'The agenda shall be determined by each House.'

The British House of Lords, and perhaps to a lesser extent the French Senate, which is elected by (indirect) universal suffrage, are still criticised for their democratic deficit and are often considered altogether as anomalies in modern democracies. As the journalist of the French left-of-centre newspaper *Libération* pointed out, 'in Great Britain, it is very simple, there are no elections, not even indirect ones as in the French Senate, but only nominations to the House of Lords.'[51] It is in fact not as simple as that, as the

Lord Speaker is elected by the whole House and the remaining hereditary peers under the Cranborne amendment to the 1999 House of Lords Act are renewed via by-elections – none of these elections being democratic in the sense that British voters are not invited to take part in any way. Such criticisms nevertheless raise the question of what makes an institution legitimate and of whether (direct) universal suffrage is the only means of turning the two Upper Houses into fully democratic institutions.

An even more fundamental question perhaps is whether the democratic deficit in terms of composition prevents the French Senate and the British House of Lords from making any (useful) contribution to the political and institutional life of their respective countries – and beyond democracy itself. Direct elections[52] would not solve the problem of the misconduct of some of their members[53] – the House of Lords having seen its reputation tarnished by the sexual misbehaviour of its deputy Lord Speaker and Chairman of Committees,[54] Lord Sewel, reviving the debate over the need for Lords reform. Yet, on that front, some significant progress has been made, since peers not only have to swear the traditional oath of allegiance to the monarch to join the House of Lords but since 2009 – in the wake of the expenses financial scandal that hit the Upper Chamber too though not in the same proportion as the House of Commons – they also have to commit themselves to abide by the new Code of Conduct by signing a written undertaking which lists seven key principles of conduct: selflessness, integrity, objectivity, accountability, openness, honesty and leadership.[55] To supplement the new scheme the position of the Commissioner for Standards was created in 2010 so as to lead the independent and impartial investigation of alleged breaches of the Code of Conduct[56].

The House of Lords and the French Senate as counter-powers and custodians of freedoms and stability

Both upper chambers are often denounced as conservative chambers, and this is also closely linked to their composition – the average age in the House of Lords in 2016 being 70, and 61 in the French Senate, with no maximum age limit[57] in both cases. The great majority of members of the Lords are life peers (with some exception such as the remaining 92 hereditary peers and the 26 Lords spiritual) which means that they can remain members of the House and take part in its work until the very end of their lives, with the exception of bishops, who retire from their sees on reaching the age of seventy and thus cease to be members of the House of Lords. The only clear requirement is that peers are not allowed actually to die in the House itself!

The French constitution for its part does not include the electoral voting system for either the Senate or the National Assembly. It hardly says anything about their composition except that, under article 24, deputies are elected by direct universal suffrage, whereas senators are elected by indirect universal suffrage. Details are in fact provided by the Electoral Code, yet the number of terms that deputies and senators[58] can serve is not subject to any particular limit, unlike the President of the Republic, who can only serve two terms in office of five years in a row. In both modern Britain and France, old age is generally considered rather negatively, more as a handicap than an asset, whereas in the past it was associated with wisdom and experience. There are however two well-known exceptions in French culture: wine and cheese!

The right-of-centre journal *The Economist* described the House of Lords in 2015 in less than flattering terms, alluding to 'the lethargy and decrepitude evident among the noble legislators … creeping along the Palace of Westminster'.[59] That was not the universal view. Yet commentators tend to forget that both the House of Lords and the Senate play an important role as counter-powers as well as custodians of civil liberties and fundamental freedoms. It is perhaps even more important in the United Kingdom, where MPs can also be Cabinet ministers. As the experts of the Commission to Strengthen Parliament observed, 'most members of Parliament are elected to support and sustain a particular government in office, and, at the same time, are members of an institution that is expected to subject to critical scrutiny that very same government.'[60]

Their much more limited numbers in the Lords as well as the presence of cross-benchers, who are not affiliated to any political party, enable the unelected Upper House to take more distance from the executive and thus exercise a more effective control over the government. Besides, the Lords, like French Senators, are very attached to their independence and feel freer than MPs to move away from the party line and from the instructions of the whips. This also facilitates the relationship between peers of different political affiliations. Until the arrival of a growing number of former ministers and MPs, debates in the Lords tended to be less partisan and adversarial than in the Commons, especially at Prime Minister's Questions, and it is still very much the case.

The French and British second chambers are not as conservative as might be thought at first sight. On an important issue in people's lives, marriage, or more precisely same-sex marriage, they even adopted a fairly progressive stance. Although they did not need to legislate to meet their obligations under the European Convention on Human Rights, the British and French governments tabled bills aiming at legalising same-sex marriage almost at the same time. Same-sex marriage was one of the key promises of the manifesto of the Socialist candidate François Hollande in the 2012 presidential election campaign that he won against Nicolas Sarkozy. In both countries supporters and opponents of same-sex marriage took to the streets to express their views and to put pressure on British and French law-makers. On 5 February 2013, the House of Commons, overwhelmingly voted to pass the British Bill legalising same-sex marriage initiated by the Conservative–Liberal coalition government headed by David Cameron by (a free vote of) 400 to 175. Labour and Liberal Democrat MPs voted massively in favour of the Bill while half the Conservative peers either rejected the Bill or abstained. The weak opposition of the bishops was swept aside.

In France the discussions and the vote on the same-sex marriage Bill (*le projet de loi sur le mariage pour tous*) proved to be particularly acrimonious. The French Bill was tabled in the National Assembly by the Socialist government, which at that time held a majority in both the National Assembly and the Senate. On 4 February 2013, the National Assembly voted for a key provision of the same-sex marriage Bill by a large majority vote of 249–97 to redefine marriage as between two people, rather than a man and a woman (thus ending the legal requirement that a marriage in France must be between two people of the opposite sex).

The French same-sex marriage Bill also included a measure to allow homosexuals to adopt children, a provision which led to a heated debate in the French National Assembly, unlike the fairly good-natured debates in the British House of Commons and in the House of Lords (which had approved this change some years earlier). In spite of the more than 5,000 amendments tabled by the French Opposition, the text was passed in the early hours of 9 February 2013. Yet, to become law, it needed to be approved in identical terms by the Senate – where the Socialists for the first time under the Fifth Republic held a majority. In April 2013, the Bill was adopted by a show of hands after sixty hours of debates by French Senators with only minor amendments – only 200 amendments were introduced by the UMP of Sarkozy. All the left-wing political groups voted for the text, whereas 131 UMP deputies out of 134 who launched a vast campaign of lobbying voted against it. Once passed by the two Houses in identical terms, the Bill was signed into law by the President on 17 May 2013.

Two months afterwards, the United Kingdom in turn passed the Marriage (Same Sex Couples) Act on 17 July 2013. The historically conservative House of Lords did not delay, let alone block, the text, in spite of Lord Dear's proposed amendment to deny the Bill a second reading. Peers overwhelmingly rejected this amendment by 390 to 148, thus allowing the text to complete its passage smoothly. It is interesting to note that the same-sex marriage law aroused much stronger opposition in France than in the United Kingdom, generally considered as a more conservative country (at least by French people) than the French Republic. The difficult passage of the Bill in France showed how influential the Catholic Church still is, as massive and sometimes violent demonstrations backed by the right-wing Opposition and by the Catholic Church were held in Paris on the Champs-Elysées, outside parliament. As for the Senate, had the Upper House not been controlled by the Socialists at that time, the outcome would have been very different. Since then, the Senate has swung back to the right, where it usually stands.

It is surprising to note how little is known of both Upper Houses despite the active role that they play in scrutinising and revising legislation as well as in holding the government to account, most notably within their respective committees. British and French people alike tend to know better members of the House of Commons and members of the National Assembly, as they have elected them, than Lords and Senators. Some of this ignorance is due to the national press, which seldom covers Lords business with much seriousness. In fact, the general feeling towards the British and French Upper Houses in the population is more ambivalent than it seems at first sight. In France, the British House of Lords generates a certain curiosity with its strange rituals and regalia. French people tend to wonder how what they sometimes perceive as a relic of feudalism has managed to survive in the twenty-first century. The Senate and the House of Lords are indeed symbols of permanence, stability and continuity as, unlike the National Assembly and the House of Commons, they cannot be dissolved.[61] If the Senate and the House of Lords are permanent chambers it does not mean, however, that they are incapable of reforming themselves. In fact, they have survived because they have been able to adapt to a changing society.

Revisiting the myth of the non-reform of the Senate and the House of Lords

The current House of Lords, defined in its standing orders as 'the second chamber of the United Kingdom Parliament' which 'makes laws, holds government to account, and debates issues of public interest',[62] is very different from what it used to be. As far as its composition is concerned, a turning point was the Life Peerages Act of 1958 initiated by the Macmillan government – completed by the Peerage Act 1963 – since the introduction of life peerages turned what remained of the aristocratic house largely based on birth into a chamber based on merit and expertise, while introducing social diversity. The new peers, were for the most part, not politicians but people of eminence who had distinguished themselves in outstanding professional careers in the civil service, academia, the law, the arts, science and media, business and industry, during which they acquired much specialist expertise and were awarded a peerage for their services to the nation. They also, of course, included women for the first time.

Today a large proportion of measures coming to the Lords have very many amendments, perhaps half of them government amendments, suggesting that the Commons has not had the time – or maybe the expertise – to examine them thoroughly, even though, as Lewis Baston and Stuart Wilks-Heeg pointed out, in the last few years there has been 'a growth in expertise and scrutiny in the Commons'[63] itself. Thus the new Lords were people who were neither aristocrats nor necessarily wealthy but who came from different walks of life and could make a positive contribution to the national legislature. For the first time, people like former trade union leaders joined the House of Lords even if they might have been fairly unfamiliar with the unusual rules and usages of the House. So the 1958 Act together with the 1963 Act widened the pool of prospective Lords and introduced some diversity in the House. Yet, successive Prime Ministers have developed the practice of privileging people affiliated to their own party from the list submitted to them to secure their own party a majority in the House and thus make sure their bills would be adopted without too much delay or dissent – though what the House of Lords decides can be overturned at the end of the day by the government via the Parliament Acts of 1911 and 1949. Thus the membership has been somewhat diminished in quality through peerages being given as rewards for long-service MPs. A person backed by a political party is more likely to join the House than a person not affiliated to any political party even if the House of Lords Appointments Commission is in charge of nominating such people for up to 20 per cent of the membership. So even if merit is the official criterion, political considerations play a role in practice, all the more as there is no cap to the number of Lords the Prime Minister can appoint. The Prime Minister's patronage over the nomination process – except for cross-benchers – led to the House of Lords being described as 'a House of Cronies' during the Blair years, though Cameron has created even more peers than Blair in half the time. This is officially a Royal Prerogative, as prospective peers receive a writ of summons from the Monarch 'to treat and give their counsel' in the affairs of the state. For the first time in the 2015–20 Parliament women were explicitly mentioned in the writ of summons. Besides, peers have to swear an oath of allegiance to the monarch before being able to sit in the House when they become a Lord, and at the beginning of each new session.

The abolition of the hereditary principle and the end of a structural Conservative majority

The House of Lords Act of 1999 was perhaps even more revolutionary than the Life Peerages Act of 1958 since it officially put an end to the hereditary principle as a means of automatically joining the House allowing peers who inherited their title by birth to be automatically granted the right to sit and vote in the House. Abolishing the hereditary principle at the basis of one of the two 'dignified parts of the constitution' – the House of Lords, in Bagehot's analysis – may very well lead one day to challenging this principle as a means of appointing the British monarch – the monarchy being the other 'dignified part of the constitution' – even though the 1997 Labour party manifesto pledged not to reform the monarchy. As was written in the latter:

> The House of Lords must be reformed as an initial, self-contained reform, not dependent on further reform in the future, the right of hereditary peers to sit and vote in the House of Lords will be ended by statute … the legislative powers of the House of Lords will remain unaltered.[64]

The statute mentioned in the manifesto became the House of Lords Act 1999 after a strenuous legislative process and a key amendment following an agreement reached between the Labour government of Blair and the Conservative Opposition[65] leader Viscount Cranborne to allow 10 per cent (92 altogether) of the hereditary peers to stay in the House during the interim period until the completion of the reform. It was the only way to overcome the strong opposition of the Lords, as is reported in a vivid account by Baroness Ruth Rendell – alias Barbara Vine – in her novel *The Blood Doctor*. Thus she wrote: 'Everyone knows the Bill's intention and what its effect will be – to get rid of us as anachronisms and white elephants.'[66]

In fact, one of the most significant effects of the House of Lords Act 1999 was to bring an end to the long-standing domination of the Upper House by the Conservative party. The Lords, in its all-hereditary days down to the 1950s, was rightly attacked as a right-wing, reactionary body with a permanent entrenched Conservative majority, whatever the government of the country. As Baroness Hollis argued, 'the Lords is effective as a revising chamber precisely and only because no government has a majority in it, and must therefore be respectful of informed dissenting opinion.'[67]

It is most certainly the case in the 2015–20 Parliament, as the Conservative party does not have a majority in the Lords despite winning a (slender) majority in the House of Commons in the 2015 General Election. The Labour party together with the Liberal Democrats hold a majority and can join forces to defeat the Conservative government. They have already done so on English Votes for English Laws and revising Commons constituency boundaries. Besides, the House of Lords includes more supporters of the European Union – and Europe in general – than the House of Commons.

Though the House of Lords Act 1999 has not turned the Upper House into a democratic institution, it has given peers the feeling that they have more legitimacy. The House has become much more self-confident and generally less inclined to yield to government bills they disapprove of or consider contrary to the general public interest or civil liberties. Thus the House of Lords has opposed bills trying to extend pre-trial detention and anti-terrorism legislation in the name of Habeas Corpus, and forced through significant amendments. As for the latest legislation on Lords reform, the House of Lords Reform Act 2014,[68] it has introduced more incremental yet important changes mainly regarding the (permanent) expulsion and suspension of members of the House. But it does not provide for the abolition of the remaining hereditary peers. Surprising as it is for an external observer, they consider themselves to be more legitimate than the rest of the Lords as they have been 'elected' – not by democratic universal suffrage but internally, either in their political party or by the whole House.[69] Perhaps even more puzzling, since their survival seems hard to defend, is the fact that there is still some resistance to their disappearance within the Lords as they are thought to be working peers making a useful contribution to the House.

In any case, the successive reforms of the Lords in the twentieth and twenty-first centuries have turned the House into a more influential chamber – it has not necessarily gained more powers but now uses its existing prerogatives more to the full to the frequent embarrassment of the government of the day. In doing so, it may threaten key conventions upon which a smooth relationship between the government and Parliament depends, starting with the Addison–Salisbury convention.[70] Under the latter, a manifesto bill that has gone through a second reading must not be subject to wrecking amendments. As is clearly explained in Barbara Vine's book, 'the Salisbury Convention postulates that any intention a political party presents in its manifesto shall be taken as the will of the people if that party is voted into government.'[71] In 2010, however, the coalition agreement was deemed to be a substitute for a manifesto. Thus the constitutional world described in traditional terms by Bagehot has collapsed, yet the still unelected undemocratic House of Lords is alive and well, with a fair claim now to be considered as 'an efficient' part of the constitution itself. At a time when the prestige of the Commons is very low, the Lords supply a thorough, less partisan forum for monitoring the quality of legislation and government.

The shorter, more democratic mandate of French senators and a better representation of urban constituencies

Similarly, the French Senate can challenge the National Assembly to think again, and effectively so, while always in the end giving way to the elected House. As far as its composition is concerned, even if it is far from having experienced the same dramatic changes as the House of Lords, the Senate has not remained unchanged. Indeed, French Senators used to serve a very long mandate of nine years – even longer than the original seven-year mandate of the President of the Republic (until 2000) – to secure their independence, sparing them the pressure and permanent campaigning which tends to be the fate of deputies who are elected for five years. The (organic) Law of 30 July 2003 reduced the term in office of French senators to six years and changed the rule concerning the partial renewal of the Senate from one-third every three years to half of its members every three years – the traditional partial renewal of the Senate aiming at preserving the continuity and stability of the Upper House. If nine years was considered far too long in France for (indirectly) elected senators, depriving them of significant accountability, the fifteen years proposed by the failed 2012 House of Lords (Reform) Bill, supported by the Liberal Democrats for the 80 per cent elected Lords of a new (mainly) elected House of Lords, would have made members of the British Upper House far less accountable even than their French counterparts. To compensate for the shortening of their mandate and in a way recompense French Senators for having agreed to reform their own House the number of senators was increased by 21 to reach 348. It was also a way of securing a better representation of urban constituencies in the Senate where thinly populated rural areas tend to be overrepresented. Among the new 21 senators, 12 were to represent French citizens living outside France – notably in London, which has the largest French community outside Paris. Yet this reform was far from meeting with unanimity as it was not always perceived as being necessary. Since the 2008 constitutional change, a cap has been enshrined in the constitution of the Fifth Republic limiting the number of senators to 348. If the French Senate seems fairly small compared with the British House of Lords (close to 800 members), it is still huge by international standards.

If at first sight a fully (directly) elected French Senate and British House of Lords would solve once and for all the never-ending question of the democratic deficit of the two chambers, it would at the same time most certainly doom bicameralism in both countries, since their second chamber would be no more than the mirror image of the other (already) democratically elected chamber. Two identical houses in terms of composition would make the second chamber somewhat redundant. In spite of the criticisms directed at the House of Lords because it is not elected, the majority of British people value the expertise of its members and its independence. Politicians in the United Kingdom and in France are held in low esteem, so replacing the current independent experts of the House of Lords by professional politicians would not necessarily improve the perception and operation of the British Upper House. It is also almost inconceivable to turn the House of Lords into a fully democratic chamber without granting it more powers, as its current ones are in fact fairly limited, and this in turn would challenge the supremacy of the House of Commons. The latter argument explains why some past and present MPs – including Lloyd George in 1911 – were not favourable to an elected House of Lords. It could lead to a Liberal-dominated Commons being fatally challenged by a Conservative-dominated Lords. A possible solution might be introducing different voting systems for MPs and for members of the Lords, as is already the case in the French parliament.

The case of the French Senate is interesting, since it combines two different voting systems.

The election process of French senators partly based on PR and the failed attempt at introducing a form of PR in the UK Parliament

In constituencies electing fewer than four senators, the voting system is the majority voting system – the equivalent of the British first-past-the-post system but with two rounds instead of one – whereas in constituencies electing four or more senators proportional representation is used. Thus 52 per cent of French senators are elected by proportional representation. The French Socialist MP for the Hauts-de-Seine department, Alexis Bachelay,[72] who criticised the Senate for being 'a chamber in essence conservative, impeded by its voting system', proposed to replace the indirect election of senators by direct universal suffrage exclusively based on proportional representation so as to represent the thirteen new regions. He also advocated a much smaller Senate composed of 100 senators instead of the current 348. By contrast, in the French National Assembly all the 577 deputies are elected by direct suffrage exclusively based on a majority system with two rounds. An attempt at introducing proportional representation under the first Socialist President of the Fifth Republic, François Mitterrand, in 1986 was quickly dropped as it led to the unexpected breakthrough of the National Front, a far-right party, whose leader was at that time the founder of the party, Jean-Marie Le Pen.

In the same way, under a proportional representation voting system in the House of Commons, the anti-European party campaigning for the independence of the United Kingdom (UKIP), which polled over four million votes in the 2015 United Kingdom General Election, would have gained significantly more seats than the single one it currently holds in the British Lower House. In fact, some attempts were made in the United Kingdom to introduce a certain degree of proportional representation – a long-time commitment of the Liberal Democrats. Although constitutional change did not rank high among the thirty-one points listed by the coalition programme for government following the May 2010 general election, some were to be given priority, such as an overhaul of the voting system from first-past-the-post to Alternative Vote, a reduction of the House of Commons to 600 MPs,[73] establishing fixed-term Parliaments, and in the longer run turning the House of Lords into a wholly or mainly elected second chamber based on some form of proportional representation.

The Conservatives led by David Cameron were not particularly enthusiastic, yet their wish to set up new constituency boundaries and the opposition of the Liberal Democrats to the first-past-the-post system gave the two parties that formed the coalition – as the 2010 United Kingdom General Election led to a hung parliament – the basis for a deal agreed during the five days of coalition negotiations in May 2010. Without this, the coalition itself might not have come into being. Though the then leader of the Liberal Democrats, Nick Clegg, saw the Alternative Vote (AV) as a poor substitute for proportional system – the latter, then holding the office of Deputy Prime Minister with special responsibility for political and constitutional reform – he made a statement announcing that the AV referendum would take place on 5 May 2011 and that the House of Commons would be reduced from 650 to 600 members. The referendum would be held on the same day as elections to the devolved legislatures in Scotland, Wales and Northern Ireland. The Parliamentary Voting System and Constituencies Act (2011) was to provide the legislative framework for the referendum on AV and further constitutional change – which was all the more critical as the United Kingdom has only a fairly limited experience of holding referendums and none before 1975, at least at the national level. British voters were invited to answer an apparently fairly straightforward question in a referendum to be held on 5 May 2011: 'At present, the UK uses the first-past-the-post system to elect MPs to the House of Commons. Should the alternative vote system be used instead?'

What might have been an opportunity to change the voting system as well as a historical event, since the referendum on 5 May 2011 was the first national referendum in thirty-six years, ended up in a humiliating defeat. Indeed, British voters rejected the argument for AV by 67.90 per cent against 32.10 per cent, but this major defeat was perceived in the press as a plebiscite against the Deputy Prime Minister. What was relatively unexpected was the scale of the defeat, as turnout proved to be higher than expected at 42.2 per cent, as shown by the report of the Electoral Commission on the May 2011 referendum.[74] One cannot deny the fact that the referendum on AV did not stir anything like the same interest as the first nationwide EEC membership referendum in 1975, where turnout reached 64 per cent and where 67 per cent of voters backed EEC membership, or more recently the 2016 referendum on the EU, where turnout reached 72 per cent. Yet the 2011 turnout for the referendum on AV shows that there was still a certain interest in electoral reform and, beyond, in politics among British voters. So, one might wonder whether voters would have backed a real proportional voting system if they had had the choice. On the other hand, the high proportion of the No vote can be interpreted as a choice for the *status quo* – the current first-past-the-post (FPTP) voting system – as if the great majority of voters were not convinced of the need for changing the voting system for the UK Parliament. The main criticism that was made against AV is that it makes coalitions more likely and therefore paves the way for a new parliamentary system altering the Westminster model of democracy. It makes it more difficult for governments to be thrown out of office, and it is probably that fear that contributed to the failure of the referendum on AV. The experience of the coalition at that time in 2011 reinforced these fears.

The mixed voting system of the French Senate is however far from being a panacea and in spite of the 2003 reform – considered by many as a superficial change – it is still criticised for its lack of diversity in terms of political pluralism and also territorial representation, the *communes* being overrepresented to the detriment of both departments and regions. The Senate is still elected by a senatorial college composed mainly of people elected locally, and many senators themselves have a double mandate, combining their senatorial mandate with a local one, very often as a Mayor. The current President of the Senate, Gérard Larcher,[75] is among those who support two different mandates for senators – a local and a national one – on the ground that local experience and a good knowledge of local politics is an asset for senators. Yet, the two organic laws enacted by parliament on 14 February 2014 aim at restricting the French parliamentarians' practice of holding multiple mandates by forbidding deputies and senators from holding a local executive mandate in addition to their national mandate as members of parliament. The objective is for the new measures to apply to the renewal of the National Assembly in June 2017 and that of the Senate in September of the same year. The experts of the Balladur Committee tried to go further in reforming the French Senate in 2008 by altering article 24 of the constitution so as to make it clear that the Senate would from then on guarantee a fairer representation of the population based on equal demographic grounds, but its proposal was dropped in the final version of the Constitutional Law of July 2008.

A French Senate-type upper limit as a potential solution for an ever-growing Lords

What could serve, however, as a source of inspiration for British constitutional reformers but also for British Prime Ministers is that under the current provisions of article 24 of the Constitution of the Fifth Republic,

'Members of the Senate shall not exceed 348.' It means that there is now an upper limit – an official cap – to the number of members of the Senate. There is one urgent reform needed in the United Kingdom which concerns the size of the House of Lords. Common sense and a genuine interest in the work of the House of Lords would dictate self-restraint on the part of British Prime Ministers in the way they use their power to nominate peers. In 2011, the independent scholars of the Constitution Unit raised the alarm bell in asking for a moratorium,[76] but to no avail. The ever-growing number of peers puts much strain on the facilities of the Palace of Westminster, which is itself in a very derelict state, and on the chamber, which is designed to accommodate no more than 400 people. It has already started to affect the good functioning of the House. The latter is especially crowded during question time before the Lords depart to their various activities. Much more seriously, it makes it more difficult for peers, especially backbenchers, to take part in debates and express their views on important topical issues, as a higher number of members means more limited speech time. Growing numbers impose certain restrictions and more rigid rules in a House which has always enjoyed and has always been attached to its self-regulation principle and where the powers of the Lord Speaker are very limited, since the latter has no power to rule on matters of order. Thus peers eager to seize the rarer and rarer opportunity to speak are more reluctant to give way to another speaker who stands up at the same time. The general atmosphere has deteriorated as Lords feel more under pressure. An additional problem is that more Lords also means fewer opportunities to join the committees themselves, though this is where an important part of the work of the House takes place. Over 150 new peers were created under the 2010–15 coalition government, essentially for political reasons to ensure a coalition majority in the Upper House, and many of these have been connected with political contributions to party funds. David Cameron, who introduced more peers than any Prime Minister since the Life Peerages Act 1958, intended to bring in more Conservative peers to make sure the House of Lords more accurately reflected the situation in the House of Commons following the 2015 General Election, though he did not explain what he means by this. Just a few months after having been reinstated as Prime Minister, Cameron was defeated in rapid succession in the Lords over Europe, devolution – English votes for English laws – and more recently tax credits. Yet attempts to match party balance to follow the result of Commons election results are bound to swell numbers even more. The political parties should be kept at arm's length and there should be a cap on Lords membership[77] as there is in the French Senate imposed through the House of Lords Appointments Commission perhaps of 400, as 400 to 450 peers only attend debates. Yet, it is unlikely that the situation will improve in the near future as Lords reform was neither part of the 2015 Queen's Speech nor of the 2016 one, although the proposed cull of MPs draws further attention to the bloated membership of the Lords.

If David Cameron or his successor (Theresa May) have not been willing to do anything about the current size of the House of Lords apart from further increasing its numbers – sabotaging the Upper House from within and perhaps leading to an institutional crisis – on the other hand Cameron promised to reduce the number of MPs to 600 in the 2015 Conservative Manifesto. This will now happen. Besides, as the Democratic Audit – an independent research organisation based at the London School of Economics – in 2010 pointed out, 'the House of Commons is too large by international standards' as it is 'the largest directly elected chamber in the European Union'.[78] The size of either the Lords or the Commons must not be decided arbitrarily but should take into account parliamentary life and work, all the more as those who are likely to be the most affected are backbenchers.

French reformers for their part were not expected to, and could not, make proposals on the number of members for each House since it has been fixed once and for all by the constitution – respectively 577 for the National Assembly and 348 for the Senate – which introduced an element of rigidity in the composition of parliament not always welcome in a constitution which is already considered too rigid, notably by the experts of the Balladur Committee. By contrast, size remains an issue in the United Kingdom.

Failed attempts at introducing PR in the French National Assembly and in the Commons

In the 2015 Conservative manifesto, Cameron committed his party to reforming Parliament,[79] promoting change and continuity at the same time. Thus, while advocating the 'introduction of an elected element in the House of Lords', without making clear how the members of the new House would be elected, it immediately added that it was not considered to be 'a priority'. As for the House of Commons, the Conservatives committed themselves to 'protecting the electoral system for the House of Commons' as it stands, promising to maintain the first-past-the-post system for the election of MPs. In France, the Jospin Report for a democratic revival published on 9 November 2012[80] pleaded for more proportional representation in the French Senate to introduce more political diversity and help minority groups. Like the Balladur Committee in 2008, the experts of the Jospin[81] Report four years afterwards rejected direct universal suffrage for the Senate based on proportional representation, yet they did favour an increase of the proportion of senators indirectly elected by proportional representation.[82] They also pleaded for the introduction of some limited proportional representation in the National Assembly, this time advocating the election of 10 per cent of deputies by proportional representation – the idea was to give voters two separate votes as in Germany, one based on the majority system, the other on proportional representation. The independent experts of the Jospin Committee also denounced what they consider a major anomaly, which is the participation, though marginal, of members of the National Assembly in the senatorial Electoral College.[83]

If the Balladur Committee in 2008 did not make any recommendations to alter fundamentally the way senators are elected, its members, however, favoured the introduction of some element of proportional representation for the National Assembly – up to 20 or 30 seats out of the current 577 seats. Its experts pointed out the difficulty of changing electoral boundaries, as no redefinition of boundaries had taken place since the law of 24 November 1986 in spite of article L125 (2) of the Electoral Code making it a legal requirement to do so in order to take into account demographic change. They therefore suggested that the division process of boundaries itself should be made more transparent and impartial.[84]

In the same way, in the United Kingdom, the Parliamentary Voting System and Constituencies Act 2011 included the reduction of the House of Commons from 650 to 600 members. There was a clear partisan motive, since many Labour-held urban seats had small electorates and Labour derived a clear advantage from this. Fewer votes were needed to elect a Labour MP. Its impact would have been fairly limited for Northern Ireland and Scotland, which would have lost respectively 2 and 7 of their constituencies. It might have had a much more dramatic effect on Wales as we have seen, and England for its part might have lost thirty-one constituencies. A statute to redraw constituency boundaries had already been passed although its opponents feared not only the merger of many small seats, notably in Wales, but also the weakening of ties between MPs and voters with a greater difference between local boundaries and parliamentary seats, leading to constituencies with little sense of identity, especially as pressure was put on Boundary Commissioners to act quickly. Yet the whole process was brought to a halt by the Liberal Democrats as retaliation against the Conservatives who had opposed the Lords reform proposed by their then Leader Nick Clegg. However, as clearly mentioned in their 2015 manifesto, the Conservatives, having won a majority – though a slender one – in the last 2015 General Election, are now in a position to go forward with the redistribution of constituency boundaries. Thus the 2015 Conservative manifesto reads: 'We will address the unfairness of the current parliamentary boundaries' and 'reduce the number of MPs to 600.'[85] Although the process of reviewing parliamentary constituency boundaries was launched in February 2016, progress is unlikely to be rapid here.

Rather than thinking in terms of numbers, which seems to lead to a dead end, including endless debates about the retiring age for members of the House of Lords, the nature of representation in each house as well as its specific needs should be taken into account. Indeed, one of the main questions which should be addressed is whether the two Houses of Parliament conceived for a unitary state – or union state in the case of the United Kingdom – are still appropriate for countries which have become either less unitary, like the French one, or have moved towards a quasi-federal system, like the United Kingdom. Perhaps second chambers in both countries could help make the transition easier to a new kind of state. As a former president of the French Senate, Christian Poncelet argued, 'without ending up with a federal structure, most states today experience some form of decentralisation process which legitimises a specific representation at the central level: only bicameralism can allow the necessary adaptation to the modern world.'[86] The two countries have become more complex, multi-layered states where subnational communities need to be better represented at the national level, and this could provide second chambers with both a new role and a new legitimacy. Rather than a series of piecemeal reforms in the United Kingdom and in France, a better solution might lie in turning the Senate into 'a Great Council of Regions' – instead of the 'Great Council of Communes' that it was under the Third Republic and still is in the Fifth Republic – and the House of Lords into a chamber representing the regions and nations of the kingdom, thus giving it a new *raison d'être*.

What makes it still possible to describe the regime of the French Fifth Republic as a parliamentary regime is that the government is accountable to parliament, in the same way, as stated in Erskine May that '(British) ministers have a duty to parliament to account, and be held to account, for the policies, decisions and actions of their departments.'[87]

Strengthening parliamentary control over the executive

As far as France is concerned, the Balladur Committee was highly critical in its findings stating that 'Parliament hardly controls governmental action.'[88] It pointed out the fact that 'for a long time parliamentary control in France was limited to the power of parliament of overthrowing the government',[89] yet since 1962 it has not been used for such a purpose. In the United Kingdom, it is now a power much more regulated under the Fixed-Term Parliament Act 2011 which could be considered as a form of rationalised parliamentarianism. It makes it much more difficult for the House of Commons to overthrow a government, even a fairly weak one. Although it is described in the 2015 Conservative party manifesto as one of its significant achievements in the 2010–15 Parliament, it has been much criticised, for it makes the whole process much more rigid, and a succession of hung parliaments could mean permanent deadlock, with the Commons suffering a kind of constitutional anomie and the reputation of Parliament falling still further.

French 'Questions to the Government' and Prime Minister's Questions in the UK

One of the most effective means of parliamentary control is via the use of questions, either oral or written, directed at the government in the Commons. Richard Kelly provides a clear definition of parliamentary questions as a way for Members of Parliament 'to seek information, to press for action and to hold the Government to account'.[90] In France, which had known *interpellations* in the Lower House, effectively deployed by individualists like Clemenceau during the Third Republic, the so-called 'questions to the government' started as a parliamentary practice under the presidency of Valéry Giscard d'Estaing before being incorporated in the constitution itself. Under article 48 of the constitution, a session of questions to the government is organised on Tuesdays and Wednesdays for one hour – members of the majority and the opposition take turns to ask questions, questions are not communicated to the government in advance, only the list of ministers who are required to attend the session is provided – the one at the origin of the question and the ministers have two minutes each. The United Kingdom has been considered as a role model by France, as a fixed amount of time each week – two fifteen-minute slots of questions each week then (since 1997, only once a week on Wednesdays for half an hour) started to be allocated for questions to the Prime Minister as early as 1961 and soon came to be known as Prime Minister's Questions. Each minister has thirty minutes, or sometimes even slightly more – it depends on the good will of the Speaker – to answer questions which can only 'relate to matters for which those ministers are officially responsible',[91] thus limiting the scope of questions to the field of expertise of ministers. The Speaker of the House of Commons, John Bercow, considered for his part in 2016 that he has 'not a deliberate policy of running Prime Minister's Questions longer than half an hour. If, by just being a little bit flexible, I can allow somebody at the end to get in then I think that, from time to time, I might want to do so.'[92]

He has also made flexible use of urgent questions to give backbenchers more opportunity to speak. Unlike France, knowing the questions in advance allows ministers, or rather their civil servants, to do all the necessary research work and thus they are, at least theoretically, well briefed on the day. In fact, they often appear more as a kind of showcase and tend to be less effective than what is generally thought on the other side of the Channel. This highlight of parliamentary life is now often seen by British people as 'increasingly a focal point for shallow political point-scoring rather than serious prime ministerial scrutiny'.[93] This is partly due to the fact that in the United Kingdom, notice of a question – either oral or written – must be given in advance to a minister and has then to be inscribed on the order paper of the day, except for urgent questions,[94] 'the order in which ministers and other members answer oral questions being decided by the government'.[95] Questions are asked in the order shown on the order paper. The Speaker of the House of Commons, John Bercow – whose mandate was renewed in the wake of the 2015 General Election despite Conservative hostility, strongly believes in reforming Parliament and since 2009, the year he became Speaker for the first time, he has devoted a lot of time and energy to this task – eager to give more say to backbenchers, speaking of the need 'to catapult the backbencher to centre stage'.[96] Whereas, under his predecessor, Speaker Martin, urgent questions were hardly ever used, they have become common practice under Bercow's speakership. In an interview, Speaker Bercow made the following comment: 'The Urgent Question really has become the new Prime Minister's Questions because it is a unique chance to seize national attention,'[97] and Parliament's effectiveness has clearly benefited. Urgent questions have also been introduced in the Lords under procedure reforms.

French and British committees as the cornerstone of parliamentary life

Yet an even more effective way of holding the government to account in the United Kingdom, and more and more in France too, was within parliamentary committees, as ministers do not know the questions in advance and as select committees are free to decide the nature of their inquiries. Today an important part of parliamentary work takes place within committees – limited to eight in the French National Assembly and seven in the Senate, so that they do not specifically cover the specific area of each department, unlike British select committees, where they are directly related to the principal government departments. They had a very bad press under the Fourth Republic[98] as they were blamed for putting the government under much pressure as they could be very intrusive in calling ministers to account. Today, they relieve the case load of parliament, but are also able to deal with more and more complex technical issues which require a high level of expertise. In the United Kingdom select committees which examine the work of a ministry or a particular issue have become an important instrument of scrutiny. Holding government departments to account has become the key role of select committees, and they have proved more effective than Prime Minister's Questions. This is especially so since the Wright Committee's 'Rebuilding the House' of 24 November 2009.[99] A turning point was the report of the Select Committee on Procedure in 1978, which recommended an overhaul of British select committees to produce a more rational structure – which is the case today, as the standing orders of each House provide the rules of procedure for committees – and allow MPs to scrutinise the activities of the main departments in a more systematic way.

Even if appearing before select committees is often seen as 'much more testing than regular questions in the Commons' – from the widely shared experience of James Arbuthnot, a former Minister of State – ministers having to explain themselves[100] and their policies, too many ministers still found ways of escaping committee vetting. Hence more and more proposals to increase sanctions against reluctant ministers who either refuse to testify or to produce potential pieces of evidence on which committees rely for their inquiry. Yet the huge committee machinery[101] now part of the House of Commons Standing Orders – compared with the eight permanent committees of the French National Assembly and seven of the Senate – was in the past criticised for its lack of independence from the government. Criticisms were primarily directed at the excessive control of the whips, and also, to a certain extent, of party leaders, over the membership and chairmanship nomination process of select committee. The Blair government was fiercely attacked in this connection. Beyond the patronage of party whips, the Commons agenda – more particularly the division of parliamentary time between the House of Commons and the government – was another source of controversy. Too much time was at the disposal of the government to the detriment of parliamentarians, most notably backbenchers deprived of control over the House agenda. Members of Parliament, who unlike their French counterparts may join more than one committee, also attacked the lack of time spent on the floor of the House to consider select committee reports. A turning point was the setting up of the cross-party Commons Reform select committee chaired by the Labour MP and University Politics professor Tony Wright during the government of Gordon Brown, which was at the origin of the most important reform of the committees system since they were introduced under Margaret Thatcher's premiership in 1979. The Wright Report, 'Rebuilding the House', issued on 24 November 2009, and aimed at strengthening the Commons as a whole, enhanced the collective capacity of the House. Along with these recommendations, the Commons committees' chairs have significantly gained in independence through being selected by a vote of all MPs in the House of Commons. Prospective committee members are elected by their own parties, then affirmed by a vote of all MPs in the Commons instead of being simply nominated by the whips, as used to be the case previously.

But without any doubt, the most important impact the Wright Report has had, has been through the establishment of a Backbench Business Committee – which started to operate in June 2011, giving backbenchers a greater say in parliamentary work and debates, allowing them to raise matters of current concern on the floor of the House and to take part in setting the agenda. This committee, able to choose the subjects that it wants to debate, has been very effective, especially in securing discussions before the House of Commons such as on dignity in dying that would not have been raised otherwise.[102] The Wright Committee had also strongly recommended the setting up of a House Business Committee which would recommend the overall agenda of the week ahead. This had the staunch support of John Bercow but did not encounter the same success – the 2010–15 coalition government, formally in the name of the absence of consensus but probably eager to avoid losing further governmental control over the Commons, decided not to pursue the setting up of such a committee. The House Business Committee is unlikely to be created any time soon, since the Conservative government of David Cameron in its 2015 party manifesto, while praising the work of the Backbench Business Committee, showed no intention of completing the unfinished business by introducing a House Business Committee in the 2015–20 Parliament. In this important respect, legislative control of the executive remains strictly limited as it has been with governments of all complexions since 1918.

If the committees of the Westminster Parliament have become more effective in holding the government to account, focusing almost exclusively on scrutinising government actions and decisions, they still play a marginal role in scrutinising legislation – unlike French standing committees – hence the value of the scrutinising and amending committee function of the House of Lords. Thus in France, the bills tabled in by the government are first sent to committees, the committee stage preceding debates on the floor of the House, unlike the British legislative process where committees are involved in a later stage, where they are scrutinised and amended; and in the end the final version of the text produced by the committee can end up being very different from the original bill. The founders of the Fifth Republic, well aware of the power of committees over the legislative process and of their weakening effect on the government, were determined to limit their number and curtail their powers as part of their policy to restrain parliament to the benefit of the government. By contrast, in the wider attempt at reviving parliament and rebalancing the institutions (in 2008), the number of standing committees has slightly increased from six to eight in the Lower Chamber and seven in the Upper House – instead of ten as proposed by the Balladur Committee – and the text examined in the whole chamber on the floor of the House is no longer the original government bill but the altered version produced by the committees themselves as in the previous Republics. It was part of the objective of the Balladur Committee to 'make parliamentary committees the cornerstone of parliamentary work' so as to strengthen – and 'emancipate' – parliament.

If what the Balladur Committee proposed regarding French committees was very much in line with the French parliamentary tradition – the first committees dating back to 1789 and the Constituent Assembly – it was much more innovative in terms of the status of the French Opposition since, as noted earlier, there is no culture of the Opposition in France as there is in the United Kingdom. Of course Opposition parties in France, unlike the United Kingdom, tended to fly to the extremes of Communism or neo-Fascism. Thus a substantial part of the Balladur Report was devoted to working on a better status for the French Opposition, whose rights were for the first time officially acknowledged in the constitution (such as in article 48) and the Westminster Parliament was used as a role-model. Thus the Balladur Committee reported that 'the party with the highest number of MPs after the governing party forms the Opposition and enjoys their own prerogatives.' Since 1937, the leader of the Opposition has had an official status in the British House of Commons. The Opposition presides over one-third of committees, including the one in charge of controlling the budget – hence the proposal in France to allow the Opposition to chair the Finance Committee. Yet the Balladur Committee acknowledged the difficulty of defining the Opposition and of trying to adopt the British model in France. The difficulty in France is that political groups which are not part of the government majority tend to reject a division between the government on the one hand and the Opposition on the other. They consider such a division as too rigid. All in all, the Balladur Committee pleaded for a 'Charter of the Rights of the Opposition'.

Conclusion

We have seen that France is discovering the virtues of flexibility, 'loosening the straitjacket' of rationalised parliamentarianism imposed by the founding fathers of the Fifth Republic, while the United Kingdom has introduced more rigidity in parliamentary life, including a fixed parliamentary year with the controversial Fixed-Term Parliament Act 2011. Yet recent constitutional change in both countries has aimed at rebalancing national institutions to the benefit of parliaments and democracy itself by improving the scrutiny of legislation – the Senate and House of Lords acting as revising chambers – but above all by developing more effective means of holding the government to account, a system which still defines the British and French regimes as parliamentary. In the wake of the 2008 Balladur committee in France, parliament has regained control of part of its agenda, while both parliaments have worked at strengthening the scrutiny and investigative powers of their committees. Both countries are now trying to make their respective parliaments both 'an efficient' and 'dignified' part of their own constitution as well as restoring faith in national legislatures.

Notes

1. P. Lauvaux, *Parlementarisme rationalisé et stabilité du pouvoir exécutif* (Brussels: Bruylant, 1988).
2. Its standing orders themselves were significantly shorter and more flexible than those of the National Assembly.

3. In its ruling of 23 August 1985, N85-197 DC, the Constitutional Council concluded that the law 'only expresses the general will insofar as the constitution is respected'.
4. Article 1, paragraph 1 of the constitution of the Fifth Republic states that 'the Rules of Procedure of the Houses of parliament shall, before coming into force, be referred to the Constitutional Council, which shall rule on their conformity with the Constitution.'
5. Cabinet Office, The Cabinet Manual, 2011, p. 2.
6. Significantly, in the Official Opening of Parliament, the Crown (as an object but also as a symbol) resting on a cushion precedes the arrival of the monarch and the reading of the Queen's Speech delivered by the monarch wearing the Crown.
7. A. V. Dicey, *Introduction to the Study of the Law of the Constitution* (1885), p. 494.
8. See Elizabeth Gibson-Morgan and Alexis Chommeloux (eds), *The Rights and Aspirations of the Magna Carta* (London: Palgrave Macmillan, 2016).
9. As Sudhir Hazareesingh explained in his book *How the French Think* (London: Allen Lane, 2015), p. 14, 'the centralization of power was the defining principle of the dominant political force of the early 1790s, the Jacobins.'
10. The Parliamentarian, 'Rights in the modern age', *Journal of the Parliaments of the Commonwealth*, 2/XCVII (2015), 80–1.
11. 'The medieval concept of the English Parliament as primarily a court of justice', May's *Treatise on the Law, Privileges, Procedures and Usage of Parliament*, p. 192.
12. It was founded by Louis XI in 1462 and was located in the Palace of *L'Ombrière*, previously owned by the Dukes of Aquitaine.
13. He is one of the front-runners in the run-up to the 2017 presidential election.
14. Alain Juppé, *Montesquieu: le moderne*, 2nd edn (Paris: Perrin/Mollat, 2015).
15. Thanks to the constitutional change of July 2008 and the new article 24 of Title IV devoted to parliament.
16. David Feldman, *Oxford Principles of English Law: English Public Law*, 2nd edn (Oxford: Oxford University Press, 2009), p. 87.
17. Most notably the *Companion to the Standing Orders and Guide to the Proceedings of the House of Lords*.
18. Cabinet Office, The Cabinet Manual, p. 3.
19. For more information see Pierre Avril and Jean Gicquel, *Droit parlementaire*, 4th edn (Paris: Lextenso, 2010).
20. It is now part of article 48 of the revised version of the 1958 constitution.
21. Lecture delivered to the political committee of the Reform Club on 20 April 2012.
22. Ruth Fox and Matt Korris, *Making Better Law: Reform of the Legislative Process from Policy to Act* (London: Hansard Society, 2010), p. 12.

23. Bagehot, *The English Constitution*, p.149.
24. Feldman, *Oxford Principles of English Law*, p. 87.
25. All the more as in the United Kingdom it is strongly believed that one of the key functions of Parliament is 'to facilitate a credible opposition', as Lord Dahrendorf pointed out. For more information see Commission to Strengthen Parliament, *Strengthening Parliament* (London: The Stationery Office, July 2000), p. 6.
26. Bagehot, *The English Constitution*, p. 185.
27. Bagehot, *The English Constitution*, p. 68.
28. In Fox and Korris, *Making Better Law*, Peter Riddell evoked the 'danger of inadequate and partial scrutiny by Parliament', especially the House of Commons (p. 5).
29. *Law for Lawmakers: A Justice Guide to the Law* (London: Justice, 2015), p. 9.
30. Sophie Boyron, *The Constitution of France: A Contextual Analysis* (Oxford: Hart Publishing, 2013), p. 127.
31. Cabinet Office, Cabinet Manual, 2011, p. 42.
32. See Bertrand Mathieu, *Constitution: rien ne bouge et tout change* (Paris: Lextenso, 2013), p. 179.
33. May's *Treatise on the Law, Privileges, Procedures and Usage of Parliament*, p. 181.
34. Magna Carta, 1215, chapter 12: 'No scutage or aid is to be levied in our realm except by the common counsel of our realm.'
35. Unexpectedly the House of Lords rejected the second reading of the budget by 350 votes to 75 at the end of November 1909, and in December of the same year the King decided to dissolve Parliament.
36. Political and Constitutional Reform Committee, Second Report of Session 2014–15, 'A new Magna Carta?', HC 463 (10 July 2014), p. 34.
37. The country is in fact the birthplace of bicameralism.
38. The preamble, of which the Declaration of the Rights of Man and Citizen has survived to this day unaltered.
39. It was as a reaction to the all-powerful Convention in 1795 and after the Second Republic of 1848–51.
40. The 'Council of the Republic', which was then the name of the Senate under the Fourth Republic though it was only an advisory body, fought hard to maintain the values of the Republic threatened by the rise of fascism.
41. It had quasi-identical powers to those of the Lower House known as the Chamber of Deputies.
42. Jean Mastias and Jean Grangé, *Les secondes chambres du Parlement en Europe occidentale* (Paris: Economica, 1987), p. 19.
43. Mastias and Grangé, *Les secondes chambres du Parlement en Europe occidentale*, p. 45.
44. Marie-France Verdier, 'Le Sénat dans les institutions de la Cinquième République 1958–1992' (unpublished Ph.D. thesis, University of Bordeaux, 1991), p. 178.

45. Jean Grangé, 'Le bicamérisme', in Yves Mény and Olivier Duhamel, *Dictionnaire constitutionnel* (Paris: PUF, 1992), p. 74.
46. May's *Treatise on the Law, Privileges, Procedures and Usage of Parliament*, p. 181.
47. Cabinet Office, Cabinet Manual, p. 39.
48. Under the constitution, financial and social security financing bills have to be tabled in the National Assembly first (articles 47 and 47-1).
49. Iain McLean, *What's Wrong with the British Constitution?* (Oxford: Oxford University Press, 2010).
50. Comité (Balladur) de réflexion et de proposition sur la modernisation et le rééquilibrage des institutions de la Cinquième République, Rapport 'Une Cinquième République plus démocratique' (Paris: La Documentation française, 2008), p. 4.
51. Michel Henry, 'Crise des perruques à la Chambre des Lords', *Libération*, 7 May 2015. Apparently, Michel Henry has not realised that members of the House of Lords no longer wear wigs, even for the State Opening of Parliament – with a few exceptions linked with specific offices.
52. The House of Commons, though being an elected House, has still not fully recovered from the 2009 MPs' expenses scandal.
53. Maybe a solution would be to strengthen the vetting of prospective Lords by the Appointments Commission as well as tougher disciplinary measures for those who breach the Code of Conduct. In France, in April 2014 the Bordeaux Law Academic Professor Mélin-Soucramanien, on the proposal of the President of the National Assembly, Claude Bartolone, was unanimously elected as the new Commissioner for Ethical Standards of the Assembly – succeeding Mme Noelle Lenoir. One of his main objectives is to make sure that deputies abide by the new Code of Conduct, and especially to prevent conflicts of interest. The new Code of Conduct is based on six key principles which are to be respected by each member of the French Parliament: general interest; independence; objectivity; responsibility; probity and being exemplary. It was inspired by the German and British parliamentary codes of conduct. (For more information see 'The National Assembly in the French Institutions', translated from the French by Declan Mc Cavana (Paris: Assemblée Nationale, Service des Affaires Internationales et de Défense, February 2013), p. 109.
54. Lord Sewel, who resigned facing potential legal proceedings, was swiftly replaced by Lord Laming, a former convener of the cross-benchers, as Chairman of the Committees at the end of July 2015; he was exceptionally 'nominated' (instead of being elected) until the end of the next session.
55. House of Lords, *Companion to the Standing Orders and Guide to the Proceedings of the House of Lords* (London: The Stationery Office, 2010), pp. 78–9.
56. In June 2016 the former President of the Law Society, Lucy Scott-Moncrieff, became the House of Lords Commissioner for Standards.

57. The minimum age to be eligible to the Senate was 30 (it has been recently lowered to 24, and the 2012 Jospin Report proposed to further lower it to 18), compared with 23 for the National Assembly and 21 to be eligible for the House of Lords.
58. The six-year term in office of French senators is (still) the longest in the French Republic, together with that of people who hold elected offices in municipal councils.
59. 'A democratic embarrassment: the House of Lords is aged, overcrowded and increasingly effective', *The Economist* (13 June 2015), 32.
60. Commission to Strengthen Parliament, 'Strengthening Parliament' (London: The Stationary Office, July 2000), p. 6.
61. As a counterpart, they cannot overthrow the government.
62. 'Companion to the Standing Orders and Guide to the Proceedings of the House of Lords', p. 77.
63. Lewis Baston and Stuart Wilks-Heeg, 'How strong is the case for having fewer MPs?', *Democratic Audit* (November 2010), 9.
64. Labour party manifesto, 'New Labour because Britain deserves better' (1997), p. 22.
65. The Conservative Opposition tried all that they could to delay the passage of the House of Lords Bill.
66. Barbara Vine, *The Blood Doctor* (London: Viking 2002), p. 175.
67. In a letter to *The Guardian* published on 31 July 2015 under the general heading 'Without Lords reform democracy will suffer'.
68. The 2014 House of Lords Reform Act contains provisions for permanent retirement and for permanent exclusion as well as cessation of membership following a session where a member does not attend.
69. When 'excepted' peers die they are replaced by means of by-election held in accordance with the standing orders of the House of Lords. The only other member of the House to be 'elected', this time by the full House, is the Lord Speaker, but once again it is not a democratic election by the people. The Lord Speaker is elected by the Lords as the Speaker of the House of Commons is by MPs, though they do not perform the same role.
70. For more information see Kenneth and Jane Morgan, *Portrait of a Progressive: The Political Career of Christopher, Viscount Addison* (Oxford: Clarendon Press, 1980). The Addison–Salisbury convention has been much criticised in recent years, especially under the coalition government of 2010–15, which had no formal manifesto at all.
71. Vine, *The Blood Doctor*, p. 53.
72. M. Alexis Bachelay, a Socialist MP for the Hauts-de-Seine department, gave an interview to the journalists of French Radio *France Inter* on 25 September 2014.
73. The reduction of the number of MPs from 650 to 600 aims at reducing inequalities of electors per seat – the idea is to equalise the size of parliamentary

constituencies to 76,640 electors per constituency, plus or minus only 5 per cent.

74. Electoral Commission. *Referendum on the Voting System for UK Parliamentary Elections*, Report on the May 2011 Referendum (London: Electoral Commission, 2011), p. 32.
75. G. Larcher presided over the Senate from 2008 to 2011. He was elected President of the Senate for the second time following the 2014 senatorial elections.
76. Meg Russell, 'House Full: Time to get a grip on Lords Appointments' (UCL: The Constitution Unit, April 2011).
77. In July 2015 there were 226 Conservative Peers out of 783 members of the House of Lords (212 Labour Peers, 101 Liberal Democrats (even though they held only eight seats in the House of Commons) and 179 cross-benchers, whose voting behaviour always contains an element of uncertainty as they are not subject to whips.
78. Lewis Baston and Stuart Wilks-Heeg, 'How strong is the case for having fewer MPs?', *Democratic Audit* (November 2010), 2.
79. Conservative party manifesto 2015, p. 49.
80. Commission de rénovation et de déontologie de la vie publique, Rapport 'pour un renouveau démocratique' (Paris: La Documentation française, 2012) – chaired by Lionel Jospin.
81. Lionel Jospin is a French Socialist politician, the son of a schoolteacher and a Protestant, who served as Prime Minister from 1997 to 2002 with the right-wing president Jacques Chirac in a coalition government. They fought each other in the 2002 Presidential election and Lionel Jospin ended up third, behind Jacques Chirac and the then leader of the National Front, Jean-Marie Le Pen.
82. Currently, 168 senators are indirectly elected via the majority system while 180 are indirectly elected by proportional representation.
83. Commission de rénovation et de déontologie de la vie publique, 'Pour un renouveau démocratique' , p. 42.
84. Comité de réflexion et de proposition sur la modernisation et le rééquilibrage des institutions de la Cinquième République, 'Une Cinquième République plus démocratique', p. 69.
85. Conservative manifesto, p. 49.
86. Christian Poncelet, 'Le bicamérisme, une idée toujours neuve', *Revue politique et parlementaire*, 1007 (July–August 2000), 2.
87. May's *Treatise on the Law, Privileges, Procedures and Usage of Parliament*, p. 201.
88. Comité de réflexion et de proposition sur la modernisation et le rééquilibrage des institutions de la Cinquième République, 'Une Cinquième République plus démocratique', p. 30.

89. Comité de réflexion et de proposition sur la modernisation et le rééquilibrage des institutions de la Cinquième République, 'Une Cinquième République plus démocratique', p. 51.
90. Richard Kelly, 'Prime Minister's Questions', House of Commons Library (9 February 2015) SN/PC/05183.
91. May's *Treatise on the Law, Privileges, Procedures and Usage of Parliament*, p. 360.
92. See Paul Waugh and Sam Macrory, 'The Independent Iconoclast', *The House Magazine* (23 February 2012), 20.
93. Stephen R. Bates, Peter Kerr, Christopher Byrne and Liam Stanley, 'Questions to the Prime Minister: A Comparative Study of Prime Minister's Questions from Thatcher to Cameron', *Parliamentary Affairs*, 67/2 (April 2014), 253–80.
94. As stated in Erskine May, 'urgent questions do not have to appear on the order of the day and may be taken immediately after the end of question time', p. 369.
95. May's *Treatise on the Law, Privileges, Procedures and Usage of Parliament*, p. 354.
96. James Macintyre, 'Getting the House in Order', *Prospect* (August 2011), 42–6.
97. See Paul Waugh and Sam Macrory, 'The Independent Iconoclast', *The House Magazine* (23 February 2012), 20.
98. Under the Fourth Republic, each chamber had 19 permanent/standing committees composed of either 44 deputies or 30 senators.
99. House of Commons Reform Committee, First Report of Session 2008–9, 'Rebuilding the House', HC 1117 (London: The Stationery Office, 24 November 2009), chaired by the Labour MP Dr Tony Wright.
100. As Andrew Tyrie explained in *The House Magazine*: 'Committees do not exist to make life easy for ministers and Whitehall' (10 July 2015), 30–1.
101. The 2009 Wright Committee Report advocated a reduction of the overall number of committees as well as in the number of MPs able to join each committee – no more than eleven per committee. Yet, no one will deny the importance of the creation of new select committees like the Committee on Women and Equalities following the recommendation of the All Party Parliamentary Group on women in 2014. Its remit is essentially to look at the work of the Government Equalities Office.
102. See the report of the House of Commons Political and Constitutional Reform Committee, 'Revisiting Rebuilding the House: The Impact of the Wright Reform' (London: The Stationery Office, March 2013).

Chapter Four

Better Protecting Human Rights and Strengthening an Independent Judiciary

The claim for justice was the rallying cry of the French revolutionaries in 1789. They wanted to break away from an elitist type of justice embodied by judges of the *ancien régime* sitting in the so-called *parlements*, who had either inherited or bought their judicial office. Many centuries before the French Revolution, in 1215 barons of Norman-French origin had rebelled against the arbitrary power of the English king, compelling him to seal a Great Charter (Magna Carta). It established for the very first time that everyone, including the king, was subject to the authority of the law,[1] and this came to be celebrated as the rule of law. One of its most famous provisions under chapter 40, which is still part of English Common Law, reads: 'To no one will we deny or delay right or justice.' Another major requirement of the rule of law in countries like France or the United Kingdom is for judges to be impartial and independent. They in turn have a special responsibility, which is to secure respect for this founding principle of democracies, whether they are republics or constitutional monarchies.

In spite of the universal dimension of the rule of law, national perceptions of justice vary on both sides of the Channel, as does the way it is delivered. This chapter will develop a comparison between justice under the French Republic – mainly perceived as a public service – and justice in the British constitutional monarchy, where the monarch is still officially the 'fount of justice'. It will be devoted to two legal cultures. The French one is based on abstract general principles where the quest for the truth is understood in absolute terms, whereas the British legal tradition tends to emphasise procedure and settlements negotiated outside the courts. It will also show that in spite of the high quality of their respective judiciaries, neither the independence of judges nor the protection of human rights can be taken for granted. Today, the access to justice of British and French citizens is jeopardised as the two countries have seen drastic cuts in legal aid as part of austerity budgets affecting the most vulnerable. But perhaps even more preoccupying are the threats to the rule of law in both countries, as their respective governments, faced with terrorism, tend to emphasise security to the detriment of human rights.

The French notion of *Etat de Droit*, both an ideal and part of substantive law, reflects the French attachment to the notion of the state, following the French eminent lawyer Carré de Malberg,[2] whose pioneer work is at the origin of this fundamental concept. It revolves around the notion of the state and is based on the necessity of limiting its power. This is how it was defined by the late Roger Errera, a former honorary member of the Conseil d'Etat and of the High Council of the Magistracy. For him, the *Etat de Droit* includes 'the separation of powers, the limitation of power, the hierarchy of legal norms, the guarantee of fundamental rights; when a right is violated it provides the right to an effective legal remedy before an independent and impartial judge.'[3]

Justice itself is an essential component of *l'Etat de Droit*. It differs from the British rule of law in that the latter is much more evolutionary, more flexible, more a process rather than being established once and for all like the French *Etat de Droit* – always a work in progress like the common law itself.[4] In France, the fifteen successive constitutions – with the major exception of the Napoleonic constitutions of Years VIII, IX and XII between 1799 and 1804 and of the 1815 Additional Act – all included a formal declaration of rights directly inspired by the 1789 Declaration of the Rights of Man and the Citizen as a major element of continuity in an otherwise disrupted constitutional history. It constantly kept alive the main legacy of the revolutionary era in terms of human rights, reaffirming its most fundamental principles.

In 2015, the United Kingdom adopted anti-terrorism and intelligence laws restricting civil liberties while France established a 'state of emergency', swiftly voted by the French parliament in the wake of the terrorist attacks of 13 November 2015, which claimed the lives of 130 mainly young people, French and foreigners.

Asserting the unity of the English judiciary compared with the French division of courts

In the United Kingdom, there is no codified constitution that clearly defines the role and powers of the judiciary. Although France does have an entrenched constitution, the status of the French judiciary is not necessarily more secure. It is still not formally considered as a power or as a judicial branch on the same footing as the French executive and the legislative.

The drafters of the 1958 Constitution deliberately devised it as a mere 'authority', its functions and duties being sparsely attributed, as part of a long tradition of suspicion of judges, in order to prevent them from becoming too powerful.[5] Significantly, in his official letter of assignment on 18 July 2007 to the former Prime Minister Edouard Balladur, President Sarkozy raised the point of discussing the opportunity of enshrining into the constitution the existence of 'a real judicial or jurisdictional power' as part of the terms of reference of the committee chaired by Balladur.

In the United Kingdom, judges have traditionally been held in higher esteem than in France, partly because of their central role in the common law, where judges *de facto* contribute to the development of the law, as opposed to the French view, under which judges are there to declare the law but in no way to create it. Yet on the British side of the Channel too, the spectre of the all-powerful judge, let alone judicial activism, emerged in the wake of the setting up of the United Kingdom Supreme Court in 2009. This suspicion is even more the case in attitudes to judges of the European Court of Justice and the European Court of Human Rights, often blamed for imposing their decisions on the United Kingdom and thus undermining its sovereignty.

In France, where so much importance is given to the unity of the Republic – and of the state – the judiciary is nonetheless divided into two main branches, as is generally the rule in continental Europe except in countries like Germany. One is the judicial branch with its own courts and tribunals, and at the very top the *Cour de Cassation* (Court of Cassation), also called the Supreme Court. It is deeply rooted in French history[6] – more precisely, in the revolutionary era – as it was originally set up as the *Tribunal de Cassation* by the Law of 27 November 1790. This introduced a cardinal principle in its article 3 according to which this jurisdiction is forbidden to hear the substance of a case. Unlike the United Kingdom Supreme Court, it cannot examine or re-examine facts but can only deal with arguable points of law. Its role is to make sure that the law has been correctly applied by trial judges of lower courts and courts of appeal, and that it is uniformly applied throughout the country. From that point of view, the United Kingdom Supreme Court fulfils the same task of unifying the law and harmonizing case law, but is deprived of the formidable power of the French Court of Cassation, which consists of quashing the judicial decisions of courts which have not applied the law correctly, thus protecting people amenable to a court from the potential arbitrary power of trial judges.

The other main branch of the French judicial system is the administrative one, with its own administrative 'tribunals' and administrative appeals courts. At its apex stands the *Conseil d'Etat* (Council of State), a legacy of Napoleon Bonaparte, the supreme authority in administrative justice which advises public authorities and adjudicates on citizens' claims against the administration. It checks that the administrative courts of appeal have applied the law correctly. In the United Kingdom, it took a long time to identify administrative law as such. Legal experts like Dicey refused to acknowledge its existence, believing in the ability of ordinary courts to deal with all aspects of the law. As a reaction to the proposal made by the British Lord Chancellor and Secretary of State for Justice, Michael Gove, in February 2016 to introduce a new constitutional court in the United Kingdom as a separate court from the Supreme Court, its President, Lord Neuberger, argued against a French-type division of courts:

> one of our great advantages compared with most of Europe is that we have a very simple system of courts and I think replicating the civil, European system of having a supreme court, a constitutional court, a supreme administrative court, is just a recipe for complication, for cost and for unnecessary duplication.[7]

But even if there is not the same formal division between judicial and administrative jurisdictions as in France, an administrative court was officially set up in the legal system of England and Wales in 2000.[8]

In the United Kingdom, unlike France, there are not two – or possibly three – Supreme Courts including the French Constitutional Council – but only one, the United Kingdom Supreme Court.[9] It is the highest court of appeal, hearing civil and criminal cases from all parts of the Kingdom – with the exception of criminal appeals from Scotland – that raise points of law of general public importance. It also deals with devolutionary jurisdictional issues previously heard by the Judicial Committee of the Privy Council. Besides, there is not one single legal system but in fact three, which are rooted in the history and the nature of the country and thus correspond to the nations forming the United Kingdom, with the notable exception of Wales. Given the development of a significant body of Welsh law following the 2011 referendum in Wales, which cleared the final hurdle in granting the Welsh National Assembly primary legislative power, a separate legal system for Wales might well be a realistic option. It would be a strong symbol for Welsh people, since law and language have since at least the tenth century been two fundamental pillars of Welsh identity, and has much sympathy from the Lord Chief Justice, Lord Thomas of Cwmgiedd.

Strengthening the independence of the judiciary in England and France

The President of the Law Society, Andrew Caplen, stated in 2015 that 'the United Kingdom has a reputation as a world leader in independence of the judiciary, the rule of law, and the provision of legal services.'[10] Though lacking a codified constitution, the United Kingdom very early on tried to protect its judges from the arbitrary power of the executive – and originally from the arbitrary power of the monarch – with the Act of Settlement 1701. The latter is generally known as the Act regulating access to the throne, but it is also a key piece of legislation affecting the status of judges since it protects them from arbitrary removal. For the first time it established that they would hold their judicial position 'during good behaviour' (*quamdiu se bene gesserint*), which *de facto* amounted to tenure in office[11] and independence. It particularly applies to senior judges, who have traditionally benefited from a form of immunity, as their removal process requires the approval of both Houses of Parliament.

In France, the constitution explicitly protects judges – at least the so-called *juges du siège* (literally 'judges of the seat'), who are installed to give decisions in court as trial judges and are independent of the state; under article 64 of the constitution, 'judges of the seat shall be irremovable from office.' The same provision is generally understood as also implicitly applying to the other category of judges, called in French *juges du parquet* (literally 'judges of the floor'), who act as state prosecutors and are placed under the authority of the Minister of Justice. There is no such distinction between judges in the United Kingdom, since prosecutors are not judges but lawyers working for the Crown Prosecution Service (CPS). Yet in France the idea of the independence of the judiciary is above all closely linked with a fundamental principle – the foundation stone of French constitutional law – that of the separation of powers, strongly influenced by the writings of John Locke, but generally associated with the French Enlightenment thinker and philosopher Montesquieu. One of the most important and famous provisions of the French Declaration of the Rights of Man and the Citizen of 1789,[12] which is now part of substantive law in France, is article 16, which reads: 'Any society in which the guarantee of rights is not enshrined, nor a separation of powers is worked out, has no Constitution.'

Under this principle, it is unlawful for judges to step into the legislative function by defining general rules. The French constitutional lawyer Carré de Malberg held the view that 'this principle of separation of the legislative from the judiciary commandingly excludes any possibility of entitling judges to state the law which has not already been established by law.'[13]

Thus, in France in spite of the growing importance of case law,[14] it is still not considered as a formal source of the law, as it would conflict with the principle of separation of powers. If, under this cardinal principle, judges are not to step into the legislative role in any way, the important counterpart is that the judiciary must be free of any pressure or interference from either the legislative or the executive.

A formal separation between the judiciary and the legislature with the Constitutional Reform Act (2005)

In the United Kingdom, although the independence of the judiciary from the executive has long been achieved, it was, however, still not formally the case between the judiciary and the legislative. Indeed, the Appellate Committee of the House of Lords, composed of Lords of Appeal in Ordinary (more commonly known as Law Lords), presided over by the Lord Chancellor, formed the highest court of appeal of the country from 1876 to 2009. By convention, the professional judges who joined the Appellate Committee were made life peers even if they refrained from taking part in the legislative work of the House of Lords out of a sense of judicial ethics.

The Constitutional Reform Act 2005 introduced the most significant reform of the British judiciary since the later nineteenth century, drastically reducing the powers of the Lord Chancellor by transferring his main legal function as head of the judiciary to the Lord Chief Justice, who presides over the courts in England and Wales. Again, he no longer acts as the Speaker of the House of Lords, given that the upper chamber now elects the Lord Speaker from within its own ranks. The Lord Chancellor, who embodied the lack of separation of powers since he belonged to all three estates, has however kept his position as a key Cabinet minister at the head of the Ministry of Justice[15] set up in 2007.[16] The UK Lord Chancellor and Secretary of State for Justice,[17] who now sits in the House of Commons, continues nonetheless to have important duties so far as judicial independence is concerned.[18] Thus under the Constitutional Reform Act 2005, 'the Lord Chancellor … must uphold the continued independence of the judiciary.'[19]

As a consequence, judicial independence in the United Kingdom is now officially enshrined in law.

The 2005 Act also introduced more transparency in the way British judges are recruited by setting up an independent commission, the Judicial Appointments Commission (JAC), in charge of the nomination process of judges. Finally, and particularly, the Constitutional Reform Act 2005 provided for the creation of a United Kingdom Supreme Court[20] acting as the highest court of appeal for the country in lieu of the Appellate Committee of the House of Lords – mentioned above. Montesquieu, himself an anglophile and admirer of British institutions, famously argued: 'there is no liberty if the power of judging is not separate from legislative and from executive power.'[21] The United Kingdom followed this precept and severed the ties between the Highest Court of Appeal of the country and the Westminster Parliament. The UKSC was to be a general high court, more accessible to the public, interpreting national statutes, not a specialised constitutional court. This means that it has a diversity of subject matter for jurisdiction. Since 2009 the Supreme Court has heard a great variety of high-profile cases – since it tries to concentrate on cases of the greatest importance – that reflect the evolution of British society. Thus British preoccupations such as *Radmacher v Granatino* (2010) about the nature of pre-nuptial agreements (where significantly the only woman, Justice Hale, expressed a dissenting opinion) and *R. v the Commissioner of Police of the Metropolis* (2011) dealing with the highly divisive issue of the retention of fingerprints and DNA by the police and its potential breach of article 8 of the ECHR protecting the right to privacy, have both received extended attention in the media. Other relevant legal landmarks were *Smith v the Ministry of Defence*, dealing with the bereaved relatives of British soldiers who had died in Iraq in 2013, and, on 25 June 2014, *R (on the application of Nicklinson and another) v Ministry of Justice*, where the lawyers of Mr. Nicklinson, who suffered from locked-in syndrome, pleaded without success the incompatibility of the 1961 Suicide Act,[22] assimilating assisted suicide with homicide, with article 8 of the ECHR. The judgments of the UKSC on those topical issues have had important repercussions on the lives of citizens and have significantly contributed to the evolution of the English common law.

Granting the UKSC powers additional to those of the former Appellate Committee of the House of Lords had was not on the agenda except for devolution issues.[23] They raised questions of constitutional importance about the exercise of devolved powers – regulated by the Scotland Act 1998, the Government of Wales Act 2006 and the Northern Ireland Act 1998

– which, until then, had been adjudicated by the Judicial Committee of the Privy Council. If the new UKSC inherited legal functions from both the Appellate Committee of the House of Lords and the Judicial Committee of the Privy Council, the two highest courts of appeal, respectively for the UK and for the Commonwealth countries, were not merged[24]. The aim was simply for a single United Kingdom-wide supreme court, to be in charge of all matters of a constitutional nature covering human rights and devolution issues.[25] As the 2014 annual report of the UKSC clearly states: 'in these and some other aspects it represents a constitutional court,'[26] and it acted as such in 2014 by upholding the policy of the Welsh Assembly in the agricultural wages case.

In 2009, the then Deputy President of the UKSC, Lord Hope, wondered whether 'the physical independence of a new building would breed a greater independence of spirit.'[27] He himself then provided an answer by describing his work in the UKSC as 'a liberating experience'. It seems indeed that the creation of a separate UKSC has led to more assertive justices, whose authority had already been strengthened by the need to interpret national statutes and ensure they comply with EU Law and the ECHR. The devolution process itself has not only increased their workload with devolution issues but has also led them to develop a new form of control over the primary legislation of devolved legislatures which has some striking similarities with the type of constitutional review that can be found in France.

The development of constitutional justice in France

The introduction of the French Constitutional Council in 1958 in the constitution of the Fifth Republic was to pave the way for constitutional justice in France, though the original aim of the court was to protect the executive from any infringement from parliament legislating beyond its remit. This was introduced as a reaction to the concentration of power to the benefit of parliament of the previous Republics. In fact, the Constitutional Council was to develop a form of constitutional control, with which the constitution of 1958 had not endowed it, through its own case law in 1971 in its famous decision on Freedom of Association. The review power of the French Constitutional Council was then significantly strengthened by a constitutional amendment in 1974 which extended the right to refer primary legislation to it to sixty members of either the National Assembly or the Senate, or more recently with the so-called *Question Prioritaire de*

Constitutionnalité (QPC) (Preliminary Ruling on Constitutionality) under the new article 61 (1) of the constitution following the July 2008 major redrafting of the constitution of 1958. It is now possible for court users involved in legal proceedings, and who claim that a statutory provision infringes their rights and freedoms guaranteed by the constitution, to refer a statute to the Constitutional Council via either the Court of Cassation or the Council of State. What is more, already enacted legislation can now be subject to constitutional review, as is the case in the United States. Thus, through a series of major constitutional changes, France has progressively moved from parliamentary sovereignty to constitutional sovereignty. If the law is still the expression of the general will of the people it is now subordinate to the Constitution itself. In 2008, the Balladur Committee in its report reasserted that 'the independence of judges is essential for the balance of every democratic society' and that 'it must be protected by the constitution, for it is the cornerstone of the respect for human rights.'[28]

Unlike the United Kingdom, it is not the French Justice Minister who is officially in charge of protecting the independence of the judiciary, but the President of the Republic himself.

The President of the Republic in France, the Lord Chancellor and Secretary of State for Justice as guarantors of the independence of justice

Under article 64 of the constitution, 'the President of the Republic shall be the guarantor of the independence of the judicial authority.' Though this can be seen as the continuation of his role as guarantor of the independence and integrity of the state and of French territory under article 5, it may be questioned whether he is the best person to fulfil such a mission, as he is the head of the executive and a politician himself. Some eminent lawyers, such as the late Roger Errera, fiercely criticised the provision. 'Assuming this independence needs a guarantor, which is very doubtful, why should it be the President of the Republic?'[29] To qualify such a statement, the same article 64 of the French constitution also states that in doing so the President of the Republic is assisted by the *Conseil Supérieur de la Magistrature* (High Council of the Judiciary). Yet, until the constitutional reform of 27 July 1993, the very independence of this body, in charge of the appointment process of judges and disciplinary measures applying to them, was itself questionable, since its fourteen members were all appointed by the President of the Republic – who also acted as its chairman while the Minister of Justice was its deputy chairman. The constitutional change of 2008 adopted in the wake of the Balladur Report went even further in enhancing the independence of the High Council of the Judiciary[30] by removing the President of the Republic as its chair as well as putting an end to his ability to attend its sessions altogether.[31] As for the French Justice Minister, even if the latter has lost the ability to co-chair the High Council of the Judiciary, he can still attend its session except when its members sit as a disciplinary committee. Unlike the British Constitutional Reform Act 2005, which fundamentally altered the status of the Lord Chancellor[32] – as seen above – the Balladur Report hardly contained any proposal regarding his French counterpart. The full title of the Justice Minister in France is *ministre de la Justice et Garde des Sceaux* (Justice Minister and Keeper of the Seals) – these seals which are strong symbols of the French state are the official Seals of the Republic.[33]

The French Justice Minister used to preside over the *tribunal des conflits* in charge of solving disputes between the judicial branch and the administrative branch of the French judiciary. This is no longer the case, for the statute of 16 February 2015 stated that its president ought to be recruited from the ranks of alternatively the Council of State and the Court of Cassation, then elected by members of the *tribunal des conflits* for three years by a majority vote. This reform was implemented in April 2015. The French Justice Minister, until January 2016 Christiane Taubira,[34] appointed by President Hollande, has extensive powers. The holder of this highly prestigious office oversees the running of the courts, public prosecutions, presidential pardons and prisons. She/he prepares and administers the budget of the Justice Ministry and is partly responsible for the management of the courts – although the latter has become much more decentralised. Public prosecutors are directly placed under the authority of the Justice Minister – as previously seen – which has raised an ongoing controversy over the lack of independence of this category of judges. Even if France's 168 public prosecutors acknowledge that progress has been made with the law of 25 July 2013, making it unlawful for the Justice Minister to provide them with individual instructions, they think that this is still not enough. They would like the High Council of the Judiciary to be granted full autonomy in the management of their careers, as is already the case for judges. One of their main claims was encapsulated by the public prosecutor of the Republic, Jean-Claude Marin, who proposed to 'incorporate into the Constitution the principle of the unity of the judiciary',[35] combining judges and public prosecutors in a single UK-type judiciary. Yet the 2008 constitutional change has not in any way clarified the status of French public prosecutors in spite of France having been sanctioned several times by the European Court of Human Rights for non-compliance with article 6 (1) of the European Convention on Human Rights, which requires an independent judiciary in order to guarantee everyone a fair trial.

French judges as symbols of Republican Law, British judges as Her Majesty's judges

The independence of justice in France – where judges are living symbols of Republican Law[36] – and in the United Kingdom starts with the training and recruitment process of judges. The assumption in both countries is that the personal characteristics of individual judges, in other words judges' political views, personal considerations or gender, are not relevant to how cases are decided. A most eminent British judge, the late Lord Bingham, defined them in the following way: 'judges are a neutral, colourless, undistorting medium through which the law is transmitted to those bound by it.'[37] In so doing, they are very powerful – not that they hold any political power, but they do possess sentencing power, which can go as far as depriving an offender, once convicted, of his most fundamental right: the right to liberty. Before 1969 in the United Kingdom and 1981 in France, judges held people's lives in their hands, as they could sentence serious offenders to death.

Judges are expected to leave their casual clothes, personal considerations and characteristics and prejudices, if any, at the door of the courtroom. The way they dress, they behave, they speak in the courtroom is highly codified. This is perhaps even more the case in the officially non-codified English common law, where judges wear the full legal regalia with wigs and gowns. While this has its importance, as it separates the judicial office from the person and thus guarantees judges' anonymity, protecting them from potential retaliation and placing them in a position of authority, this strange world, with its own codes, practices and rituals, may appear somehow frightening, not to say dehumanised, in lay people's eyes. Unlike Members of Parliament and many American state judges, judges are not, of course, elected representatives, and their judicial decisions are not based on political considerations. In the same way, they are not supposed to represent any particular category or subgroup of the population.

Thus, they are people with a special status and specific duties and responsibilities encapsulated in the oath they take before being able to sit as judges. Unlike French judges, British judges have to swear a double oath: an oath of allegiance to the monarch, as they are Her Majesty's judges, officially appointed by the monarch by letters patent; and a judicial oath swearing that they will 'well and truly serve their Sovereign in their office and will do right to all manner of people after the laws and usages of this realm, without fear or favour, affection or ill will'. French judges, who are formally appointed by the President of the Republic under article 13 of the 1958 constitution, have only to take a judicial oath under which they swear, 'to fulfil their office well, to keep the secrecy of deliberations and of the votes even after the end of their term in office and to behave in everything as a dignified and loyal judge'.[38] Both French and English judges are under a legal obligation of confidentiality. Yet secrecy seems more deeply rooted in the practices of the United Kingdom than in France, as its judges were recruited until fairly recently on the basis of secret soundings under the patronage of the Lord Chancellor. This reflects the confidential ethos of British public life as a whole.

The lack of diversity in the higher judiciary in the UK and in France

For long, the judiciary in France and the United Kingdom had the common characteristic of being a male preserve. Men were a majority in law schools and in the legal profession. But French law faculties are very different now from what they used to be, as there has been a massive feminisation not only of students – two-thirds of law students are women – but also of members of academic staff, except for university vice-chancellors. The British Queen's Counsel, Helena Kennedy, has observed the same phenomenon in the United Kingdom, noting that 'over 50 per cent of students in law schools are female' and that 'women are more visible in courts.'[39] In 2016, for the first time ever, a woman was appointed Lord Chancellor and Secretary of State for Justice in the United Kingdom. The second female Prime Minister in the history of the country, Theresa May, a Conservative, who succeeded David Cameron who resigned as Prime Minister and as Leader of the Conservative party in the wake of the 2016 referendum on Britain's EU membership, reshuffled the government in July 2016. She appointed Elizabeth Truss as the new Justice Secretary. Her nomination raised a controversy, not so much because she is a woman but because she is not a lawyer. On 21 July 2016, after a week of debate about the suitability of her appointment and some fierce criticisms – notably from the former Shadow Justice Secretary and Lord Chancellor, Lord Falconer – Elizabeth Truss, a forty-year-old former accountant, was sworn in as Lord Chancellor and Secretary of State for Justice at the Royal Courts of Justice. She is the third non-lawyer – after Chris Grayling and Michael Gove – to be appointed Lord Chancellor under the process of the Constitutional Reform Act 2005. Her only experience of the justice system was when she served on the Commons Justice Committee as an MP. A former Lord Chancellor himself, Lord Falconer explained: 'in any government, the Lord Chancellor has a duty to ensure that judges are properly protected from political attacks and are able to act independently and that the government itself always acts in accordance with the law.' Since the Constitutional Reform Act 2005, the holder of the post of Lord Chancellor, which is now combined with Justice Secretary, does not have to be a lawyer. The controversy around the nomination of the new Lord Chancellor put to the fore the problem of the status of the office. It has become too much politicised, combining the traditional role of the Lord Chancellor with that of Justice Secretary at the Head of the Department of Justice. It seriously compromises the independence of this office holder. As Helena Kennedy suggested, it would be preferable to appoint the Lord Chancellor in a much more impartial way through an independent appointments commission. As she argued in her letter to *The Guardian* on 28 July 2016, 'the strength of the traditional role of the Lord Chancellor was that it was filled by a very experienced lawyer who had no further ambition and would therefore fearlessly defend the rule of law and the independence of lawyers and judges.' Yet since the Constitutional Reform Act 2005, there has been a lack of legal expertise of the Lord Chancellor.

France for its part has had not one but three women *Garde des Sceaux* – Minister of Justice and Keeper of the Seals. Elisabeth Guigou[40], born in Morocco, was the first woman ever to become *Garde des Sceaux* in 1997 in the *cohabitation* government of the Socialist Lionel Jospin under the presidency of Jacques Chirac. Ten years afterwards, in 2007, Rachida Dati, a former graduate from the French Judicial Training College (the Ecole Nationale de la Magistrature, ENM), was nominated for this prestigious office by the then President, Nicolas Sarkozy. She thus became the highest-ranking person of North African descent in France.[41] In the wake of the 2012 presidential election, the Socialist President, François Hollande, appointed Christiane Taubira,[42] a black woman from Guyana, as *Garde des Sceaux*, a staunch supporter of minorities' rights,[43] who resigned on a rights issue in January 2016 and was replaced by a white man (Jean-Jacques Urvoas).

While the United Kingdom is trying to move on from a predominantly white male judiciary with only 23 per cent women judges, the massive feminisation of French judges, with 64 per cent of women, well over the European average of 48 per cent, is starting to cause concern as some fear that male judges in France might become extinct.[44] In fact what is really at stake is the quality and efficiency of justice, including access to justice. Indeed, a more gender-balanced judiciary is essential to the quality of justice along the lines suggested by Lord Falconer, who claimed that 'if judges are insufficiently diverse, then their quality declines,'[45] even if he failed to redress the problem himself.

In the French Republic, which has a fully professionalised Bench, becoming a judge is a career choice made by students once they have acquired their basic legal qualifications. Would-be judges aiming to join the judicial branch sit the entrance examination for the *Ecole Nationale de la Magistrature* (ENM), whereas future administrative judges sit the entrance examination for the *Ecole Nationale de l'Administration* (ENA) – a highly prestigious *Grande Ecole*. Would-be judges will usually not practise as a lawyer first, but instead have to prepare for a fierce competitive examination which, if they are successful, will allow them to be trained as judges in the ENM in Bordeaux, attached to the Ministry of Justice. France is proud of its tradition of competitive examinations, which are a requirement for anyone who wishes to join the French civil service. It can be traced back to the 1789 Declaration of the Rights of Man and the Citizen, which states in its article 6 that 'all citizens … shall be equally eligible to all high offices, public positions and employments, according to their ability, and without other distinction than that of their virtues and talents.'

Judges themselves are civil servants, though of a particular kind, since they are sworn in and enjoy special statutory protection from the executive. The ENM is responsible for the initial and ongoing training of French judges and prosecutors, and each year the school trains some 200 new so-called *auditeurs de justice* – trainee judges – as part of their initial training.[46] Once they have qualified as a judge, they will sit in junior posts and then hope to be promoted up the judicial ladder.

French women are particularly successful,[47] whereas fewer men apply, and those who do so tend to perform less well in the entrance examination. One reason may be that French men prefer to become lawyers, which, in France is a different career from the judiciary, partly because, in private practice, they can earn far more money than judges. Jean-François Thony, the former head of the ENM, explained that women law students prefer to be judges, while men tend to go for the legal jobs that carry power (e.g. as prosecutors) or earn a lot of money, (e.g. jobs in corporate or taxation law).

Also, women in France seem to be more attracted than men to the ideals of the judiciary and more motivated by the idea of serving the state.[48] The French public service is based on values and principles such as equality and neutrality. The French way of selecting future judges officially guarantees transparency and fairness as well as equality of opportunities, since all candidates are on the same footing; it is also considered a very independent process since it is not under the patronage of the executive. So in the French Republican tradition, there has been a long-established, officially fair recruitment and training process to secure a high-quality judiciary and to enable the best law students to succeed. Besides, the appointments of most judges have to be approved by a special institution, the High Council of the Judiciary, in which representatives of judges but also lay people sit.

This long-established recruitment process was however seriously challenged by what became one of France's most famous miscarriages of justice – the Outreau case (2004) – involving a young investigating judge with hardly any legal professional experience at all: Judge Burgaud was confronted by a case where children falsely pretended that they had been sexually abused. It is interesting to note that this young male judge gave much importance to the children' s testimonies, not only giving them the benefit of the doubt but also placing the highest priority on their own welfare and interests – as is in fact required in the United Kingdom under the Children Act 1989.This judicial case acted as a reminder of the fallibility of judges and led to serious questioning of the recruitment process of judges allowing very young people in their late twenties or early thirties to become judges without the need for any professional experience beforehand apart from internships lasting only a few months. It was thought that there was something seriously wrong in this recruitment process, and the uproar in French public opinion was such that the abolition of the ENM was even envisaged. An indirect consequence of the Outreau miscarriage of justice was to bring closer the training of would-be judges to that of lawyers-to-be which, until recently, was totally separate in France. Thus French trainee judges now have to spend six months in lawyers' chambers to complete their initial training, while some would-be lawyers can attend the lectures normally exclusively aimed at future judges. It is interesting to note that this French reform was largely inspired by the training and recruitment process of English common law judges.

Although in the United Kingdom there is no specialised judicial school as in France, merit is today equally important, and it is now an official criterion for the selection of English would-be judges. As the former Lord

Chancellor, Lord Irvine, said, 'yes, it is true that many judges today are white, Oxbridge educated men. But, it is also true that they were appointed on merit, from the then available pool, at the time the vacancies arose.'[49]

This state of facts could first of fall be explained by the absence of a formal judicial career structure in the UK of the kind found in France. Indeed, appointment to the English Bench is generally regarded as an end in itself following a successful career as a lawyer – preferably a barrister – as a founding principle is: 'The better lawyer you are, the better judge you will be.'

Traditionally, English judges were chosen primarily from the English Bar, as good reputation at the Bar was associated with independence and impartiality, considered as two key requirements for joining the Bench. The Courts and Legal Services Act 1990 officially broke the monopoly that the Bar held on all superior judgeships in order to allow non-barristers, especially solicitor-advocates,[50] but also people who read law without necessarily having practised as lawyers, such as law academics, to join the judiciary and thus widen the pool of would-be judges. It seems, however, that the barristers' monopoly over the Bench has not completely disappeared. This is notably the view of Lady Hale,[51] a former university academic and the only woman in the United Kingdom Supreme Court. She has pointed out that 'our divided legal profession is one of the principal differences between the UK and most of the rest of the Common Law world and is one of the main reasons for the continuing lack of diversity in the Higher Judiciary,' adding that 'top jobs are reserved for the top Barristers.'

In fact such a division is less and less justified, as barristers are no longer the only ones with rights of audience in higher courts and now can themselves have direct access to clients, which used to be only possible for solicitors.

However, the process of judicial appointments has improved significantly in England and Wales since the Constitutional Reform Act 2005 which, as far as the judiciary is concerned, aimed at increasing both equality and diversity. Part 4 provided for the creation of an independent statutory body free from the patronage of politicians, the Judicial Appointments Commission (JAC). The latter started to operate in April 2006. It was introduced 'to widen the range of applicants for judicial appointment and to ensure that the very best eligible candidates are drawn from a wider range of backgrounds'. Appointments were to be made solely on the basis of merit and solely on the recommendation of the newly constituted JAC,[52] with a reduced role for the Lord Chancellor,[53] thus guaranteeing a fair and open selection process closer to the French type of recruitment. Before the creation of this independent commission,[54] senior judges were recruited by way of invitation from the Lord Chancellor. Because the judicial appointments process relied on the soundings of the senior members of the judiciary and profession, it tended to be very conservative and unbalanced, especially towards women and minority groups, but also often to solicitors. Yet the Judicial Appointments Commission has failed to fulfil its initial objectives and therefore to improve diversity in the judiciary, especially in higher courts among senior judges. To try to put an end to the lack of gender balance in the judiciary an 'Equal Merit Provision' was inserted into section 63 of the CRA 2005 by the Crime and Courts Act 2013. Under this new provision, 'selection solely on merit does not prevent the selecting body, where two persons are of equal merit, from preferring one of them over the other for the purpose of increasing diversity.'[55]

But the practice, as cautiously laid out by the President of the Supreme Court, Lord Neuberger, still seems impervious to reform. In both countries, there is still much progress to be made to achieve judicial diversity and thus to have judges who are more reflective of society. One might wonder whether introducing a French-type career judiciary in the United Kingdom would be a feasible and desirable solution to secure a more gender-balanced judicial profession. For, as Lady Hale argued, the lack of such a judiciary is detrimental to women and to non-barristers. She is far from being the only one to favour a career judiciary for the UK. The House of Lords Constitution Committee, which launched an inquiry into the judicial appointments process in 2011,[56] examining gender balance within the judiciary from a constitutional perspective, proposed 'a judiciary in which lawyers are appointed to junior judicial roles at a much earlier stage in their career',[57] as in France. The idea would be to turn the Judicial Studies Board, initially set up in 1979 – responsible for judges' training in England and Wales, running seminars on sentencing, providing courses for newly appointed judges as well as refresher courses for more experienced judges – into a Judicial Training College like the institution in France.

The case of France, however, shows that a career judiciary does not necessarily guarantee equality between men and women judges, as the glass ceiling still exists. Besides, the French type of career judiciary tends to lead to a form of corporatism. Many efforts have been made in the United Kingdom, including the creation of the Judicial Appointments Commission, to abolish the existing corporatism based on the 'old boy network', where judges were – and still are – tempted to recruit people like themselves, white, middle-class and from the public schools. Lady Hale is among the English judges who think that the UK puts too much emphasis on legal professional experience rather than taking more into account legal ability, personal skills and potential. But, as previously seen, this can be a handicap for future judges. If there is undoubtedly a need to rejuvenate the judiciary in England and Wales, significant experience as a legal practitioner is what France still lacks. Yet it has started emulating the United Kingdom by encouraging more and more legal practitioners with at least some fifteen years of legal practice who want a career change, such as former advocates or prison governors, to join the Judicial Training College, and it has proved a change for the better.

The importance of local justice in the UK and in France with the lay Bench

It would be unfair not to mention the importance of the lay Bench (with 17,552 lay magistrates)[58] in the UK, which is well gender-balanced, as 53 per cent are women, and which very much depends on a strong sense of commitment of lay magistrates to their community. Unlike the professional Bench, they come from a wide range of backgrounds and occupations. They very much embody a local type of justice, close to citizens geographically, and also socially, morally and perhaps politically. They are the face of justice in the UK and a guarantee of its humanity. If France is praised internationally for the quality of its career judges, its lay judges remain largely unknown, though – as Roger Errera explained – not only do they almost double professional judges' numbers[59] but they are also part of a long-established tradition, at least in specialised courts at the local level. They can be found dealing with labour and social-law matters – in industrial tribunals and social security courts, as well as in commercial courts where justice is delivered by people who are either elected or nominated in relation to their belonging to specific socio-professional categories. In addition, like jurors in the United Kingdom, French citizens with no criminal record can be selected at random from electoral registers to hear the most serious crimes, those liable to custodial sentences for more than five years or life imprisonment, in the Assize Court – which is the equivalent of the Crown Court in England and Wales. But if combining career judges with non-professional judges in the composition of French courts is deeply rooted in French legal culture, it is far from being an ideal type of justice, as the decisions of non-professional judges are often challenged, let alone overturned, partly through lack of proper training and legal qualification of the French lay Bench.[60]

Soon after her nomination as the head of the French Ministry of Justice in 2012, Christiane Taubira launched a vast consultation process called 'Justice in the twenty-first century' (J21) to see what measures could be introduced to better assist French court-users and also to put French citizens at the core of justice in order to develop a people's justice in the spirit of the French Republic.[61] It is in a way a continuation of the recommendations by the Balladur Committee which paved the way for the 2008 constitutional change. In its report, the committee pointed out the need to grant French citizens new rights as part of the final, and far from least important, aspect of its constitutional change proposals.[62] These included the ability for court-users to make a referral to the French Constitutional Council via the Council of State or the Court of Cassation (under the new article 61-1) – *Question Prioritaire de Constitutionnalité* (QPC), Priority Question of Constitutionality – or the possibility for a person awaiting trial to approach the High Council of the Judiciary (under the redrafted article 65) to make justice more accessible. Thus attempts have been made effectively to make the French legal system more accessible and more intelligible to ordinary citizens. Yet, at a time when much emphasis is put on restoring people's confidence in justice, access to the latter and the rule of law are seriously deficient in both the United Kingdom and France.

Human rights under threat: a French state of emergency and British inroads into civil liberties

On 13 November 2015, eight suicide bombers triggered the bombs they carried around their waists to kill a maximum of civilians – mainly young people – around them in a famous concert hall in Paris known as the Bataclan, in Parisian cafés and restaurants in the fashionable Xth and XIIth districts, and outside the football stadium, the Stade de France, where the French President was attending an international match. These attacks claimed 130 lives and numerous casualties. After three days of official mourning when French flags were flown at half-mast, the national anthem sung at many public events and places, including universities, to pay homage to the victims and their families, François Hollande, the President of the Republic, who, under article 5 of the Constitution, is the guarantor of national independence, territorial integrity and the continuity of the French state as well as the functioning of the institutions, took the rare decision of assembling the two Houses of parliament – the National Assembly and the Senate – for a joint session as the French *Congrès* in Versailles.[63] Taking the floor before parliament, he declared that France was at war, and that given the exceptional circumstances that the country faced in terms of imminent serious threats to the security of its citizens and its territory, exceptional measures were required. This war rhetoric was very different from his call for national unity, cohesion and solidarity after the massacre of the journalists of the satirical magazine *Charlie Hebdo* in January 2015,[64] but might be explained by the new scale of terrorist attacks which hit French people at random and where the President himself could have lost his life. Hollande thus declared that he would ask for the State of Emergency to be officially established – which would need urgent legislation and a revision of the constitution itself, as it does not include provisions for a 'state of emergency'. The President called on the assembled law-makers to change the constitution in order to better protect French people and the country at large.

The President criticised current constitutional arrangements dealing with a 'state of crisis' as no longer adapted to the new exceptional circumstances, alluding more particularly to sections 16 and 36 of the constitution of the Fifth Republic. The first gives the President of the Republic full emergency powers when the functioning of the institutions, the territorial integrity and the independence of the nation are under serious and immediate threat, and was used by President de Gaulle to deal with the Algerian crisis in 1961. To his credit, President Hollande decided to use the 1955 law on the state of emergency rather than section 16 of the constitution, which would have given him the full powers as President of the Republic – that is to say, exceptional emergency powers. As for the second, it is a short, laconic though crucial article as it deals with the 'state of siege'. It is simply stated that the latter 'has to be decreed in the Council of Ministers; and that its 'extension thereof after a period of twelve days may be authorized solely by parliament'. Yet, the constitution itself did not specify under which conditions the 'state of siege' could be used. As for the 'state of emergency', it was nowhere mentioned in the constitution of the Fifth Republic.[65] In fact, since that constitution was drafted in 1958 in a very different context, it does not contain any provisions on terrorism. The only piece of legislation that existed was a law – that of 3 April 1955 on the state of emergency passed during the Algerian war which contained exceptional measures, such as imposing curfews, banning public meetings, allowing the police to carry out searches and seizures in private homes without search warrants and without judicial oversight, but also controlling the media in order to deal with exceptional circumstances like war or armed insurrection.

Within just a few days following the terrorist attacks, the French parliament voted massively and hastily a new law – the Law of 23 November 2015 Reinforcing the State of Emergency – with immediate effect, making it lawful to extend the state of emergency from the initial twelve days authorised by the law of 3 April 1955 to three months. Indeed, under the provisions of the law of 1955, 'any extension of the state of emergency beyond twelve days must be authorised by law.'[66] Yet, it did not only extend the state of emergency, but it also introduced further restrictions on the freedom of movement of people[67] considered as a threat to public order and security, to the right to privacy and freedom of speech, thus expanding the provisions of the 1955 State of Emergency Act and security measures,[68] to the great concern of French judges and lawyers. Judges of the judicial branch more particularly condemn the fact that they are deprived of their usual prerogatives under the state of emergency, not to say totally sidelined, to the benefit of prefects, who embody the executive in French departments, and the police. An essential legal safeguard in France is that the police must always work under the control of a judge. Yet, the new Law on the State of Emergency has significantly strengthened the state's police powers. The situation is hardly better for judges of the administrative branch, who can only perform an *ex post* type of control of house arrests.

No one can dispute the need to better protect French people and territory from potential new terrorist attacks. However, what might be debatable is the proportionality of the measures[69] adopted, since a whole array of laws dealing with security already existed. Some of the new derogation measures seem to be out of proportion, and even questionable. They have been used against people whose connection with any terrorist activity was doubtful, such as environmental activists during the United Nations Summit on climate change held in Paris from 30 November to 12 December 2015 in a country still in a state of shock. Although, to avoid any possible delays, the new Law on the State of Emergency was not submitted to any preliminary constitutional review by the Constitutional Council before its promulgation by the President of the Republic, the question of its compliance with the constitution was raised, at least in connection with its article 6, once the law had been enacted, by some environmental activists placed under house arrest under the new law. The legal argument put forward by the claimants was that article 6 of the new law, stating that the Interior Minister can decide to put someone under house arrest as long as he has 'serious reasons to think that the person's conduct is a threat to security or public order' breaches their right 'not to be detained arbitrarily', as guaranteed by article 66 of the constitution. The same article also says that the judicial authority is the guardian of the freedom of the individual, which implies that for every deprivation of personal liberty, the judicial authority must be involved – the problem being that in the state of emergency detention is carried out outside judicial control.

The Constitutional Council in its own case law[70] imposed strict legal safeguards on any measures depriving individuals of their liberty to avoid potential abuses, ruling that it must be provided by statute, it must be necessary – and must only last while it is considered necessary – and, perhaps even more important, it must be supervised by a judge, preferably a trial judge rather than a public prosecutor. Article 6 of the Law of 3 April 1955 as amended by the new Law on the State of Emergency was also challenged via another priority question of constitutionality (QPC), this time by the League of Human Rights on 11 December 2015. Yet in its decision of 22 December 2015 the Constitutional Council ruled that the first paragraphs of article 6 of this law were consistent with the constitution. However, the official go-ahead from the Constitutional Council has neither fully reassured the legal community nor settled the question of how to reconcile the state of emergency with the rule of law.

Two additional proposals put forward by the French government to tackle the issue of terrorism – mentioned by the President in his November 2015 speech before the two Houses of the French parliament – have raised arguable points of law. One was to change the constitution in order to incorporate the state of emergency into its provisions, even though many lawyers questioned the necessity of such a constitutional change. The other would consist of stripping French-born citizens convicted of acts of terrorism[71] of their French nationality. Although this would only apply to binationals (otherwise the individual would become stateless), it would be a major change, as for now only people who have acquired French nationality by naturalisation can have their French nationality removed. The Defender of Rights,[72] Jacques Toubon, firmly expressed his opposition to stripping binational people born in France of their French nationality. This is in no way surprising, as French nationality is deeply rooted in the *jus soli* – that is to say French citizenship is mainly determined by the fact of being born on French territory. This led to the resignation of Christiane Taubira in January 2016. The following month she published a book entitled *Murmures à la jeunesse* (Paris: Philippe Rey), firmly condemning the new provision stripping French citizens of their nationality – in fact, in the end, the latter was dropped.

Moreover, for French people, such a proposal came as a grim reminder of the sinister Law of 23 July 1940 under the Vichy regime aimed at stripping of their nationality French citizens who had left France between 20 May and 30 June 1940 without the authorisation of the government, targeting people like de Gaulle and Mendès-France, who had joined Free France, and later applied by Pétain to deport Jews sent to German concentration camps. On 30 March 2016, after consulting the Speakers of the National Assembly and the Senate, President Hollande announced he would abandon his constitutional reform proposals to enshrine in the constitution the state of emergency and enable judges to strip convicted terrorists of their French nationality. Faced with growing divisions within his own Socialist party and the fierce centre-right opposition to his scheme, he soon realised he would not be able to reach the three-fifths parliamentary majority required to change the constitution.[73] The controversy over the possibility of stripping French-born people of their nationality was in some respects similar to the one in the United Kingdom around the ability for the then British Home Secretary, Theresa May, to revoke the British citizenship of dual nationals and of some foreign-born Britons she considers to be a threat to national security through a deprivation order. Besides, the new controversial Counter-Terrorism and Security Act 2015 contains provisions about the possible refusal to issue certificates of naturalisation.

In their fight against terrorism, France and the United Kingdom have adopted very similar security arrangements, which also include new laws on intelligence to develop the means available to intelligence services to track terrorists or alleged terrorists and to give the state wide surveillance powers. Thus, on 24 July 2015, in the wake of the *Charlie Hebdo* terrorist attacks, President Hollande promulgated France's new Surveillance Law,[74] which, though endorsed by the Constitutional Council except for three sections, is considered by many in the judiciary and among human rights associations as a threat to the right to privacy and free speech. It has been criticised for transferring investigatory powers such as wiretapping, data and mobile phone calls interception and access to people's communications from the police to intelligence services on a wide scale, which could lead to a form of mass surveillance outside judicial control. This echoes, in some sense, part three of the United Kingdom Counter-Terrorism and Security Act 2015 devoted to data retention, including internet data. The British Counter-Terrorism and Security Act, which received Royal Assent on 12 February 2015, in its draft version contained provisions for the introduction of a new statutory duty to address the risk of being drawn into terrorism – what was to become Part 5 of the Act. It originally placed a statutory duty on specified authorities (including prison governors and providers of probation services, educational institutions such as schools, colleges and universities and health and social care authorities and the police) to prevent people from being drawn into terrorism, the so-called Prevent Strategy. It included a provision about freedom of speech and academic freedom which was so controversial that, after protests in the House of Lords, it was removed from the final version of the text, as far as universities are concerned. Initially, universities were to be required to have policies on extremist speakers introduced – the objective being to try to silence people inciting terrorism and stop radicalisation on campuses. It was greatly modified in the end as it seemed to be difficult, not to say impossible, to reconcile it with the current statutory duty of universities under section 43 (1) of the Education Act 1986 'to take such steps as are reasonably practicable to ensure that freedom of speech within is secured for members, students and employees of the establishment and for visiting speakers'.

The parliamentary Joint Committee on Human Rights firmly opposed this original drafting of the text – and proved to be very influential in its withdrawal, arguing that 'universities are the places where there should be open and inclusive discussion of ideas,'[75] and therefore had to be removed from the Bill. As noted earlier, pre-trial detention (currently for up to fourteen days) had been included in earlier Counter-Terrorism Acts.

Conclusion

The James Bond film *Spectre* was released in 2015 and very favourably received by French and British audiences. Yet when fiction becomes reality, that is to say, when mass surveillance threatens to invade people's fundamental rights to privacy, it is likely to be fiercely opposed by the people. On a more serious note, French history offers reminders of how dangerous it can be to give intelligence services and/or the police means that they do not normally have under ordinary circumstances and to give the executive extensive powers, while extremist parties such as the far-right National Front – as the regional elections of 6 and 13 December 2015 once again showed when they won 7,000,000 votes – are on the rise. There is more than ever a need to strike the right balance between protecting the community and respecting the rule of law. On 16 November 2015, President Hollande concluded his address to both Houses of parliament by saying, 'terrorism will not destroy the Republic, the Republic will destroy terrorism.' Yet as Michael Ignatieff, the former head of Harvard's Centre for Human Rights, pointed out, 'it is the response to terrorism, rather than terrorism itself that does democracy most harm.'[76] Indeed, democracies seem particularly powerless and vulnerable as they cannot use the same tools as terrorists precisely because of what makes them democracies: their attachment and respect for human rights and fundamental freedoms. They must react according to their values, rules and rights, or they would not be much different from terrorists. Few people question the fact that terrorist threats require some appropriate proportionate answers, including legislation when there is a gap in the law, but that should not undermine the fundamental values and principles on which democracies are built. States can and do respond to terrorism by the enactment of special laws or the modification of certain rules. Yet any changes or responses to terrorism which are introduced must comply with the rule of law. The UK has to look to common law and the Human Rights Act 1998, and France to its constitution, all the more as terrorists, as non-state actors, are not waging war in the sense acknowledged by current international law.

After the terrorist attacks in France in both January and November 2015, British people reacted with spontaneous empathy and extraordinary solidarity towards France and its people, which deeply moved the French and revived their morale.[77] It is essential to keep this solidarity between France and the United Kingdom alive, and the best way of doing so and of facing terrorism is to strengthen bilateral intelligence and judicial cooperation.

Notes

1. Magna Carta did not put an end to the inequalities between men and women. See the article by David Carpenter in *The Guardian* entitled 'Magna Carta: 800 years on', published on 2 January 2015.
2. R. Carré de Malberg, *Contribution à la théorie générale de l'Etat* (Paris: Sirey, 1920–2; new edn Dalloz, 2004).
3. Roger Errera, *Et ce sera justice. Le juge dans la cité* (Paris: Gallimard, 2013), p. 15.
4. Thus, it is always very difficult to find an appropriate translation in French – *Etat de droit*, *règle de primauté du droit*, *la prééminence du droit* – none of them is fully satisfactory.
5. Thus, under Title VII of the 1958 constitution the judiciary is referred to as the 'judicial authority', and only a few provisions are explicitly devoted to it from article 64 to the new article 66-1.

6. One of the first steps of the 1789 French revolutionaries was to break the power of the twelve regional royal courts, called *Parlements*, by the Law of 16–24 August 1790 prohibiting ordinary courts from reviewing administrative action. Its article 13 stated that 'judicial functions are distinct and will always remain separate from administrative functions.' Their objective was to put an end to a bad practice that had characterised the *ancien régime*, the excessive interference by the *Parlements* in matters of government and public administration.
7. Frances Gibb, 'Towards a New Supreme Court?' *The Times Law Supplement* (4 February 2016).
8. Besides, Cardiff itself is rated as one of the most active administrative centres in the country and thus has a high reputation in terms of administrative law.
9. This however may change in the future, as Gove raised the point of setting up in the UK a German-style constitutional court in charge of examining European legislation and its compliance with the British constitution – able to strike it down if necessary – while he was giving evidence to the EU Justice subcommittee in February 2016.
10. *The House*, Parliament's Magazine, 37/1517 (29 May 2015), 291. Caplen was succeeded by Robert Bourns as President of the Law Society of England and Wales in July 2016.
11. British judges are not appointed for life, as they have to retire at seventy.
12. Apart from its very first article, which states that 'men are born and remain free and equal in rights. Social distinctions may be based only on considerations of the common good.'
13. Carré de Malberg, *Contribution à la théorie générale de l'Etat*, p. 741.
14. It is *de facto* an indirect source of the law for it can exercise some influence over French legislators.
15. The Ministry of Justice was introduced as a result of the fusion of key functions previously performed by the Home Office with those of the former Department of Constitutional Affairs, which had replaced the Lord Chancellor's Department.
16. It is interesting to note that in France proposals have been recently made to split some of the functions currently fulfilled by the French Justice Ministry with the Home Office – the reverse of what has happened in the United Kingdom.
17. The combination of the role of Lord Chancellor with the position of Secretary of State for Justice has even given him additional authority.
18. There is currently a controversy as to whether the Lord Chancellor should be required to have legal training. It was raised in the case of Chris Grayling, the former Lord Chancellor, who was appointed by David Cameron, as he was a former journalist of the BBC, thus breaking a long-established convention under which the Lord Chancellor – as the head of the judiciary – had to be a former judge or QC.

19. See Constitutional Reform Act 2005, part 2, 'Arrangements to modify the office of the Lord Chancellor, 3 (1)': 'Guarantee of continued judicial independence'.
20. The Constitutional Reform Act (CRA) passed in 2005 started to be implemented in 2006. The United Kingdom Supreme Court (UKSC) was only officially inaugurated in 2009.
21. Montesquieu, *The Spirit of the Laws*, ed. and trans. A. M. Cohler, B. Miller and H. Stone (Cambridge: Cambridge University Press, 1989).
22. A Private Member's Bill, the Assisted Dying Bill [HL] 2013–2014, sponsored by a former Lord Chancellor, Lord Falconer of Thornton, was introduced in the House of Lords on 15 May 2013, to depenalise assisted suicide and thus make active euthanasia lawful.
23. Devolution jurisdiction was granted to the Judicial Committee of the Privy Council with the revival of the devolution process in 1999. It performed that judicial role until it was allocated to the United Kingdom Supreme Court in 2009.
24. Thus, the United Kingdom acquired the appeal jurisdiction of the House of Lords and the devolution jurisdiction of the Privy Council.
25. Even if the UKSC and the Judicial Committee of the Privy Council are located in the same building in Parliament Square (the Middlesex Guildhall), and if the same justices sit in the two courts, they remain two separate courts. Although the Judicial Committee of the Privy Council has lost its devolution jurisdiction to the new Supreme Court, it has kept its Commonwealth jurisdiction, and it is in this capacity that it is housed in the Supreme Court building.
26. United Kingdom Supreme Court, Annual Report and Accounts 2013–2014, HC36 (London: The Stationery Office, 2014), p. 107.
27. Lord Hope, 'The view from over the square', *The House of Lords Magazine* (2009), 14–15.
28. Comité de réflexion et de proposition sur la modernisation et le rééquilibrage des institutions de la Ve République, 'Une Ve République plus démocratique', p. 78.
29. Roger Errera, 'The recruitment, training, evaluation career and accessibility of members of the Judiciary in France', in Giuseppe Di Federico (ed.), *Recruitment, Professional Evaluation and Career of Judges and Prosecutors in Europe* (University of Bologna, 2005), p. 59.
30. Under the new article 65 which was totally redrafted in the wake of the Balladur Report, the High Council of the Judiciary is divided into two sections: one in charge of the appointment process and disciplinary measures involving judges, the other dealing with public prosecutors' nominations and potential sanctions.
31. It replaced him on the one hand by the Chief President of the Court of Cassation to preside over its section dealing with judges, and by the Chief Public Prosecutor of the Court of Cassation as the new president of its section in charge of public prosecutors.

32. The former Lord Chancellor and Secretary of State for Justice was Michael Gove, a former Education Minister, appointed by David Cameron in the 2015 Conservative government.
33. Apart from sealing constitutions themselves, such as the constitution of the Fifth Republic, it is now commonplace for significant constitutional changes to be sealed – such as the Balladur Report or more recently the Jospin Report – in sealing ceremonies. For more information see Louis Rouvier, *La Chancellerie et les Sceaux de France* (Marseille: Moullot, 1950), pp. 87–9.
34. The Guyanese-born Christiane Taubira is a former regional councillor for the French overseas territory of Guyana, a former member of the French National Assembly and of the European Parliament. She is on the left of the Socialist party and ran as a candidate for the Left Radical Party in the 2007 presidential elections. She became the new Justice Minister in 2012 under the presidency of Hollande. She is also well known in France for two laws named after her of particular significance: the so-called *Loi Taubira* of 21 May 2001 which recognises the slave trade and slavery as crimes against humanity, and the *Loi Taubira* or *Loi sur le mariage pour tous* (the law on same- sex marriage) of 23 April 2013. On 27 January 2016 she resigned as Justice Minister over the government's proposal to strip convicted French-born terrorists of their citizenship if they have a second nationality, and was succeeded by Jean-Jacques Urvoas.
35. Jean-Baptiste Jacquin, 'La colère gronde chez les procureurs sous pression', *Le Monde* (28 January 2016).
36. The *loi républicaine* (Republican Law) is an important notion in France which expresses the symbolic dimension of the law above the parties and above political divisions.
37. Thomas Bingham, *Lives of the Law: Selected Essays and Speeches 2000–2010* (Oxford: Oxford University Press, 2011), p. 128.
38. In French, judges' judicial oath reads: 'Je jure de bien et fidèlement remplir mes fonctions, de garder le secret des délibérations et des votes même après la cessation de mes fonctions et de me conduire en tout comme un digne et loyal magistrat.'
39. Helena Kennedy, *Eve was Framed: Women and British Justice*, rev. edn (London: Vintage Books, 2005), p. 1.
40. She did much to strengthen the presumption of innocence during her three years as *Garde des Sceaux*.
41. She was trained as a judge in the Bordeaux Judicial College in 1997.
42. She was fiercely attacked for having sponsored what became the 2013 Law on Same-Sex Marriage in France mentioned in chapter 3.
43. She has herself written on the topic of equality and diversity, including a book entitled *Egalité pour les Exclus: Le Politique face à l'histoire et à la mémoire coloniale* (Paris: Le Temps Présent, 2009).

44. Owen Bowcott, 'UK among worst in Europe for employing female judges', *The Guardian* (20 September 2012).
45. Speech to the Association of British Women Barristers delivered in 1998.
46. It lasts 31 months altogether, of which 11 months are spent at the judicial school and 20 in the courts, in lawyers' offices, with investigators, private companies or public administration.
47. Their growing success dates back to the 1950s, when the old-boy network ruled and an overwhelming majority of judges were ageing men. The Justice Ministry's answer was to set up, just after the Second World War, the ENM, which is now the gateway to a career in the judiciary or the state prosecution service.
48. Brenda Hale, 'Women in the Judiciary', Fiona Woolf Lecture, 27 June 2014. It is known in French as the *Conseil Supérieur de la Magistrature* (CSM).
49. Lord Irvine's speech before the Association of British Women Barristers, The Barbican, London, 11 February 1998.
50. They are solicitors who after additional training obtained an advocacy certificate allowing them to plead not only in lower courts but also in higher courts just like barristers-at-law.
51. She is the Deputy-President of the United Kingdom Supreme Court.
52. The Judicial Appointments Commission (JAC) makes recommendations to the Lord Chancellor, and no one may be appointed whom the commission has not selected.
53. Although the Lord Chancellor retains the ultimate power to decide whom to appoint, or to recommend to the Queen for appointment, and thus maintains parliamentary accountability, his discretion has been tightly circumscribed by the provision of the Act. Besides, because of its power to recommend one candidate for a post, whom the Lord Chancellor would have extreme difficulty in rejecting, the JAC has become in effect an appointing body. Thus the role of the Lord Chancellor has become purely formal.
54. Members of the JAC are appointed by the Queen on the recommendation of the Lord Chancellor; it is composed of fifteen members – six must be lay members, five must be members of the judiciary, two must be members of the legal profession, one must be a tribunal member and one a lay magistrate.
55. Judicial Appointments Commission, 'Equal Merit Provision: JAC Policy' (April 2014).
56. More recently, in March 2017 the Constitution Committee of the House of Lords launched a follow-up inquiry on judicial appointments, hearing evidence from the Lord Chief Justice, the President and the Deputy-President of the Supreme Court.
57. House of Lords Constitution Committee, Twenty-Fifth Report, 'Judicial Appointments' (7 March 2012).

58. House of Commons, Justice Committee, 6th Report of Session 2015–16, 'The Role of the Magistracy', HC 165 (London: The Stationery Office, 19 October 2016).
59. The *Conseils des Prud'hommes*, i.e. industrial tribunals themselves, account for 15,000 non-professional judges in France.
60. Thus, the French Justice Minister Christiane Taubira launched the proposal of replacing non-professional judges by career judges in industrial tribunals, but this seems to be very controversial, notably because French people are very attached to the current composition of the tribunals, as they feel those judges are closer to the population.
61. Following a long consultation process the Bill on Justice in the Twenty-First Century on class actions and the organisation of justice was adopted by the French Senate on the first reading on 5 November 2015. The previous day, the Senate had adopted the Bill on the independence and impartiality of justice and for a more open justice.
62. It followed its recommendation for a better-controlled executive and a strengthened parliament, which were to form part one and part two of the constitutional reform.
63. Under article 18 of the constitution, the President of the Republic can convene the two Houses of parliament to address members of the National Assembly and the Senate in person when he has an important message to convey. In addition, under article 89 the President can decide to launch a revision of the constitution before the two Houses of parliament gathered as the *Congrès*.
64. You could hear people saying that they were proud of being French and of belonging to the French Republic, which does not happen very often in France.
65. The controversial draft Bill tabled in the National Assembly in February 2016, which was to become the Act on the Protection of the Nation, aims at incorporating the state of emergency into the constitution of the Fifth Republic under a new section (article 36-1), which was dropped in the end because it was too unpopular and no consensus was reached on the need to change the constitution.
66. The draft Bill of February 2016 (now Act) further extended the state of emergency ending on 26 February 2016 for another three months. The state of emergency was then extended for a further three more months to protect people, especially football players and supporters, during the 2016 Euro (European Football Championship). On 20 July 2016, following the Nice terror attack on the Promenade des Anglais, the National Assembly voted overwhelmingly for further extending the state of emergency.
67. Under the new law, it is possible for example to put people under house arrest for up to twelve hours per day instead of eight; to use electronic tagging for people who are under house arrest and who have already been convicted of acts of terrorism, and/or to block social networks and websites glorifying acts of

terrorism – to cite but a few of the exceptional means that are now available. Yet, the press and radio control provided by the original Act on the State of Emergency has not been retained in the 2015 Act.

68. Under the state of emergency, administrative searches can be undertaken – that is to say, under decisions made by French prefects outside the supervision of judges instead of decisions made by judges themselves; private homes of people suspected of terrorism can be searched outside the normal schedule from 6 a.m. to 9 p.m. under ordinary law, i.e. at any time of day and night.
69. According to the facts and figures provided by a journalist from the newspaper *Le Monde*, Jean-Baptiste Jacquin in his article 'L'état d'urgence soumis au Conseil Constitutionnel' (14 December 2015), one month after the implementation of the State of Emergency, 2,575 searches and seizures outside judicial control had been carried out, 273 people put into custody and 354 people under house arrest.
70. Official Journal of the Republic (JO) (11 January 1980), 84 [no. 79-109 DC].
71. Under the wording of the February 2016 draft Bill on the Protection of the Nation, such a measure would apply to 'any person convicted of a crime or misdemeanour seriously affecting the life of the nation'.
72. The third chapter of the Balladur Committee, aiming at strengthening people's rights and giving them new rights, included the proposal of a kind of ombudsman called the *défenseur des droits* (the Defender of Rights) to replace the Mediator of the Republic, introduced by the Law of 3 January 1973. This proposal was adopted and led to the introduction of a new title in the constitution of the Fifth Republic – Title XI (bis) – composed of one single article solely devoted to the Defender of Rights (article 71-1). Under this new article, the Defender of Rights is appointed by the President of the Republic, together with a parliamentary hearing, for a non-renewable term of six years. He is in fact accountable to both the President of the Republic and parliament, and is in charge of guaranteeing the due respect of rights and freedoms by state administrations, territorial communities and, more generally speaking, all bodies carrying out public services.
73. Deputies and senators were to be convened as the French *Congrès* to examine those constitutional changes in April 2016.
74. Law of 24 July 2015 on Intelligence.
75. House of Commons/House of Lords Joint Committee on Human Rights, 5th Report of Session 2014–2015, 'Legislative scrutiny: counter-terrorism and Security Bill', HC 859/HL Paper 86 (London: The Stationery Office, 7 January 2015), p. 26.
76. 'The Freedom Paradox: Liberty has been the first victim of the war fought in its name', *The Economist*, Special Report (31 August 2006).
77. Including a special concert given by the Parliament Choir of Westminster in Paris (Notre Dame) on 3 May 2016, in which the present writer took part.

Chapter Five

Devolution in the United Kingdom, a Decentralisation Process in France

At first sight, any attempt at developing a comparative approach between devolution in the United Kingdom and the French decentralisation process seems almost impossible as each one of them is considered unique. French people like to speak of French decentralisation as the French exception as the British do with devolution.[1] The latter has always been difficult to define.[2] It is neither federalism nor regionalisation as such. Besides, although the two countries are still officially classified as unitary states, their territorial organisation is very different. France for centuries stood for the archetype of the unitary state, the French Republic being one and indivisible, as stated in article 1 of the constitution. As opposed to the French one-nation state, the United Kingdom is a union formed of four different nations or a multinational state. It all started with England, the original founding nation, to which three additional nations congregated or were conquered at different times and under different circumstances. One nation, the English, dominated the constitutional arrangements from the start. Besides, the British constitution, even before devolution, combined a single ultimate source of authority, stemming from a sovereign national Parliament, with considerable variations in the territorial arrangements for its component nations and regions. It did not develop as a unitary state based on unity and indivisibility like sixteenth-century France under François I but rather as a Union state or an asymmetrical multi-nation state with some degree of autonomy allocated to its four different nations. The United Kingdom has survived to this day as a union owing to permanent adjustments between central government and the periphery – or Celtic fringe as it is sometimes referred to. France, for its part, has always, including under the Fifth Republic, privileged the centre[3] to the detriment of the periphery, denying it any significant responsibilities or liberties – at least until the constitutional reform of 28 March 2003.

The French tradition of a highly centralised state dates back to the 1789 Revolution which has made its mark on the complex territorial organisation of the country, which has remained largely unchanged to this day, at least as far as the *communes*[4] are concerned. The French *communes* or municipalities were built on the former parishes and still represent the first level of territorial government in France characterised by a huge fragmentation. The territorial organisation which emerged from the 1789 Revolution has led to two contradictory characteristics of French territory – uniformity and fragmentation[5] – or what can be described as the French territorial paradox. The passion for equality which drove French revolutionaries in 1789 also shaped their conception of French territorial organisation, as recalled in the 2009 Balladur Report. The same rules had to apply to all territorial communities and they had to be on an equal footing. Thus there was, and still is, no link of subordination between *communes* and *départements*. Equality between territorial communities is now a key principle of the constitution of the Fifth Republic and has acquired full constitutional value as it was incorporated in the new article 72 during the second phase of the French decentralisation process in 2003 – more than twenty years after the Deferre Laws which introduced decentralisation in France (more commonly known as Act 1 of French Decentralisation).

This chapter does not aim at dealing with the complex technicalities of French decentralisation and the devolution process, but will rather focus on some common general trends and patterns. Neither of them has been a linear process but each has been based on constant adjustments in the distribution of competences between central government and devolved or decentralised authorities. The main objectives of the French decentralisation process were reasserted by the 2009 Balladur Committee on French local communities, as they were then called. This committee was set up by President Sarkozy, to complete the 2008 constitutional reform on modernising and rebalancing the institutions of the Fifth Republic, and it was modelled on the previous Balladur Committee. This time the idea was to rebalance territorial government, or rather to try to rationalise and optimise French territorial government while strengthening local democracy. Balladur described France's territorial organisation as 'ancient, complex and made of successive additional layers' in the foreword to his 2009 report.[6] Clarity, simplicity, stronger local democracy, enhanced territorial solidarity were the official goals – or rather the arguments used both by the French and British governments to gain the support of doubtful voters. It was notably the case in Wales at the end of the 1970s where the majority of people saw devolution as involving unwanted and undesirable elements of divisiveness. They were still not fully convinced in 1997, as the referendum held that very year with its minute majority for devolution showed. On 18 September 1997, 50.3 per cent of the people who voted in Wales supported devolution and 49.7 per cent did not.

Piecemeal territorial reforms in France and the UK: common trends and patterns

Devolution and the French decentralisation process have given rise to an array of reports, laws and regulations and have both been piecemeal arrangements rather than a coherent whole. They have also undergone permanent adjustments which make it difficult for an external observer to draw any coherent conclusions. However, in the array of primary and secondary instruments, some common trends and patterns can be identified. If the two procedures remain largely in the making, they have gone through three main phases, dictated by distinct objectives which make them significantly different in nature from what they were originally meant to be – in 1982 in France and in 1998 in the United Kingdom. However, throughout the whole decentralisation process in France and devolution in the UK, some common priorities do stand out in terms of division of competences and of finance. The origin of these profound changes in both countries, and then their legal and financial frameworks, will be examined before focusing on what lies ahead for both countries. Whatever the option they will, in the end, adopt for themselves – be it federalism or an advanced form of regionalism – they have, and will become, less and less easy to classify as unitary states.

Whereas the United Kingdom has tried to better take into account its original diversity by granting a limited autonomy to its Celtic nations while trying to maintain the coherence of the whole, the French Republic has progressively moved away from its initial indivisibility – some would say uniformity – towards some limited form of diversity. Many criticisms have been made during the decentralisation process in France as it was blamed for adding complexity to the already multi-layered institutional structure more commonly known in France as the *millefeuille*. Although the official goal of decentralisation has always been to simplify French territorial government, it has led to overlapping competences, to cross-financing and to unscrupulous local officials taking advantage of their multiple elected offices.

In the United Kingdom, devolution, far from being limited to administrative and managerial considerations, has touched on fundamental issues in terms of identity, fuelling nationalist feelings in Scotland especially. On

18 September 2014, the United Kingdom as a union of four different nations was seriously challenged when Scotland held a referendum asking the Scots whether they wanted their nation to become independent. This referendum[7] could have transformed the country's constitutional arrangements and the entire Union in an irrevocable way by putting an end to the political and parliamentary union between Scotland and the rest of the country established in 1707 via an official Act of Union. The Scottish nationalists of the SNP under the leadership of Alex Salmond had never come so close to independence. In the United Kingdom, the key to almost every issue is the rise of nationalism in Scotland and to a lesser extent in Wales, and the possibility of the UK ceasing to be a unitary state. As Tom Shuller explained, 'in the United Kingdom, the result of the Scottish referendum has set in motion pressures for further devolved powers within Scotland, but also within Wales, Northern Ireland and within England itself.'[8]

France for its part is under a different, yet no less worrying, kind of pressure – of an economic and financial kind – as unemployment[9] continues to grow especially among the young, so that decentralisation today is more driven by managerial and financial considerations than by the will to strengthen local democracy. In France and the United Kingdom, decentralised communities and devolved administrations have been affected by the reduction of the national block grants on which they rely for their finances as central governments try to cut back expenditure at all levels. Thus the Act 3 or third phase of the French decentralisation process initiated under Hollande's presidency focuses on the reduction of *régions* from twenty-two to thirteen, not only to achieve economies of scale, but also to enable them to better compete with their European counterparts in attracting inward investment.

If devolution in the United Kingdom and the French decentralisation process have developed at a different pace using different means,[10] they have both raised fundamental questions about the role of the state, the division of competences between central governments and devolved or decentralised communities, as well as the way of financing the whole process. In addition, the reforms have not been isolated national processes but have both been influenced by the emergence of a Europe of regions to different degrees. Devolution in the UK and decentralisation in its latest stages in France did not come out of the blue but were associated with the development of the European integration process, to the point that today it is hardly possible to speak of either devolution or decentralisation without speaking of Europe.

More precisely, it was linked to the importance and recognition given to the sub-state bodies of European countries. Spain has, like the UK, been confronted with a combination of historic nationalist demands for self-government and economic pressures for greater autonomy and has initiated an evolutionary process of asymmetrical devolution, especially powerful in Catalonia. More generally, from the 1980s onwards regions turned to a more positive engagement with Europe. With their own historic, cultural or national identities they even began to see it as an opportunity to increase their own autonomy, to pursue their own distinct interest and to project themselves as more than mere dependencies of the state. The Scottish historian Christopher Harvie wrote of 'a regional Europe'.[11] Originally the very existence of sub-state bodies was not emphasised, in the name of the key principle of the non-interference of the European Communities with the constitutional and territorial arrangements of their Member States. But as they became more numerous, many experiencing forms of a regionalisation or decentralisation process, the European Communities themselves adapted to those territorial and institutional changes. In fact, sub-state bodies, regions or bodies assimilated to regions, including small nations, started to be taken more seriously as potential active participants in the European building process. A turning point was the Treaty of Maastricht (1992), which set up the Committee of the Regions, with a cultural as well as a political dimension, even though the latter remained an advisory body and relatively inactive. The unitary nature of the French and British constitutions and Westminster's parliamentary sovereignty have been challenged from above through the European integration process transferring powers upwards to the EU at a supranational level. But it has also been challenged from below – and from within France and the UK themselves – with the French decentralisation process and devolution. It is thus essential to inquire what lies ahead for both France and the UK in these times of uncertainty as their destinies are intertwined in Europe.

The origin of contemporary devolution in the UK and decentralisation in France

Following the landslide victory of the French left in 1981 and the election of François Mitterrand as the new President of the Republic, a major reform of French territorial organisation was launched as part of the political will to introduce a new society. Thus from the start, French decentralisation has been associated with the left as part of the Socialist vision of society based on equality of opportunities, including in local government. The Law on the rights and liberties of *communes*, *départements* and *régions* of 2 March 1982 and the Law of 22 July 1983 on the division of competences between *communes*, *départements*, *régions* and the state, more commonly known as the decentralisation laws or Deferre Laws, named after the Interior and Decentralisation Minister of Mitterrand, Gaston Deferre,[12] were introduced in the wake of the report 'Vivre Ensemble' of the Guichard Committee.[13] The Laws of 1982 and 1983 were to form *l'Acte 1* – phase 1 – of French decentralisation. They aimed at strengthening local democracy and improving territorial government as well as taking decisions closer to the people. Like devolution in the United Kingdom, French decentralisation has not been an event but a process, a permanent work in progress with neither a clear starting point nor a well-defined final objective.

The 1982 and 1983 decentralisation or Deferre Laws: a minimalist form of devolution

Although the Deferre Laws left largely unchanged the deeply rooted historical territorial communities known as *communes* and *départements*, they departed from traditional prejudices against an intermediary territorial level between *départements* and the state inherited from the 1789 Revolution. They now introduced *régions* as full territorial entities with the same status as *communes* and *départements*, including a democratically elected council. The new *régions* were larger-sized territorial communities mainly in charge of territorial planning and vocational training. But perhaps even more important, not only did the new laws officially prevent each category of territorial communities from controlling the other, but they also replaced the control of the prefect – embodying the state – over acts of territorial authorities performed before their implementation by an *ex post* judicial review. In addition, territorial communities were allocated the power to control their own budgets.

Act 1 of the decentralisation process was in fact the implementation of a project that had originally failed when it was submitted by General de Gaulle to French voters in 1969 in a referendum. This attempt at formally introducing French *régions* had failed partly because it was associated with the highly unpopular reform of the French Senate in the same referendum. Another possible explanation is that French people were not ready for some form of regionalisation at a time of social instability, as they were not convinced that it would benefit them and the country at large.

Decentralisation was initially introduced in France without changing the constitution, though it was to have a significant impact on the division of competences between central government and territorial communities. Although French decentralisation was mainly administrative without including transfers of sovereignty – it was conceived in and for a unitary state – it did challenge the principle of the unity and indivisibility of the Republic. For the first time ever, the constitutional change of 28 March 2003 incorporated the notion of territorial diversity – even though strictly controlled – into the French constitution[14].

If the French decentralisation process was originally officially established as a way of strengthening democracy at the local level, it consisted mainly in 'transferring administrative competences from the central government to territorial communities'[15] – known as *les collectivités territoriales* under Title XII of the constitution – with their own democratically elected municipal, regional or general councils. They were granted limited administrative and financial autonomy while being subject to judicial review as seen above. The 1982 decentralisation laws started to loosen the grip of the state over local communities by transferring executive powers from the prefects as representatives of the state to the presiding officers of general councils in departments, and to regional councillors elected by universal suffrage. Yet, it would be much too limited to think of decentralisation in France in purely administrative terms. Like devolution in the UK, it was in essence a highly political process. Territorial government could not have made much progress, if it had not been underpinned by a strong political will at the central level. In the preliminary remarks to his 2009 report, Balladur pointed out that 'territorial government is a highly political matter.'[16] If the decentralisation laws of 1982 and 1983 did not fundamentally overhaul French territorial organisation, they set in motion a process stretching over more than thirty years with successive waves of transfers of new powers as well as innovative policies and instruments of local democracy.

Act 1 of the French decentralisation process at the beginning of the 1980s was thus closer to the minimalist type of devolution that was initially introduced in Wales by the Government of Wales Act 1998 than to devolution in Scotland. The Act, an executive not a legislative measure, devolved very limited powers to Wales. It exercised conferred, not reserved powers. Its second part, devoted to the functions of the new Welsh Assembly, only granted it functions previously exercised by the Secretary of State for Wales. Besides, under the Act, the Assembly's legal status was nothing more than a body corporate, with no formal separation between the legislative and the executive. There was no recognised cabinet. Unlike the Scottish Parliament, the Welsh Assembly did not have tax-raising powers or the power to pass primary legislation, but only secondary powers. This meant that the Westminster Parliament in England continued to legislate for Wales.

In fact, devolution in the United Kingdom, even in its more advanced form in Scotland, was not to depart from the doctrine of parliamentary sovereignty, and devolved authorities, whether governments or elected assemblies, were all conceived as subordinate to Westminster. In France and the UK alike, those fundamental doctrines contained an element of rigidity and set limits to how far the transfers of powers could go without fundamentally altering the nature of the British and the French states.

The Kilbrandon Report (1973) as the catalyst for devolution in the UK

Devolution as a principle of providing local community government had been on the British public agenda since the Kilbrandon report in 1973. An attempt at introducing devolution legislation failed under the Labour government of James Callaghan following unsuccessful referendums in Scotland[17] and Wales in 1979. But it was then taken up by another Labour leader, Tony Blair, in his party manifesto in 1997 as part of a package of constitutional reforms aiming at modernising and democratising the UK constitution by bringing the government closer to the people. Yet the reasons for devolution were different for each of the three now devolved areas of the UK. In Northern Ireland its purpose was to reconcile the two religious communities, in conflict for centuries. It was based on nationalist sentiment in Scotland[18] and the will to give Scottish people their own representative body – their own Parliament – along the lines of the Scottish Constitutional Convention assembled to that effect. Whereas the issue of the less intense separatist Welsh identity, as embodied in its own language and in legislation, such as the Welsh Intermediate Education Act 1889 and the Disestablishment of the Church Act 1919, provided the background to the Welsh devolution process, Wales did not possess the Scottish sense of citizenship to the same degree. So devolution in Scotland appeared as a kind of compromise to calm down nationalist claims and deflect the cry for independence.

Devolution was never intended to be a transfer of sovereignty but limited transfers of executive and/or legislative competences. Thus there remains one sovereign Parliament which can legislate for the whole country: the British Parliament. Besides, England, Scotland and Wales are not sovereign states but nations, and Northern Ireland only a region, albeit with its own legislature and civil service. Yet, the devolution process revived by the Blair government through the 1998 three Devolution Acts of Parliament – respectively for Scotland, Wales and Northern Ireland – was to further emphasise, and indeed intensify, the asymmetrical character of the Union and strengthen Scottish and Welsh national consciousness, while having a chequered success in Belfast at Stormont.

The legal framework: no clear division of competences

The first striking aspect of devolution in the UK – especially for foreign observers – is the fact that it was initially introduced by simple Acts of Parliament, though they since have been acknowledged as constitutional statutes;[19] that is to say, they are not subject to the doctrine of implied repeal. The latter means that a new statute clearly and officially aiming at their repeal would be required to abrogate them. So if technically and legally they could be repealed by the Westminster Parliament, their abrogation would inevitably lead to a major political and institutional crisis. Thus once the approval of the people in the Celtic nations had been obtained *ex ante* and the legitimacy of devolution secured via different referendums in Scotland, Wales and Northern Ireland in the autumn of 1997,[20] instead of imposing the new territorial organisation from the top or central government like French decentralisation in its early days, pragmatic reasons led to the adoption of three separate constituent devolution statutes, the Scotland Act 1998, the Northern Ireland Act 1998 and the Government of Wales Act 1998, introducing three new devolved assemblies, the Scottish Parliament, the Northern Ireland Assembly and the National Assembly for Wales, and allowing the first elections to be held for the new institutions in 1999. Each assembly was to have a different size and composition with a different set of powers, but each operated under the sovereignty of the British Parliament. The devolved systems of government are modelled on the Westminster system in which the executive is drawn from Parliament and accountable to it. However, there are some key differences between the Westminster Parliament and the Welsh Assembly, as proceedings in the latter must be bilingual – in English and Welsh.

Although, even more surprising, in a country like France where so much importance is given to the codified constitution, decentralisation was not provided by a constitutional law but by ordinary legislation – the 1982 and 1983 Deferre Laws, as seen previously. Decentralisation was not part of the constitution until the constitutional change of 28 March 2003. This added to the very first article of the constitution that 'it [France] shall be organised on a decentralised basis.' In spite of numerous statutes – the Laws of 7 January and 22 July 1983 amended by the Laws of 25 January 1985 and 6 January 1986, together with the Law of 13 August 2004 on local liberties and responsibilities – as well as a code (the *code général des collectivités territoriales*) regulating territorial communities, the division of competences between the state and territorial communities, and also between the different levels of territorial communities, has never been clearly defined in France.

The French general competence clause and British transfers of competences to separate devolved governments

In the French decentralisation process, the division of competences is characterised by a lack of specific powers allocated to each particular level of territorial communities, so that the absence of a specialisation principle and the widespread shared competences have been the source of great confusion between the French territorial communities and central government. The Law of 7 January 1983 provided for the transfer of so-called blocks of competences (*blocs de compétences*) and a general competence clause. The latter allows territorial communities to intervene freely in all fields in territorial government matters – except state powers – provided they can claim a local public interest. It reflects a long tradition of self-government at the local level in France, and has encouraged territorial communities to intervene in various local matters. The downside, however, is that it has led to overlapping competences and much inconsistency generally. As Michel Verpeaux pointed out, 'except for professional training allocated to *régions*, social services to *départements*, urban planning to *communes*, the majority of competences are shared competences.'[21]

To take but one significant example, higher education is a state prerogative but secondary education is shared between *régions* (in charge of *lycées*) and *départements* (in charge of *collèges*), while the *communes* are in charge of primary schools. Besides, freedom of administration, traced back to the Law of 5 April 1884, which gave *communes*[22] and *départements*[23] their status as local communities[24] (*collectivités locales*), means that each territorial community must have its own democratically elected council[25] and must be able to implement its policies in territorial matters thanks to its own secondary power and financial autonomy.

A fundamental breakthrough for French territorial communities was the incorporation into the constitution, under article 72, of the principle of subsidiarity by the constitutional change of 28 March 2003. It means that competences have to be carried out at the most appropriate level, as close as possible to the territories and people they apply to, and must only be transferred to a higher level if no alternative is possible. It is modelled on the principle of subsidiarity introduced at the European level by the Maastricht Treaty, which favours multi-level governance. Under this principle, sub-state authorities were allowed their own representative offices in Brussels and given the possibility of representing their interests in the Council of Ministers without conflicting with the official position of their own state. Under article 5 of the EU Treaty as revised by the Lisbon Treaty, which further strengthened the subsidiarity principle, 'the Union shall act only if and in so far as the objective of the proposed action cannot be sufficiently achieved by the member states … but can rather … be better achieved at Union level.' The objective is to determine the best level of action in areas that do not fall within the exclusive competence of the EU. It also lies at the heart of the devolution process in the UK. In the Brussels deal which paved the way for the June 2016 referendum on the UK's EU membership negotiated by the British Prime minister on 19 February 2016, David Cameron obtained the power for national parliaments to oppose EU legislation potentially undermining the subsidiarity principle.

In the United Kingdom as in the French decentralisation process, the 1998 Devolution Acts neither contained any general statements of principles nor clear division of powers. Devolution as it was introduced by the three Acts of 1998 provided no clear definition or separation of powers between the national level and the devolved administrations. Indeed, they did not include provisions detailing the arrangements that were to govern the relationship, not only between the newly created institutions themselves but also between Westminster, Whitehall and the devolved administrations. What devolution initially did for Wales as well as for Scotland was to transfer the different sets of competences formerly exercised from within central government by the territorial departments (the Scotland and Wales Offices), that is to say a system of territorial administration, to separate devolved governments. It was based on the adoption of a set of separate reforms, asymmetric ones, with no legal guarantees of devolved competence. If part of the explanation in the UK can be found in the importance given to the doctrine of Westminster's parliamentary sovereignty acting as an impediment to a clear division of powers, in France the long tradition of the omnipotence and omnipresence of the state, where everything derives from it and is kept under its control, is a powerful obstacle to any attempt at transferring part of its powers to territorial communities.

A reserved-powers model for Scotland, a conferred-powers model for Wales

Still, in spite of the ill-defined nature of the division of competences under devolution in the UK, two main types of transferring powers – known as the reserved-powers model[26] and the conferred-powers model were respectively introduced for Scotland and Wales. In Scotland, always the driver of the devolution process, under the original Scotland Act 1998 the decision was taken to specify only reserved powers, i.e. the powers reserved to the Westminster Parliament, concerning the constitution, political parties, foreign affairs, public services and defence, but also competition law under Schedule 5 of the same Act. This meant leaving Scotland with a general competence over all other matters (under clause 27) – a principle different from that of 1978 and the great achievement of Labour Shadow Secretary Donald Dewar – so that wide-ranging primary legislative power was granted to the Scottish Parliament (Holyrood), as participants in the Scottish Constitutional Convention had wished. By contrast, a minimalist approach to devolution was chosen for Wales, as seen previously – partly justified by historical and legal reasons – as the Welsh nation was only granted conferred powers in twenty areas in a way reproducing at the subnational level the European principle of conferral. Besides, the original Government of Wales Act (GOWA) 1998 gave the Welsh people not a legislating Parliament but an Assembly. Although these different models could be justified on historical and legal grounds, they increased the potential of tensions between central government and Welsh devolved institutions and became a major source of growing frustration and controversy in Wales for two decades to come.

In France, the constitutional change of March 2003 led to more clarity and generally improved the status of local communities, notably by officially acknowledging the subsidiarity principle as a pillar of French decentralisation – now part of the constitution. Decentralisation until then had very much been imposed by the state from above in the Jacobin Republican tradition. In the same way, in the UK a better regulation of the relationships between the different levels of government was introduced. Following some key recommendations in 2005 from the Commission on the Powers and Electoral Arrangements of the National Assembly for Wales, chaired by Lord Richard, the Government of Wales Act 2006 introduced a better separation of power by creating a separate executive drawn from the Assembly termed the Welsh Assembly Government. Under the 2014 Wales Act it is now called the Welsh Government or Llywodraeth Cymru. The Act also provided for the incremental expansion of the Assembly's legislative power through Legislative Competence Orders (LCOs), also called Orders in Council, a type of secondary legislation which identified and transferred specific powers from the Westminster Parliament to the Assembly.

After a successful referendum on Assembly powers, held in March 2011 following the Jones–Parry Report, Orders in Council under part 3 of the GOWA 2006 ceased to have effect, and the Assembly was able to pass legislation known as Acts, though only within its specified devolved fields. So if it meant that the Welsh Assembly no longer needed to seek the Westminster Parliament's agreement on a case-by-case basis, it still did not give it the same general power to legislate as the Scottish Parliament. As stated in the Assembly of Wales guide to the legislative process, 'the National Assembly for Wales is the democratically elected body that represents the interests of Wales and its people, makes laws for Wales and holds the Welsh Government to account.'

Besides, the success of the 2011 Welsh referendum was interpreted as a sign of a more politically mature Welsh nation. So the Government of Wales Acts of 1998 and 2006, the 2011 Welsh referendum and the 2014 Welsh Act show how much has been achieved in the Welsh devolution process in the last seventeen years or so, and how the concept of devolution is now firmly embedded in the life of Wales.

Abolishing French régions *or* départements*: a permanent dilemma*

In France, if *départements* on the whole have benefited the most from the successive transfers of competences[27] since 1982 and are generally praised for their contribution in terms of social services – including social housing – and social cohesion, they are now under threat. Indeed, there have traditionally been two schools of thought among French territorial experts: those who supported the abolition of *départements* and those who favoured the abolition of the much more recent *régions*. Yet both had in common the will to simplify French territorial organisation by removing one layer from the *millefeuille*. The current trend is to give priority to French *régions*. This was clearly the case in the Balladur Report in 2009, which concluded that, although the priority was to reduce the number of territorial communities, it would be a mistake to abolish either the *communes*, for they can deliver services at a much more local level than all the other territorial communities and are closer to the people, or the *régions*, as they are the only bodies able to compete with European regions. On 8 April 2014, the French Prime Minister, Manuel Valls, in his statement of general policy, unveiled the next phase of the decentralisation process, the future Act 3, aiming at 'simplifying the territorial *millefeuille*'.[28] It was to be a preliminary to the submission of two draft Bills to the Council of Ministers of 18 June 2014, respectively on the new map of French *régions*, replacing the twenty-two existing ones by thirteen super-*régions*,[29] and on their competences. They are modelled on the German *Länder* and are supposed to reduce costs by some fifteen billion euros,[30] although there is no consensus on the figures. Part of the scheme is also to abolish the *départements*[31] and their elected councils in 2020 (after the next presidential election), their competences being transferred to other territorial communities. The official objective is for the new *régions*, in charge of economic development, to be the driving force of economic growth and employment, but it is a very controversial reform.

Indeed, the new division of French territory was hastily decided behind closed doors without consulting local elected officials. Not only does it break with French history, cultural identity and heritage, but it is also considered by many an artificial, not to say arbitrary, reorganisation of French territory. It was introduced for mainly economic, but also political, reasons in the run-up to the December 2015 regional elections, traditionally favourable to the far-right National Front. French geographers like Jean-Luc Boeuf not only denounce the fact that the reform does not take into account citizens' preoccupations, but question the real motives behind it. They say that 'in France, we pretend to believe in regionalisation but the state controls everything.'[32]

The new regional map of France has kept some *régions* like Brittany and Corsica while introducing seven super-regions,[33] merging existing *régions* like Aquitaine[34] with Poitou-Charentes and Limousin. The latter is generally considered fairly satisfactory, as the new super-region does have a historic, cultural and also linguistic coherence as its various components have in common the Occitan culture and language.[35] Similarly Brittany was kept free from merger with Val de Loire. However, Act 3 of the French decentralisation process, mainly driven by financial considerations and imposed by the central government, contains the seeds of discontent. By contrast, the *communes* until now have been the least affected by the decentralisation process and are therefore still highly fragmented. Hence experts often speak of the impossible reform of the (36,000) *communes*, a huge majority of which have less than 3,000 inhabitants. It is a territorial level to which the great majority of French people are attached, the one which caters for their everyday needs and services and with which they identify with the most naturally.[36]

Pressing for more decentralisation in France and more devolution in the UK

The general trend in France is towards the specialisation of each level of territorial communities and more diversity, generally speaking, in terms not only of status, but also of areas of responsibilities and finance. The 2009 Balladur Report for its part advocated maintaining the general competence clause[37] only for the *communes*, while granting all other territorial communities, more clearly defined, specific competences. France seems to be moving progressively away from the one-size-fits-all model towards more flexible territorial government. If state controls have been formally abolished over territorial communities, central government has found other, perhaps more subtle ways of controlling them, especially financially. A French legal expert, Professor Brisson, explained that France is in fact only partly decentralised. He describes it as 'a semi-decentralised system', adding that the French state 'has not in any way yielded any of its strategic responsibilities in favour of local communities'.[38] French territorial communities, like devolved institutions in the United Kingdom, are still not considered as partners but as subordinate bodies. There are strong pressures for more decentralisation in France especially from politicians with a local mandate. In the same way, there are persistent claims for still more devolution in the UK, even if the latter has made much more progress than decentralisation in France, most notably in Wales since 2006. Central government is back – or rather has never really renounced its prerogatives. France, in spite of its three main successive phases of decentralisation between 1982 and 2016 is still a mainly centralised state, with Paris enjoying overwhelming weight. The capital has even been allocated its own specific status now known as *Grand Paris*, comparable to the devolved role of London in the UK. In the same way, in the United Kingdom central national institutions (Westminster and Whitehall) have remained largely unchanged. England remains highly centralised, and London is now considered a city-state. Indeed devolution in England is still an unsolved enigma, with an English Parliament, regional assemblies and intercity 'power-houses' all having their advocates, and the House of Commons implementing the controversial idea of 'English Votes on English Laws'. Tom Schuller for the Franco-British Council[39] pointed out that 'London has a much more unbalancing impact regionally than Paris does.'[40] However, Paris with its 11,000,000 inhabitants can also be considered a global city like London and still dominates French territory.

The House of Lords Constitution Committee has severely criticised the loose system governing intergovernment relations. However, the post-devolution UK for its part has shown an extraordinary potential for adaptation and expansion, thus avoiding significant intergovernmental disputes. In fact, three options could have been used to adjust devolution: the use of law; via legislation, standing orders or parliamentary resolutions, written, but not legally binding agreements; or arrangements such as protocols, concordats or informal practice held to be conventions. In day-to-day relations between central government and devolved administrations there has been a great reliance on informal and bilateral links, relying on much good will and shared political efforts. In Wales, the Second Report of the Commission on Devolution (or Silk Commission), 'Empowerment and Responsibility: Legislative Powers to Strengthen Wales'[41] in March 2014, was devoted to the review of the (non-financial) powers of the National Assembly. Some of its key provisions dealt with the Welsh model of devolution – as noted above, a conferred-powers model setting out what is devolved (in twenty different areas) and with intergovernmental relations.[42] Over the former it advocated a reserved-powers model, as in Scotland and Northern Ireland, as a clearer, more coherent one than the one based on conferred powers. As for the latter, it suggests the introduction of a statutory code of practice for intergovernmental relations as well as a Welsh intergovernmental committee to oversee the devolution settlement. It also revived some of the proposals of the Richard Commission such as a bigger Assembly for Wales, one of the smallest legislatures in the world. While acknowledging the success of Welsh devolution, it concluded that the *status quo* is not sustainable owing to its lack of clarity and coherence. Wales is trying to catch up with the devolution process in Scotland, thus making devolution less asymmetrical in nature and outlook, a process of competitive emulation which many constitutional commentators find disturbing for the existence of the Union.

The financial framework: devolved administrations' and territorial communities' limited fiscal responsibility

Transferring further competences from central government to British devolved administrations and French territorial communities without at the same time providing them with the necessary financial resources has too often deprived them of effective decision-making power. They are both underfunded and still financially too dependent on central government. In France, local costs represent 20 per cent of the whole public expenditure and have grown faster than the national wealth due to the new transfers of competences from central government.

Before the constitutional change of March 2003 there was a gap in the law affecting local finances. The constitution did not originally include any provisions on the resources of local territorial communities. The French decentralisation process did not therefore initially include financial autonomy. However, significant improvement was made when the principle of financial autonomy was incorporated into the constitution under article 72, paragraph 2 by the empowering statute of 29 July 2004. Article 72 (2) states: 'Territorial communities shall enjoy revenue of which they may dispose freely in the conditions determined by statute.' The same article also provides them with their own resources – article 72, paragraph 3 explicitly refers to 'tax revenue and other own revenues of territorial communities', adding that they 'represent a decisive share of their income'. French territorial communities' own resources have proved insufficient to cover their growing expenses, even when much higher than in their European counterparts. When the Balladur Report was issued, they raised 49 per cent of their total income (against 15 per cent for the UK), well above the average of 27 per cent in EU Member States.[43] The constitutional change of March 2003 introduced a form of financial charter for local finances aiming at increasing the financial accountability of territorial communities, yet it did not put an end to the complex and obsolete character of French local finances. As the experts of the Balladur Committee explained, 'The same project can be co-financed by different categories of local communities',[44] and also by the state. This is closely linked to the shared competences of French territorial communities. So cross-financing tends to be the rule and leads to delays and conflicts as well as slow decision-making mechanisms.

The other structural problem of French local finances is that they are dreadfully outdated. The main taxes and duties that French territorial communities can directly levy at the local level, representing two-thirds of local taxation, have largely remained unchanged except for the business tax. Until the Finance Law of 2010, which replaced the business tax with the territorial economic contribution, and a series of new local taxes in the wake of the Balladur Report, there were four direct local taxes: the housing tax; the French equivalent of Council Tax; the property tax on built and unbuilt property; and the business tax (now the territorial economic contribution). Even if French territorial communities seem to enjoy significant financial leeway, since under the article 72 (2) they 'may be authorised by statute to determine the basis of assessment and the rates' of local taxes, they are still *de facto* very dependent on central government. France has a long history of state interventionism, and this is also the case in local finances. The Balladur Report has put forward a paradox in the French decentralisation process, which is the growing part of the state contribution in direct local taxation, notably through the General Operating Grant (DGF).[45] The 2014 Finance Law has led to an unprecedented reduction of the General Operating Grant, thus seriously challenging the principle of the financial autonomy of French territorial communities. The same trend can be observed in the United Kingdom – or rather in England: the funding of councils is largely determined by central government as it is based on limited grants and Council Tax is subject to a cap. There is much less flexibility than in France for raising local taxation, as local government has traditionally relied on revenue-support grant.

Faced with a long-lasting financial and economic crisis following the 2008 'credit crunch' in the banking system, France and the UK have both adopted national austerity measures, leading to significant reductions in central government funding for local communities and putting great strain on their finances, to the extent that in England some local councils are almost bankrupt. The rise in Council Tax necessary to cover the cost of the national living wage announced by the Chancellor of the Exchequer in the Spending Review of November 2015 to finance care for the elderly will put further pressure on local finances and local representatives. Supporters of local government such as the Liberal Democrat Baroness Pinnock[46] advocate French-type solutions to free local government from central control, such as allowing local councils to raise local taxes. They also explore other forms of taxation, such as some form of local income tax, while allowing the use of the Value Added Tax (VAT) locally to fund local services. Land taxes have also been debated since Lloyd George's budgets of 1909 and 1914. Beyond the financial aspect, what is really at stake in France and in the UK is independent local decision-making and local democracy itself. In the same way, taxation is more than ever at the core of the devolution process in Scotland and Wales.

Scotland, which already had a more advanced form of devolution than Wales under the Act of 1998, was granted further fiscal and financial powers in the 2012 Scotland Act, thus moving closer to a form of economic autonomy. A cross-party commission of Opposition parties within the Scottish Parliament chaired by Sir Kenneth Calman was set up in 2008 by Gordon Brown's Labour government with the aim of securing Scotland's place in the Union. It was to review the provisions of the Scotland Act 1998 in the light of the first ten years' experience of the Scottish Parliament and to consider how devolution for Scotland could further develop. In its report, entitled 'Serving Scotland Better: Scotland and the United Kingdom in the 21st century', published in June 2009, it recommended a whole range of new devolved powers over taxation. The objective was to make the Scottish Parliament not only politically accountable – as it was already the case with MSPs having to face elections – but also financially accountable. It would provide an alternative to independence in order to strengthen devolution and the Union itself. The Calman Report was largely followed up by the Conservative–Liberal Democrat coalition government after the May 2010 General Election, and strongly influenced the content of the Scotland Act 2012, creating a new Scottish rate of income tax, and was in place for Scotland's fifth devolved Parliament in 2016. The 2012 Scotland Act aimed at strengthening the devolution settlement in Scotland and increasing the financial accountability of the Scottish Parliament. Its objective is to increase the Scottish Parliament's ability to make autonomous choices and to be accountable for these choices. It is designed to reduce Scotland's dependence on UK tax and revenues. Some provisions in the Act are directly derived from the Commission on Scottish Devolution or Calman Commission; others have been left out, such as the recommendations for social security and welfare reform. The Act is divided into four parts: Part 1 concerns the Scottish Parliament and its powers, while part 2 concerns the Scottish ministers and their powers. Part 3 covers finance, whereas part 4, entitled 'Miscellaneous', contains a clause on sentencing policy as well as matters such as interpretation and commencement. The 2012 Act in all includes 39 clauses, of which 9 set out finance provisions, including 6 clauses relating to changes to the tax system that will be implemented by secondary legislation. All the other clauses are devoted to constitutional issues. Even if part 3 is shorter, it is one of the most sensitive ones, as it deals with a strategic and highly sensitive issue, finance, as well as being a strong symbol of sovereignty. It is all the more important in the current context of financial crisis where governments try to steer their economies out of the recession. Part 3 covers not only taxation – different kinds of Scottish taxes falling within the scope of the Scottish Parliament's power to legislate – but also borrowing by the Scottish ministers. Thus key elements of taxation will be devolved, there will be a reduction in the block grant and extended borrowing powers will be introduced. It should be noted that Scotland's important financial services, notably the banks, were severely damaged by the 'credit crunch' in 2008. However, the structure and thresholds of the wider UK income tax system, which remains a reserved matter, were retained as well as the national block grant operating under the Barnett Formula, highly favourable to Scotland. Some commentators feared that core elements of the social union and the economic ties that bound the Union together were now being fundamentally damaged.

Despite its shortcomings, the Calman report, followed by the 2012 Scotland Act, served as a catalyst for Wales. It emboldened the Welsh government to ask for similar devolution of fiscal power. Thus, in October 2011, a Commission similar to Calman in Scotland was set up in Wales, the Commission on Devolution in Wales, or Silk Commission – with the support of the Welsh Government and all three opposition parties in the National Assembly for Wales – to look at the financial relationship between Wales and Westminster and to provide a wider review of devolution in Wales. The Silk Commission[47] completed its work on the fiscal side of Welsh devolution and published its first report on November 2012 entitled 'Empowerment and Responsibility: Financial Powers to Strengthen Wales'. It advocated devolving taxation and borrowing powers to the National Assembly for Wales and to the Welsh government. Although the UK government delayed its official response to the Silk Commission's report, in October 2013 the British Prime Minister and his Deputy Prime Minister announced in Cardiff that the Welsh government would eventually be offered some power over income tax, subject to a referendum.

A few months later, on 18 December 2013, a draft Wales Bill was published 'to amend the Government of Wales Act 2006; to make provision about local housing authorities in Wales and about the Law Commission in relation to Wales'. The draft measure, which became the Wales Act 2014, thus gave effect to many of the key recommendations of the first report of the Commission on Devolution in Wales. It aimed at giving Wales some fiscal autonomy by granting the Welsh Assembly, which until now had no taxation competences, the power to set a Welsh rate of income tax subject to the approval of the Welsh people via a referendum. Interestingly, on 28 February 2016 the Secretary of State for Wales, Stephen Crabb, conceded that the 2016 Wales Bill, introduced after the European referendum, would be used to remove the referendum requirement. Its objective is also to give Welsh ministers some borrowing powers, but inferior to the ones granted to their Scottish counterparts under the Scotland Act 2012 which has already led to criticisms, notably on the part of the Labour party denouncing the lack of fair funding for Wales under its current provisions owing to the perceived injustices of the Barnett Formula.[48]

The Commission set up in the wake of the 2014 Scottish referendum, chaired by Lord Smith of Kelvin, produced its report very rapidly in November of the same year. Three proposals stand out which are likely to have a significant impact on the current constitutional arrangements of the United Kingdom, starting with more fiscal devolution. The objective of the Commission is to go beyond the provisions of the 2012 Scotland Act and thus move further towards the full fiscal autonomy that the Scottish nationalists are claiming. Under the terms of the Smith Report, the Scottish Parliament will be responsible for setting all the rates and bands of income tax on earned income for Scottish taxpayers while the UK will continue to levy income tax on savings and dividends. It means that around 60 per cent of the money the Scottish Parliament spends will flow directly to it. Echoing the promise made by the SNP in its 2015 manifesto, the Smith Report also includes a degree of welfare devolution to Scotland. The idea is for Scottish ministers to have the flexibility to develop their own priorities for welfare spending within certain limits to avoid significant distortions between the different parts of the United Kingdom. This again is a serious diminution of the cohesive force of the Union. In the same way, in France there is a strong attachment to 'equalisation mechanisms intended to promote equality between territorial communities' – now enshrined in article 72 (2) of the constitution – which still justifies a form of state intervention as a way of fighting inequalities between people and also between territorial communities.

The way ahead: a revisited Union and a more diverse Republic

The Union of four different nations has rarely been under so much strain as Scottish nationalists' centrifugal forces try to pull the Kingdom apart while the English nationalists of UKIP show stirrings of independence of the European Union, compromising the survival of the United Kingdom as a cohesive whole. To avoid such a catastrophic scenario – and answer some of the Scottish nationalists' claims – the Smith Commission recommended that the Scottish Parliament and government be made permanent institutions and the Sewel Convention for ongoing legislative continuity placed on a statutory footing. Yet, as the report of the Bingham Centre for the Rule of Law explained, the problem with the Smith Commission's approach is that 'it perpetuates the notion that devolved institutions are subordinates of Westminster, not partners in the governance of the United Kingdom.'[49]

A few months afterwards, in January 2015, the UK's government issued its official response in a Command Paper entitled 'Scotland in the UK: an enduring settlement',[50] containing draft clauses for a Scotland Bill to be introduced in the first session of the new Parliament. The latter, after having been through pre-legislative scrutiny, was tabled in the House of Commons on 28 May 2015. The Scotland Bill, brought from the Commons on 10 November 2015 (receiving Royal Assent on 23 March 2016, thus becoming the Scotland Act 2016), 'a Bill to amend the Scotland Act 1998 and make provision about the functions of the Scottish Ministers; and for connected purposes' – focuses mainly on constitutional arrangements. Its first part is devoted to the permanence of the Scottish Parliament and Scottish government and to the Sewel Convention, while its second deals entirely with taxation (income tax and VAT). Its third main section is about welfare benefits and employment support. SNP ministers, determined to retain as much of the Barnett Formula as they could, delayed their support for the Bill until they had sufficient guarantees about maintaining the national block grant. They were particularly eager to keep it, as they worried about the impact of the collapse of oil revenues on Scotland's economy and finances and the subsequent blow dealt to the financial forecast of the Scottish First Minister, the SNP Nicola Sturgeon.

In the 2015 Command Paper, two particularly important draft clauses received particular attention and are now part of the Scotland Act 2016. The first provides that after section 1 of the Scotland Act 1998 is to be inserted, 'the Scottish Parliament and the Scottish Government are a permanent part of the UK's constitutional arrangements.' It adds that, under Part 1, 63 A (1), 'the Scottish Parliament and the Scottish government are not to be abolished except on the basis of a decision of the people of Scotland voting in a referendum.' Part 1 of the 2016 Scotland Act also provides that after section 28 (7) of the Scotland Act 1998 will be added: 'but it is recognised that the parliament of the UK will not normally legislate with regard to devolved matters without the consent of the Scottish Parliament.' If in both cases, the aim was for the Westminster Parliament to be unable to disestablish the Scottish Parliament without the consent of the Scottish people, the new provisions are not to be legally binding and thus not judicially enforceable before the courts. At best, they will be politically binding which means that though they represent a strong symbol of the permanence of Scottish institutions their scope will be limited even if they might move the current constitutional arrangements further in a federal direction in the long run. It will still be legally and technically possible for the Westminster Parliament one day to abolish provisions which are only of a statutory nature, even if the prospect of a political and constitutional crisis would deter national legislators from doing so.

The most imminent risks are not only bringing in more constitutional changes to try to satisfy Scottish nationalists' claims, but also having very fragmented constitutional debates. The independent experts of the Bingham Centre for the Rule of Law pointed this out in an alarmist tone. If rethinking the constitution has undeniably been going on for some years, including within the King's College London Constitutional and Political Reform Centre formerly chaired by Professor Robert Blackburn, the pace has accelerated under the pressure of the Scottish referendum and now been affected by the EU referendum. The objective should not be to propose yet more constitutional changes to satisfy nationalist claims, while the last devolution statutes, the 2012 Scotland Act and the 2014 Wales Act, have not even been implemented. The 2014 Wales Act followed the release of the second report of the Commission on Devolution in Wales, 'Empowerment and Responsibility: Legislative Powers to Strengthen Wales', published in March 2014, devoted to the review of the non-financial powers of the National Assembly. Some of its key provisions dealt with the Welsh conferred-powers model of devolution and with intergovernmental relations. Regarding the former, it advocated a reserved-powers model as in Scotland as a clearer, more coherent model than the one based on conferred powers. On the latter, it suggested the introduction of a statutory code of practice for intergovernmental relations as well as a Welsh Intergovernmental Committee to oversee the Welsh devolution settlement. As for the 2016 Wales Bill (now the 2017 Wales Act), it provides the Welsh nation with a long anticipated reserved-powers model. Though it is supposed to introduce more clarity in who does what between central government and the Welsh devolved administration, it will be difficult to implement. The draft Wales Bill on the future of devolution in Wales published in October 2015 aimed at introducing a clearer, stronger and fairer Welsh devolution settlement as well as at devolving new powers to the National Assembly and the Welsh government. Yet, some experts on Welsh devolution would have liked the subsidiarity principle to be given more prominence as well. The Welsh reserved-powers model is shackled by no less than 195 exceptions. In some ways, the powers of the Welsh Assembly appeared to be curtailed rather than gaining equality with the Scottish Parliament.

The desire for more devolution in Wales is partly directed towards more devolution to the local level. Wales lacks influence in Whitehall at the national level; hence the call made by the Welsh Affairs Committee of the House of Commons to Whitehall 'to think about Wales' in its pre-legislative report on the Welsh draft Bill published on 28 February 2016. The latter proposed a number of improvements to the Bill in order to facilitate the move in Wales from a conferred-powers model to a reserved-powers model. Members of the committee[51] were especially worried about the long list of reservations which would make it difficult in practice to implement the new model of reserved powers. They also focused on whether Wales should have its own jurisdiction in the future, examining the various arguments for a separate or distinct legal jurisdiction. The question was asked previously under the 2014 Wales Act whether the police and justice should be devolved to Wales. However, not only is there an absence of cross-party consensus on the need to devolve justice, but the Silk Commission itself concluded that justice – especially civil and criminal law – 'are better exercised on a non-devolved basis'. The First Minister for Wales, Carwyn Jones,[52] explained when giving evidence to the House of Lords Constitution Committee in Cardiff in January 2016, 'I do not think that people necessarily understand what the different levels of government actually do.' There are currently key debates on legal matters – unlike Scotland, Wales does not have its own separate law, legal system (including its own criminal system) or legal profession. For the moment, there is a shared legal jurisdiction for England and Wales which limits the ability of the Welsh Assembly to legislate on criminal law matters, and the 2016 Wales Bill (now the 2017 Wales Act) 'is built on the idea that there should be minimal divergence in the law between England and Wales', as Carwyn Jones explained; that is to say, the law and legal system would be considered as reserved powers and Wales accorded its own legal jurisdiction. The rapid growth of Welsh law, allied to a reserved-powers model, would seem to lead to that conclusion.

The National Assembly is now firmly established as a legislature with primary legislative power – the origin of a growing body of Welsh law – and one would expect a separate Welsh jurisdiction to follow. The Lord Chief Justice, Lord Thomas of Cwmgiedd, and Carwyn Jones hold the view that it would be better for Wales to have a distinct rather than a separate jurisdiction, while keeping a shared court system, penal system and legal profession, as it would otherwise be costly not only in terms of money but also in terms of legal qualification. The House of Commons Welsh Affairs Committee defines the latter – a distinct jurisdiction – as 'a unified court system encompassing Wales and England but applying two distinct bodies of law: the law of Wales and the law of England'.[53] Wales having its own indigenous institutions operating locally and meeting the needs of its citizens had the sympathy of the distinguished late Lord Bingham.

The other source of uncertainty about the 2017 Wales Act concerns tax devolution. Even if the need for a referendum on the partial devolution of income tax – which was part of the 2014 Wales Act – were removed, how new taxation power would be transferred and how the new scheme would work has not been clearly defined. Though, by general agreement, the 2017 Wales Act has been badly drafted without a proper consultation process for the main actors in Wales's institutional, political and economic life, the First Minister, however, believes that it contains at least one positive point, which is that 'it would allow the Assembly to change its name to a Parliament.' He adds that 'people understand better what Parliament does because they are used to the term.' In any case, under the new reserved-powers model for Wales provided by the 2017 Wales Act, the single jurisdiction of Wales and England, together with constitutional arrangements, foreign affairs and defence, will all fall under the category of reserved powers. The 2017 Wales Act was introduced early in the second legislative session of Parliament as announced by Stephen Crabb,[54] the former Secretary of State for Wales, on 28 February 2016 with a working party to consider a distinct Welsh jurisdiction. It was part of the legislative programme put forward by the government in the 2016 Queen's Speech. It stated that the government would work 'in cooperation' with the devolved administration to 'establish a strong and lasting devolution settlement in Wales'.[55]

However, what is also essential is to concentrate on constitutional issues which have not yet been dealt with, i.e. the gaps in constitutional reform such as the English exception in the devolution process, England remaining for its part highly centralised. England is still very much undevolved, and no clear solution has yet been advocated. Until recently, though the English were on the whole favourable to devolution to the Celtic nations, if unexcited by it, they were hostile to devolution for themselves. Westminster and Whitehall have largely remained unchanged. One of the main, yet highly controversial, options for England would be English Votes for English Laws. It was originally part of David Cameron's notorious referendum 'vows' – more commonly known as EVEL,[56] and it was enshrined not in a statute but in a new provision to the Standing Orders of the House of Commons on

22 October 2015 that govern the procedure of the House of Commons. If the way it was introduced is already in itself questionable, it remains more than ever a divisive issue. It was introduced without there being a political consensus, for which it was sharply criticised by the Lords Constitution Committee in October 2016. The objective is to ensure that Bills, certified by the House of Commons Speaker as affecting only England – or England and Wales – will only be adopted if approved by a majority of English (or English and Welsh) MPs. The first Bill that was for the first time ever submitted to EVEL, that is to say to a grand committee stage where English – or English and Welsh MPs – formally consent to the Bill, was the controversial Housing and Planning Bill.[57] The First Minister for Wales, Carwyn Jones, is sceptical about EVEL because he believes that 'it is very difficult to have an institution where members are allowed to vote only in certain circumstances: it is either a UK Parliament or it is not!'[58] Scottish nationalists have claimed it would prevent a Scottish Prime Minister from taking office and would create two distinct classes of MPs, some of whom (notably the Scots) would not have full equality of status..

Even before EVEL, the Westminster Parliament was already *de facto* both a British Parliament where all the four nations are represented – at least in the House of Commons – and an English Parliament in the sense that the great majority of its 650 MPs (533) represent English constituencies.[59] This is also true of the House of Lords, which has a majority of peers from southern England. One of the numerous problems that English Votes for English Laws would entail would be to create two tiers of MPs, undermining the principle of equality between them. Besides, the status of MPs whose voting rights would be limited would also have to be dealt with as well as the impact of such fundamental changes on the House of Lords. Another solution to the English question, perhaps less controversial and more pragmatic at the same time, is to focus on some form of decentralisation for England based on existing institutions, city deals and strengthening local government – a Cities and Local Government Bill to this purpose was included in the 2015 Queen's Speech. The Cities and Local Government Devolution Act 2016[60] received Royal Assent on 28 January 2016 – 'A Bill [now an Act] to make provision for the election of Mayors for the areas of, and for conferring additional functions on combined authorities established under Part 6 of the Local Democracy, Economic Development and Construction Act 2009'. It set up combined authorities and provides for transfers such as transport by central government on condition that elected mayors be accepted. Yet it will be difficult for the so-called Northern

Powerhouse to compete with London and its 8.6 million people living in Greater London. And, of course, it would depend on the Treasury in Whitehall for its funding.

It is all the more urgent to tackle the English question since English nationalism too is on the rise. In this connection, the party for the independence of the United Kingdom from the European Union (UKIP) is now very much part of the political landscape. Though it won only one seat in the 2015 General Election under the first-past-the-post voting system, which is not favourable to small political parties in general, UKIP was supported by no less than four million voters. The great majority are in England. Perhaps more surprisingly, UKIP seems to be making its way in Wales. A YouGov Poll for ITV Wales/Cardiff University on 30 November–4 December 2015[61] suggested that UKIP could gain from zero Assembly seat to nine in the Welsh Assembly election in May 2016 thanks to the voting system, which is partly based on proportional representation. If UKIP intended to appeal to traditional supporters of the Labour party by campaigning on the reintroduction of grammar schools, they mainly exploited the fear of a wave of immigrants to try to attract Welsh voters. UKIP did win its first seats in the Welsh Assembly on 5 May 2016 – seven altogether, including the two former Conservative MPs Neil Hamilton and Mark Reckless – partly to the detriment of Labour, which, although it remains the dominant party in Wales, fell short of a majority, with twenty-nine seats. As for the Welsh nationalists of Plaid Cymru, they became the second party after Labour,[62] with twelve seats in the Assembly, relegating the Conservatives (with eleven seats) to third place. Thus UKIP has not lost its momentum since the last European elections.[63] Moreover, the campaign for the in/out EU referendum gave it an opportunity to progress and to promote the withdrawal of the United Kingdom from the European Union with a serious threat to the Union of the Kingdom as a result.

Various proposals have thus already been made to achieve a more stable, coherent constitutional framework for the United Kingdom as a whole. They are all based on the need to redefine the purpose and core values of the Union in what is now identified as constitutional unionism. Those values were not promoted – not in a sufficiently clear way – during the 2014 referendum campaign as the Unionist parties, and more largely the supporters of the Union, never satisfactorily explained why it was 'better (to stay) together', and took it for granted. It is the more regrettable since in the words of Gordon Brown, who campaigned powerfully in favour of the Union 'no Union can survive without unionists.'

Some constitutional analysts favour a royal commission on the future of the Union, but the majority support a United Kingdom-wide multi-party constitutional convention. What is important is to make sure that it is a representative, open forum instead of a series of discussions between constitutional experts behind closed doors. What the Welsh constitutional experts of the project United Kingdom's Changing Union recommend is for such a convention to be composed of elected members drawn from the four United Kingdom legislatures. The idea is to involve both the United Kingdom government and the territorial governments, all the more so as there has been a serious lack of intergovernmental and interparliamentary dialogue until now. The aim is not only to 'meet the aspirations of all four constituent nations in the common interest of the Union as a whole' but also to meet the aspirations of citizens themselves, the difficulty being to define the level and the form of direct public involvement. Too often, they have been the great absentees, whereas it is essential for them to be associated with the whole process. It must be a real national conversation such as the one which preceded the setting up of the Scottish Parliament. The Scottish constitutional convention, which was established in the middle stages of the devolution process, could serve as a source of inspiration once again.

Among the numerous proposals that have been put forward by legal and political experts regarding the future of the Union as a whole and the form its constitutional arrangements could take, two are particularly worth examining. The first is in fact a joint Welsh initiative based on an active collaboration between the Wales Governance Centre at Cardiff University, the Institute for Welsh Affairs and 'Tomorrow's Wales'. After three years of intensive work they published a report in 2015 entitled 'UK's Changing Union'. This Welsh initiative is all the more important as the constitutional debate until now has been very much Scottish-centred. This can partly be explained by the fact that the Welsh nationalists are not considered as a threat to the Union. Plaid Cymru achieved no breakthrough in the 2015 General Election, nor indeed has it ever done. In the 2015 election the self-styled party of Wales only managed to maintain their three seats in the House of Commons and came in fourth in the overall vote. Wales is still a Labour stronghold. Significantly, the leader of the Labour party in Wales and First Minister, Carwyn Jones, has himself called for 'a UK-wide constitutional convention'.

The other major scheme is an initiative based on the collective work of the Bingham Centre for the Rule of Law and the British Institute of International and Comparative Law. They issued their report in May 2015 entitled 'A constitutional crossroads: ways forward for the UK' around the idea of a 'Charter of Union'[64] as a first step towards a codified British constitution 'to lay down the underlying principles of the UK's territorial Constitution'. What is of interest is that the drafters of the Charter for the Union partly based their proposals on the arguments used during the Scottish independence referendum campaign. Their other main source of inspiration was the findings of the Kilbrandon Report (1973), the original foundation of the devolution process.[65] However, if this project seems at first glance very ambitious, the term 'charter' – partly inspired by the Magna Carta, the Great Charter – can be misleading. Indeed, the so-called Charter for the Union would in fact be 'set up by a statute of the UK Parliament interpreted and enforced in the courts'. So it would only have the legal value of an Act of the Westminster Parliament and at most be a constitutional statute, not subject to implied repeal. It would mean that it could itself be one day abrogated by a new Parliament, like the devolution statutes of the Human Rights Act of 1998, instead of being fully entrenched.

Among the core values of the Charter for the Union – also part of the Welsh constitutional project – would be social and economic cohesion between the four nations; subsidiarity; and a decentralised England within a much less asymmetrical Union. The Welsh and English projects both focus on the UK as a Union state and explore a federal or confederal option based on a codified UK constitution. In the nineteenth century, the constitutional authority A. V. Dicey did not think that federalism was a desirable option for the country. A Liberal Unionist, he argued that 'federalism revolutionises the whole constitution of the UK; by undermining the parliamentary sovereignty, it deprives English institutions of their elasticity, their strength, and their life.'[66]

A federal United Kingdom would not only mean a fully written codified constitution but would involve fundamental changes regarding the existing national institutions. The Upper House of Parliament could be turned into a territorially elected chamber providing formal political representation at the centre for the nations and regions of the UK, while the United Kingdom Supreme Court would act as a constitutional court with constitutional review power, which it has hitherto resisted. Of course, a fundamental weakness would be that one of the four elements in the federation – England – contains 85 per cent of the population. Federalism is even less an option for France – except for the territory of New Caledonia[67] – still a highly centralised country, than for the UK. Both countries have rejected it for themselves, as they also did for Europe.

However, neither the 2015 Conservative manifesto nor the 2015 Queen's Speech included any proposal or Bill dealing with parliamentary reform or the reform of national institutions. The 2016 Queen's Speech for its part only announced that the government would 'uphold the sovereignty of Parliament and the primacy of the House of Commons'.[68]Thus turning the House of Lords into an elected House based on a territorial form of representation is not on the agenda, any more than a reform of the voting system for the House of Commons. What will arise is change to the constituency boundaries (deferred until 2018) to reduce the number of seats from 650 to 600, which would make it harder for the Labour party to win seats in the Commons. The 2015 Queen's Speech and the 2016 one were dominated by the European issue, focusing on the need to renegotiate the UK's relationship with the EU. Significantly, neither the 2015 Queen's Speech nor the 2016 one[69] included any Bill on the repeal of the Human Rights Act 1998, which would have further alienated the central government from the nations and regions and undermined the whole devolution legal framework.

Conclusion

Of the two nations, the UK seems further in 2016 from restoring order to its constitutional complexities. The 2014 referendum on the independence of Scotland did not come near to resolving the Scottish Question – or indeed the future of Wales. It also revived the English Question more intensely than ever. The positive way to look at those constitutional issues would be to see them as a new beginning, not only for Scotland but also for the Union as a whole. There will be more devolution granted to Scotland under the 2016 Scotland Act, and to Wales under the 2017 Wales Act, even if the hasty promises (or 'vows') made by politicians in the count-down to the Scottish referendum were not to be entirely fulfilled. In any case, aggravating the asymmetrical nature of the current devolution process can only fuel resentment and nationalist feelings in both England and Scotland and is bound to lead to a new referendum on independence in Scotland. Constitutional reform should not be exclusively based on ever more devolution adopted piecemeal but also on the modernisation and democratisation of national institutions, and a more positive emphasis on the Union. Thus British democracy would benefit from a more streamlined House of Commons and a more democratic British Upper House based on territorial representation – even if it acted as a very efficient counter-power defeating the government on the highly sensitive issue of tax credits in 2016 – as well as a UK Supreme Court with a wider devolution jurisdiction and one or two Welsh Justices, as a move towards a formal Welsh law. To use the expression of *The Guardian* journalist Simon Jenkins, this is 'an exciting new era' in a country with a rich and complex constitutional and political history.

It is without doubt a challenging time, especially for constitutional lawyers, following the 23 June 2016 referendum where the people of the UK voted to leave the European Union. It raises many complex – and, for some, unprecedented – constitutional issues. Now is the time for the UK to seize the day and adopt a fully written constitution which would entrench devolution and better protect human rights for the benefit of all four nations and the British people. The 2014 Scottish Constitutional Bill, which was to be the blueprint of the new independent Scottish state, did propose a fully written constitution for that nation. Its effect would be to create a United Kingdom more diversified, but also perhaps more truly united than ever before. Salvation could come, therefore, not from the English centre but from the margins, the so-called Celtic fringe. It would be an anti-Diceyan irony to be treasured.

As for France, the 2009 Balladur Report in its own conclusion advocated more diversity and pragmatism,[70] which are in fact two key features of British devolution, to improve the French decentralisation process, although the report did not have much impact. In any case, rather than merely thinking in terms of competitiveness and profitability, when examining the future of decentralisation in France more importance should be paid to implementing the innovative instruments of participatory democracy at the local level now part of the constitution, such as the right of petition, allowing citizens to take part in defining the agenda of their territorial community and the use of local referendums associating citizens with the decision-making process.

Notes

1. Devolution was defined by Vernon Bogdanor as 'a process that involves the dispersal of power from a superior to an inferior political authority and which consists of the transfer to a subordinate elected body on a geographical basis, of functions at present exercised by parliament'; V. Bogdanor, *Devolution* (Oxford: Oxford University Press, 1979), p. 2.
2. No better translation in French has been found apart from *la dévolution*, even if Professor Gicquel for his part has proposed to translate it by *la décentralisation maximale* (in other words 'decentralisation max').

3. This type of territorial organisation was very well encapsulated in the expression coined by a French geographer Jean-Francois Gravier in a landmark book *Paris et le désert français*, published in 1947 (Paris: Flammarion, new edition 1958).
4. In September 1789 a special committee was set up by the Constituent Assembly which emerged from the *Tiers Etat*, initiated by Abbé Sieyès, in charge of carrying out a thorough review of territorial government. Six months afterwards, it produced its report recommending the division of the territory into some 80 units accessible within a day on horseback, which were to form the so-called *départements*, while maintaining, yet with different names, the former parishes to form the new *communes*. This new territorial organisation was part of the birth of the new French nation.
5. Comité pour la réforme des collectivités locales (presided over by Edouard Balladur), 'Il est temps de décider' (Paris: La Documentation française, 2009), p. 7.
6. Balladur Report, 'Il est temps de décider', p. 5.
7. A clear majority of Scottish people (55 per cent), asked whether 'Scotland should be an independent country', rejected independence for Scotland, whereas 45 per cent expressed their attachment to an independent Scotland – especially young people aged sixteen and seventeen, who were allowed to vote for the first time, fully aware that their vote could make a difference.
8. Tom Schuller, 'The impact of devolution on Franco-British Relations: Regional challenges and opportunities', Franco-British Council (BFC) Seminar, Lille (France), 9 February 2015.
9. The French unemployment rate is at an eighteen-year high of more than 10 per cent, though President Hollande has made the fight against unemployment one of his official priorities.
10. French decentralisation was initially imposed by the state, whereas separate referendums were held in Scotland, Wales and Northern Ireland before the 1998 Devolution Acts.
11. Christopher Harvie, *The Rise of Regional Europe* (London: Routledge, 1993).
12. Gaston Deferre was the former Socialist Mayor of Marseille.
13. It was set up by the former President Valéry Giscard d'Estaing and published its report in November 1976.
14. Act 2 of the French decentralisation process, launched by the 28 March 2003 constitutional change, introduced some flexibility in the territorial organisation of the Republic, allowing territorial communities to experiment with new competences as a temporary measure and in a specific area, introducing for the first time some diversity into the French constitution. Thus, under the totally redrafted article 72, new territorial communities with a specific status can be established by law.
15. Pierre Avril and Jean Gicquel, *Lexique de droit constitutionnel* (Paris: PUF, 2003), p. 37.

16. Balladur Report, 'Il est temps de décider', p. 7.
17. Scotland of course approved devolution in March 1979, but not by a big enough margin under the Cunningham amendment (moved by a Scottish Labour MP), which required 40 per cent of the electorate to endorse it.
18. In the 1974 General Election, the SNP secured 30 per cent of the Scottish vote and 11 out of its 71 seats in Westminster.
19. The original Scotland Act (1998) in the decision *R v HM Advocate* 2003 was described as 'a major constitutional measure which altered the government of the UK', the Privy Council, then acting under its devolution jurisdiction, suggesting that the Scotland Act 1998 might be read as a constitutional document which provides a complete system of rights, obligations and remedies as regards the devolved governance of Scotland. Wales received the same recognition under the St David's Day Agreement of 2015.
20. Instead of being consulted after the adoption of a national statute, and rather than imposing devolution on Scottish, Welsh – and Northern Irish – people by Westminster, great emphasis was placed on obtaining their consent via referendums in each of the three territories involved. This is a very novel practice at the national level (where only two referendums had been held, in 1975 on Europe and in 2011 on the Alternative Vote), and not a natural device in a parliamentary regime. British people are – or rather were – not familiar with referendums, unlike the Swiss. Not only were the three 1997 referendums a way of testing the popularity of devolution, but they also aimed at securing legitimacy for devolution. To take but one example, Wales has had no less than three referendums on devolution – in 1979, 1997 and 2011. Under the provisions of the Wales Act 2014 Welsh people were to be invited to express their views in a new referendum 'about commencement of income tax provisions'. This was later rescinded by the then Secretary of State for Wales, Stephen Crabb, in early 2016.
21. Eric Landot, Bruno Malhey and Michel Verpeaux, *La Réforme des Collectivités Territoriales* (Paris: Berger-Levrault, 2011), p. 100.
22. Under the Statute of 5 April 1884, *communes* were allocated a general competence – and it is still the case today. Though it would be almost impossible, or at least wearisome, to list them all, *communes* play an important role, providing a whole range of services such as education (especially primary schools), social services (notably for the elderly), highway maintenance and refuse collection, but also law and order, as French Mayors, who are elected, are the representatives of the state (in that capacity they can also act as registrars). Besides, they carry out important missions as far as town planning is concerned.
23. *Départements* play a key role in social services, including social housing, and the social cohesion of the whole community.
24. They were originally called local communities (*collectivités locales*) but are now referred to as territorial communities (*collectivités territoriales*). As is explained

in the 2009 Balladur Report, once the Republican nature of the regime had been secured under the Third Republic, *communes* and *départements* were granted the status of local communities, which means that they could administer themselves freely via councils democratically elected. They were however to be supervised by the state, or rather its representative, the prefect, introduced by Napoleon Bonaparte.

25. Municipal councils for *communes*, general councils for *départments* and regional councils for *régions*.
26. The basic components of the original devolution arrangements for Scotland were significant, since devolution gave it one of the widest ranges of competences of any devolved government in Europe – except at the time full fiscal powers. It was the consequence of the decision to specify only the reserved powers – the powers reserved to Westminster concerning the constitution, political parties, foreign affairs, public service and defence, and also competition law under Schedule 5 of the Scotland Act 1998 – leaving Scotland with a general competence over all other matters.
27. Since 2004, French *départements* have also been in charge of roads.
28. Hélène Bekmezian, 'Petites histoires autour d'un grand marchandage', *Le Monde* (5 June 2014), 6.
29. The new map of *régions* is due to be implemented on 1 January 2017.
30. Kim Willsher, 'Plus ca change: outcry at latest effort to redraw map of France', *The Guardian* (4 June 2014), 16.
31. As seen previously, modern France was built around the *départements* introduced at the time of the 1789 Revolution, highly respectful of the geographical and also cultural and religious identities of French territorial communities.
32. 'Retricoter la France', *La Vie* (26 June 2014), 18–21.
33. The proposal to merge Nord-Pas-de-Calais with Picardie was highly controversial as Picardie is a stronghold of the National Front. The latter obtained its best results there at the 2014 European elections.
34. The Aquitaine region which dates back to 1959, with its capital Bordeaux, is composed of five *départements* – Gironde, Dordogne, Lot-et-Garonne, Landes and Pyrénées Atlantiques. It used to be known as Guyenne. It experienced its most prosperous time under the Black Prince (1362–72).
35. The new region will include twelve *départements* representing one-seventh of the national territory and 5.8 million inhabitants.
36. French Mayors, being democratically elected, are close to the people, and French citizens do not hesitate to contact them directly to express their claims. Like British MPs, they have their own 'surgeries'.
37. The general competence clause was abolished in 2010, then re-established by the Socialists in 2013.
38. In Antoinette Hastings-Marchadier and Bertrand Faure (eds), *La décentralisation à la française* (Paris: LGDJ, 2015), p. 157.

39. He did so in his report of the conference held in Lille on 9 February 2015 on the impact of devolution on Franco-British relations.
40. As mentioned in the seminar in Lille on 9 February 2015 held by the Franco-British Council on 'the impact of devolution on Franco-British relations', projects in common around culture have been elaborated by the (former) Conservative Mayor of London Boris Johnson and the Socialist Mayor of Paris, Anne Hidalgo – a woman Mayor for the first time ever in the history of the French capital. Besides, the French Parisian transport company RATP has won a contract to run London buses.
41. Commission on Devolution in Wales, 'Empowerment and Responsibility: Legislative Powers to Strengthen Wales', Second Report, March 2014 (Cardiff: Commission on Devolution in Wales, 7 March 2014).
42. Wales has now been granted its own reserved-powers model under the new 2017 Wales Act, although a complex controversial one given the wide list of powers reserved to the Westminster Parliament.
43. For more information see 'Les collectivités territoriales dans l'Union européenne: organisation, compétences et finances' (DEXIA, November 2008).
44. Balladur Report, 'Il est temps de décider', p. 20.
45. The Decentralisation Law of 1982 introduced a block grant from the state to finance local communities and thus to help finance local schemes.
46. Baroness Katherine Pinnock was one of the speakers of the Lloyd George Society weekend school, 20–1 February 2016 in Llandrindod Wells. Her lecture was on 'The future of local government'.
47. It was named after its chairman, Paul Silk, a former clerk to the National Assembly for Wales from 2001 to 2007.
48. However, the Chancellor of the Exchequer, George Osborne, announced in the 2015 Autumn Statement that the implementation of a funding floor for Wales would be within the range recommended by the Holtham Commission.
49. Bingham Centre for the Rule of Law, 'A Constitutional Crossroads: Ways Forward for the United Kingdom' (London: British Institute of International and Comparative Law, May 2015), p. 8.
50. Cabinet Office, 'Scotland in the UK: an enduring settlement', Cm 8990 (London: The Stationery Office, January 2015).
51. House of Commons Welsh Affairs Committee, 'Pre-legislative scrutiny of the draft Wales Bill', First Report of Session 2015–2016, HC 449 (London: The Stationery Office, 28 February 2016).
52. Following the May 2016 Welsh Assembly elections, the Opposition parties – Plaid Cymru, the Conservatives and UKIP, with the exception of the Liberal Democrat AM – formed an informal coalition to block the return of Labour leader Carwyn Jones as First Minister, as Labour did not win a majority (securing 'only' 29 seats in the Assembly instead of its previous 30 seats). Yet after an agreement reached between the Welsh Labour party (the first biggest party)

and Plaid Cymru (the second biggest party), Carwyn Jones remained as the First Minister, but of a minority government.

53. House of Commons Welsh Affairs Committee 'Pre-legislative scrutiny of the draft Wales Bill', p. 25.
54. Stephen Crabb succeeded Iain Duncan Smith as Secretary of State for Work and Pensions in March 2016 following the resignation of the latter over further cuts in disability benefits and as a staunch supporter of Brexit. Alun Cairns was appointed Secretary of State for Wales on 19 March 2016 following Stephen Crabb's promotion.
55. Queen's Speech to both Houses of Parliament delivered on Wednesday, 18 May 2016.
56. Government bills that have a Second Reading in the Commons, once certified by the Speaker as England-only in their entirety, would then be considered only by English MPs at Committee stage, then go to Report stage as normal. However, for bills containing English, or English and Welsh, provisions, a new stage would be added taking the form of a Legislative Grand Committee, which would consider a Consent Motion (for any clauses certified as only English, or English and Welsh, by the Speaker). At this stage, no amendments to the text of the bill could be made. If clauses of the bill are vetoed by the Legislative Grand Committee there will be a reconsideration stage when further amendments can be made and this is followed by a second Legislative Grand Committee. Then the bill continues to the normal Third Reading. The legislative process in the House of Lords will remain unchanged. See House of Lords Select Committee on the Constitution, 'English Votes for English Laws', HL Paper 61 (31 October 2016), pp. 2–3.
57. Under the Housing and Planning Bill due to become law in April 2017, families with a total income of £40,000 per year in London, and £30,000 outside the capital, will have to pay the market rental rate, the additional money thus raised going to the Treasury instead of local councils. Welsh MPs were invited to vote on the Housing and Planning Bill though it does not affect Wales, where very different rules and regulations apply in this area.
58. Carwyn Jones giving evidence to the House of Lords Constitution Committee in Cardiff on 21 January 2016.
59. Except 59 seats for Scotland, 40 seats for Wales and 18 for Northern Ireland – the question of a double mandate for Welsh MPs who are also Assembly Members has been examined by the Silk Commission, which has recommended the abolition of such a dual mandate as it might lead to conflict of interests and a waste of energy and effort.
60. The development of city-regions such as Sheffield, Manchester and Liverpool is based on cooperation between local metropolitan councils.
61. Steven Morris, 'UKIP sees Wales as second chance for sea change', *The Guardian* (Monday 11 January 2016), 8.

62. Labour lost its minister Leighton Andrews (Rhondda) to Plaid Cymru leader Leanne Wood.
63. It won twenty-six council seats in the May 2016 local elections in England.
64. 2015 being the 800th anniversary of Magna Carta/the Great Charter – different versions of a 'new Magna Carta' have been proposed, notably by King's College London.
65. Yet its rejection of federalism as an option for the UK has been widely criticised.
66. A. V. Dicey, 'Home Rule from and English Point of View', *Contemporary Review* (July 1882).
67. At the time of the French Revolution of 1789 people even died for supporting the idea of a federal France.
68. Although the government is determined to respond to Lord Strathclyde's report on delegated legislation.
69. The 2016 Queen's Speech only announced that the government would bring forward proposals for a British Bill of Rights. These rights would be based on the rights included in the European Convention on Human Rights, combining them with the common law tradition.
70. Balladur Report, 'Il est temps de décider', p. 118.

Chapter 6

The European Dimension: France and the UK, Partners in Europe

A day will come when you will no longer wage war … on that day you will be conscious of a common thought, common interests, and a common destiny … a day will come when we shall see those two immense groups, the United States of America and the United States of Europe, stretching their hands across the sea … to reap the well-being of all.
Victor Hugo[1]

Constitutional change in France and the United Kingdom has since the 1960s had a European as well as a purely domestic dimension. However, trying to understand the relationship of the two countries inside Europe, and also towards Europe, is a major challenge. This chapter provides reflections on Europe from both sides of the Channel. France and the United Kingdom joined the European Community – now European Union – at different times, under different circumstances and on different grounds. Whereas France was one of the six founding nation-states which signed the Treaties of Rome of 1957, the United Kingdom only joined the European Community sixteen years later, on 1 January 1973, under a Conservative Prime Minister, Edward Heath. Since then, France and the United Kingdom[2] have shared a common European membership, and thus a common destiny, as two of the key players, together with Germany, of the European Union, given their political, cultural, economic, military and strategic importance. Together, over forty-three years they have overcome several major crises that the European Community has gone through over its long history, including the difficult ratification process of the Maastricht Treaty (1992), which led to a more political type of European integration with the official birth of the European Union. After the 2016 referendum in Britain, this phase will come to an end, at least in its present form.

France and the United Kingdom are two proud countries with a well-established sense of national identity and sovereignty. This strong attachment to their national independence is deeply rooted in their past as former colonial empires. However, they sometimes find it difficult to live with their colonial legacy. Thus during an official visit to Haiti[3] in May 2015, President Hollande presented his apology on behalf of France for its slave practices as a colonial power, while erecting a slavery memorial in Haiti to honour the memory of Toussaint l'Ouverture and French slaves. He also launched a revision of the national curriculum of French pupils to put more emphasis on the countries and people who suffered under French colonial rule. In the United Kingdom, the prestigious academic world of Oxford – usually peaceful – was agitated by a controversy initiated by students in South Africa from the University of Cape Town who asked for – and were granted – the dismantling of the statue of Cecil Rhodes in April 2015 as a symbol of colonialism backed by academics. Yet their objective did not just target one man but aimed at denouncing colonialism and revising the national education programme to fight what they perceived as institutional racial discrimination in South Africa. This protest movement soon spread to Oxford University and the students of Oriel College in turn called for the removal of the statue of Cecil Rhodes from their own college. However, unlike their South African counterparts, and in spite of their majority vote, the college authorities, starting with its Provost, Moira Wallace, backed by many alumni, stood firm.

If history sometimes strikes back, it is always essential to understand the present. This is certainly true of Europe and the respective positions of France and the United Kingdom towards the European construct. The explanation of these demands an analysis of the European idea as it evolved following the Allied victory in 1945.

Among the most influential statesmen who best embodied their countries' attachment to national pride and sovereignty during and after World War II were Churchill and de Gaulle, who both played a critical role in the fate of the United Kingdom and France, the first as Prime Minister, the latter as leader of Free France with his headquarters in London. The mixture of admiration and distrust that the two men felt for each other was symptomatic of the relationship between their two countries, and also between them and Europe. They both believed in strong nation-states and could not conceive any kind of Europe – or international organisation – other than one based on such states. Both had been key war leaders and thought that they needed a strong military endowed with deterrent nuclear weapons for their country to be powerful and have a say in the European and international community.

War powers and parliamentary consent in France and the United Kingdom

Defence and foreign policy were considered by General de Gaulle to be the reserved areas of the President as Head of the French state, all the more so as they are strongly connected with national sovereignty. They are closely linked with the President's missions as guarantor of national independence and territorial integrity, as well as of respect for international treaties. In the United Kingdom, 'the Prime Minister is the minister responsible for National Security and matters affecting the Secret Intelligence Service.'[4] Among the prerogative executive powers – powers that are exercised on the sovereign's behalf by ministers – are powers in relation to foreign affairs and deployment of the armed forces which in France belong to the President. Thus, as experts of the Fabian Society clearly stated, 'the powers of executive government, exercised by the Prime Minister, flow from the Royal Prerogative rather than from Parliament.'[5] So war powers which are part of the monarch's residual non-statutory powers can be used in an 'unconstrained' fashion by the Prime Minister as 'the government does not need to have Parliament's authority to engage in these activities,'[6] whereas in other countries like France declarations of war require parliamentary approval. Unlike Britain, where the British Prime Minister benefits from much leeway in the deployment of the British armed forces and more generally the use of war powers, in France it is now compulsory for the French President not only to inform parliament of a French military intervention abroad as early as possible but also to obtain parliament's consent regarding any military engagement of French troops lasting more than four months.[7] Thus article 35 of the constitution now reads: 'Where the said intervention shall exceed four months, the government shall submit the extension to parliament for authorization.' It was part of the efforts made by the 2008 French constitutional reformers to strengthen parliamentary control over the executive, notably over the President of the Republic. In the same way, following the controversial intervention of the British military in the 2003 Iraq War, a convention was established in the United Kingdom under which military force was to be subject to prior parliamentary approval except in cases of emergency. In 2011, the then Foreign Secretary of the coalition government of David Cameron (2010–15) announced that this convention would be enshrined in law so as to strengthen Parliament's role over war-making powers. Yet, on 18 April 2016, the Defence Secretary in the Conservative government (2015–17), Michael Fallon, issued a written ministerial statement aiming to end such a commitment in order not to constrain military action.

There are, indeed strong military ties between France and the United Kingdom. They opposed each other over the centuries in numerous wars[8] until the French defeat in Waterloo in 1815. They collaborated as a unified military force in 1914–18. There has also existed effective cooperation between their armed forces,[9] especially since the 2010 Lancaster House Treaty.[10] France and the United Kingdom were – and still are – the only EU member states with a nuclear deterrent force, and the only ones in the closed circle of the five permanent members[11] of the United Nations Security Council, whose aim is to secure peace in the world, arbitrating in international conflicts when necessary. Its composition reflected the balance of power after World War II, and each country had a veto. In Churchill's view, often expressed in ambiguous language, the United Nations was itself to pave the way for a united Europe. He pursued the matter within another framework, the North Atlantic Treaty Organisation (NATO).[12] Both the United Kingdom and France were among its founding members in 1949: its objectives were not only to contain the Soviet Union during the Cold War, but also to facilitate European political integration. Yet it is also in the name of the protection of France's national nuclear independence and security strategy that de Gaulle decided to withdraw France from the integrated military command of NATO in 1966 while remaining part of the organisation[13] – being one of the main contributors to its budget – whereas the United Kingdom has always given it more importance than France, and sees it as part of its supposed 'special relationship' with the United States. France fully reintegrated all the structures of NATO in April 2009 under the presidency of Nicolas Sarkozy during the celebrations marking the sixtieth anniversary of the organisation.

The United Kingdom traditionally relied heavily in military and economic terms on its Empire (later the Commonwealth), most notably during the two World Wars, while France for its part was very dependent on its own former Empire, the so-called French-speaking countries, what the French call France's *pré-carré* or 'traditional preserve' in Africa. Both nations then followed the same course, abolishing conscription, first the United Kingdom in 1960, then France in 1996 under President Chirac – limiting the size of their armed forces and cutting their defence budgets as well as their financial contributions to NATO. The United Kingdom is faced with an additional theoretical difficulty since its four nations do not share the same position on the United Kingdom's nuclear policy. Scotland in particular has expressed its wish to become a nuclear-free zone. At least, this is the position of the SNP, which included its views on military policy in its blueprint for independence, then campaigned on an anti-Trident message – Trident is a United Kingdom nuclear submarine system based in Scottish waters at Holy Loch – in the 2015 UK General Election, which revived the controversy about the cost for the UK of remaining a nuclear power. The Labour Party also has radically opposed views on Trident amongst its membership.

Two military episodes have more specifically highlighted the main differences in the military decision-making process in France and the UK, also in terms of divergent 'cultural' approaches regarding war and the conduct of foreign affairs.

The first was the 2003 war in Iraq. From the start, and in spite of strong pressure from the United States threatening to boycott French products, the then President of the French Republic, Jacques Chirac, who belongs to the parliamentary right-wing party claiming de Gaulle's legacy, very early on took the decision not to send French troops to Iraq. He considered it an unlawful war against a sovereign state which had not directly and seriously threatened French territory or its people. He was backed by the great majority of French people, though he faced strong opposition not only from the United States but also from the British government. French 'bashing' in the British media and among members of the then British government reached a peak, but then subsided. Rarely in modern history had there been so much tension and lack of understanding between the two countries as at the time of the Iraq invasion. It was one of the most courageous decisions that Jacques Chirac took under his presidency backed by Dominique de Villepin in the United Nations. Even if he was later involved in legal proceedings which tarnished his reputation, he will always be remembered as the President who opposed the war in Iraq. One might wonder what decision de Gaulle himself, as a general and President of the French Republic, would have taken. He would most certainly not have followed the United States, as he had always been eager to protect French independence from the United States and its influence, including in Europe.[14]

The United Kingdom, for its part, under the Labour Prime Minister Tony Blair, acted probably against the will of the majority of British people, who took to the streets in massive historic numbers. Blair, with no personal experience of war, proved more belligerent a Prime Minister than Thatcher, victor in the Falklands, and waged war in Sierra Leone, Kosovo and finally Iraq. The decision of the British Prime Minister to send troops there followed secret talks between him and the then American President George W. Bush in early 2002 in Texas. The Chilcot inquiry, whose report was eventually published in July 2016, examined what precise role the British government played. This revived the debate about the lack of control over the use of war powers in the British constitution and the need for Parliament to give its consent before any military intervention. This important question was not settled as originally intended for by the Constitutional Reform and Governance Act 2010 as, contrary to the original Bill initiated by the government of Gordon Brown, it did not contain any provision regarding war powers, but only a provision on ratifying international treaties.

Ten years after the Iraq invasion, in 2013, France and the United Kingdom in a way switched roles. The French Socialist President Hollande, often denounced as lacking decisiveness in domestic policy, had dispatched French forces to Mali. Now he was determined to send troops to Syria and tried to convince the American President Barack Obama to do the same. The French President's decision was motivated by the revelation of the use of chemical weapons by the Syrian army against the people. By contrast, bearing in mind the unpopular decision of Tony Blair and its aftermath, the then Labour leader of the Opposition, Ed Miliband,[15] played a pacifying role. He joined the campaign against the war in Syria in Parliament, which forced the British coalition government of David Cameron to back down following the passage of a motion of the House of Commons against British military intervention. This encouraged President Obama, not to intervene militarily in Syria, and war was then avoided. This episode showed how Parliament, in this case Westminster, could flex its muscles when necessary and influence decision-making over war powers. It has become an assumption that this will dictate similar crises in the future. It now needs to be clearly enshrined in the British constitution to ensure that Parliament is formally consulted and gives its consent on the use of war powers. To that effect, Professor Blackburn and his team at King's College have proposed to include in a codified British constitution a provision requiring 'the prior approval of either House of Parliament'[16] – this presumably means by statute – before declaring war or committing the British forces to enter into armed conflict abroad. In France, as previously mentioned, the 2008 constitutional change introduced in the wake of the Balladur Report is already a significant step forward towards more transparency in the use of war powers. Under article 35, not only must the French parliament be informed by the government of its decision to commit French troops abroad 'at the latest three days after the beginning of the military intervention', but parliamentary consent must be given for any military intervention lasting more than four months. It is a way of placing the executive war powers under parliamentary control and could be a source of inspiration for improving the British constitution in such a strategic area.

A tradition of human rights in common within the Council of Europe

As seen in previous chapters, France and the United Kingdom are not usually perceived as military powers, but as countries with a long tradition of human rights committed to promoting fundamental freedoms and civil liberties. One of the key purposes of every constitution, whether fully or only partially written like the British constitution, is to protect fundamental rights and freedoms against the potential arbitrary power of the state or the Crown. Unlike France, which has had declarations of rights[17] built on the Declaration of the Rights of Man and the Citizen of 1789 and its four fundamental rights – the right to equality, liberty, security and property – as part of its fully written constitutions, the United Kingdom has never had an official Charter of Rights in the French meaning of the word. The Declaration of 1789 consists of a list of individual rights and freedoms such as equality, freedom from arrest, freedom of conscience, freedom of expression, freedom of religion, right to property, and presumption of innocence in criminal proceedings, and also rights of the nation. The Declaration of 1789, followed by the 1791 constitution, emphasised the principle of separation of powers even if, in the French revolutionaries' perception, it was essentially meant to prevent the judiciary from obstructing parliament. Yet, not only does the constitution of the Fifth Republic mainly refer to the Declaration of the Rights of Man and the Citizen of 1789 as alluded to in the preamble of the 1946 constitution, but the constitution for the most part protects institutions themselves rather than individual rights. It focuses predominantly on the institutional arrangements of the Republic. Apart from a few articles like article 66, which protects individuals from arbitrary detention,[18] and article 66-1, which protects them from the death penalty and against any attempt at reinstating it – stating that 'no one shall be sentenced to death' – rights are essentially to be found in the preamble of the constitution rather than in the body of the document.[19]

On the other side of the Channel, Dicey was very hostile to formal declarations of rights such as the French Declaration of 1789, as he believed that fundamental rights and values were already well protected under common law by ordinary courts and judges. Indeed, in the United Kingdom, long before the incorporation of the European Convention on Human Rights into British domestic law,[20] judges themselves identified new rights through their case law in a very creative way. Key statutes were also passed by Parliament which established fundamental rights and have long been part of British constitutional arrangements, notably the Habeas Corpus Act (1679), protecting individuals from arbitrary arrest and detention, and the Bill of Rights (1689) ten years later, which secured parliamentary control over the monarch, thus protecting people from arbitrary royal power. Dicey's own suspicions of formal Declarations of Rights were fairly common. They were expressed by Edmund Burke in the later eighteenth century, and still have not fully disappeared. French contemporary legal experts like those on the Veil Committee in charge of revisiting the preamble of the constitution of the Fifth Republic argued that 'those in favour of a Declaration of Rights still represent a minority in England because it is considered as incompatible with the principle of parliamentary sovereignty,' adding that 'the Human Rights Act 1998 is the first text since the Bill of Rights (1689) to have provided for a statutory protection of fundamental rights.'[21]

Yet, the United Kingdom has its own founding constitutional document, Magna Carta, which has gained a universal dimension to the point of being widely acknowledged throughout the world by constitutionalists and those who believe in democracy. All democracies owe to it the rule of law, and not only common law countries. Magna Carta and the rule of law are still fundamental pillars of the United Kingdom's constitutional arrangements together with the sovereignty of Parliament, even if it is still nowhere clearly defined, not even in the section 1 of the Constitutional Reform Act 2005. In fact, Magna Carta and the 1789 Declaration form part of a common constitutional heritage between France and the United Kingdom.

As the Veil Committee pointed out, 'the French constituent power has always built incrementally adding layers of new rights to existing ones.' Thus in the French tradition of human rights, the policy is not to replace rights but to build on them. This in turn could inspire those in Britain, mainly politicians, who propose to repeal the Human Rights Act 1998 in order to replace it by a new British Bill of Rights without providing clear legal arguments for it. Experts of the Veil Committee also noted in their report, 'the body of fundamental rights has significantly increased thanks to the jurisprudence of the Constitutional Council and its creative interpretation of the preamble of the Constitution.'[22]

In its ruling on Freedom of Association of 16 July 1971, the Constitutional Council for the first time established the constitutional value of the principles and rights contained in the 1789 Declaration of the Rights of Man and the Citizen – dealing mainly with the rights of individuals – but also in the preamble of the 1946 constitution[23] protecting collective and social rights. Since then, the Constitutional Council has also ruled that environmental rights included in the 2004 Charter for the Environment, part of the preamble of the constitution of the Fifth Republic, had also the same constitutional value as the provisions of the rest of the constitution. So in a country where case law is still not considered as an official source of the law, it has become an essential point of reference for French legal practitioners.[24]

Part of the remit of the Veil Committee was in fact to examine whether it would be necessary and useful to codify – that is to include in the preamble of the constitution – the new rights emerging from the case law of the Constitutional Council – for the sake of clarity as well as for a better understanding of those rights. Besides, it would have given them full constitutional value as it is now the case for the rest of the preamble of the Constitution and would have made it more difficult not to abide by them. In its eventual findings the Veil Committee ruled out such a codification on various grounds, such as the absence of a national consensus and the risk of introducing too much unnecessary rigidity. The Veil Report concluded that 'too rigid rules can quickly become obsolete and can even compromise the future,'[25] and that case law and ordinary legislation were ample to protect those new categories of rights. Yet it made one major exception over 'the principle of equal dignity', arguing that 'as the cradle of human rights, France should include an explicit reference to the principle of dignity in the preamble of the constitution.' The idea was more precisely to add it to article 1 of the constitution, which describes the main characteristics of the French Republic – that is to say, 'indivisible, secular, democratic and social' – as well as the principle of 'equality of all citizens before the law'. It would have read: 'France recognises the equal dignity of all', but in the end this was not included in the 2008 constitutional change as there was no consensus.

Finally, in addition to their national rules and regulations as well as constitutional arrangements regarding human rights, France and the United

Kingdom[26] contributed to the founding of the Council of Europe, a regional intergovernmental organisation located in Strasbourg whose members have in common and promote human rights, including the protection of national minorities, the rule of law and pluralist democracy. Even if it is not one of the EU institutions it is a very active human rights organisation, notably through the work of its committees such as the committee for the prevention of torture and the committee for social rights ,which provides legal advice to countries throughout the world and has also issued fundamental international statements such as the convention on preventing and combating violence against women and domestic violence. One of its most important achievements was its fight for the abolition of the death penalty, which is now part of the European Convention on Human Rights, under its sixth protocol, a prerequisite for any applicant member to the Council of Europe or to the European Union. The very existence of such a body contributes to the strengthening of human rights and democratic values in Europe and in the international community.

Both France and the United Kingdom have freely and willingly ratified the European Convention on Human Rights,[27] as Member States of the Council of Europe, even if in both cases it took them a fair amount of time to agree to incorporate it into their own domestic law. It is very much a Franco-British text, as eminent lawyers such as, on the French side, Pierre-Henri Teitgen and, on the British side, Sir David Maxwell-Fyfe (later Lord Kilmuir)[28] played a key role in the preparatory work in the early 1950s, and in the drafting of the European Convention. Whereas the United Kingdom was the first country to ratify it as early as 1951, France surprisingly was the last one to do so in 1974 under the presidency of Georges Pompidou, a staunch supporter of European union, and only allowed individuals the right to individual petition before the European Court of Human Rights in 1981. This was thanks notably to the perseverance of the then French Justice Minister, Robert Badinter, a former lawyer and law academic. It took the United Kingdom much longer than France finally to incorporate the European Convention on Human Rights into its domestic law, Mrs Thatcher being resistant in the 1980s, with the Human Rights Act voted in 1998 and implemented in 2000.The context of quasi-civil war in Northern Ireland in the seventies, which led to the reinstatement of direct London rule in 1972, caused serious problems. This followed a failed attempt at devolution; resulting in terrorism on the part of Catholic and Protestant paramilitary groups, as well as repressive means used by the police and the military. It delayed the incorporation of the European Convention as it was impossible for the United Kingdom at that time to meet its requirements. France itself also had its own grey areas difficult to reconcile with the provisions of the European Convention, most notably regarding the treatment of suspects in police custody.[29] Yet, the Convention can in no way be considered a substitute for failing national arrangements in terms of human rights, since cases can only be referred to the European Court of Human Rights when all other legal national means have been exhausted. Indeed, the main responsibility for protecting fundamental rights and civil liberties lies primarily with the French and the British authorities. This aspect emphasises the strong relevance of the European connection for the course of constitutional change.

Constitutional issues triggered by a common EU membership

If both Churchill and de Gaulle were averse to the very idea of sharing or pooling national sovereignty, since both thought that it was inherently indivisible, they were however determined to secure peace and stability in post-war Europe. Both had played a key role for their country in combating and defeating Nazism. In the speech that he delivered in Zurich as early as 1946, Churchill famously pleaded for the 'united states of Europe' – which led to divergent interpretations, notably in France. Even if Churchill did not include the United Kingdom in such a visionary project, as he believed that the future of the post-war United Kingdom lay in its relationship with the United States as well as with the British Empire – later the Commonwealth – he was also highly sympathetic to a united Europe. The idea was not new. Long before him, Victor Hugo, a former member of the Constituent Assembly set up in the wake of the 1848 Revolution, delivered a landmark address at the International Peace Conference in Paris on 21 August 1849 where he spoke of a 'united states of Europe', inspired by a profound humanism and pacifism.

Because of its leading role in World War II fighting Nazism and other totalitarian regimes, culminating in the Battle of Britain of 1941, the UK was expected in France to lead the post-war European building process. As James Callaghan, an intermittent Eurosceptic, wrote in his memoirs, 'Britain threw away a glorious opportunity, freely offered to her by Europe, to take the lead in restructuring the devastated countries of the Continent,'[30] both economically and politically. At the same time, the post-war French regime was eager to find a role for itself and for the country trying to break away from the humiliation that France had experienced after the 1940 debacle and the sombre years of the Vichy regime, and also having been excluded from both the Yalta and the Potsdam conferences held in 1945. France was considered a defeated, occupied country by its allies, whereas the United Kingdom, represented by its Prime Minister, Churchill, one of 'the big three' at Potsdam, was fully associated to the post-war negotiations over the redrawing of borders. Apart from the wish to rehabilitate France by giving it a better, more honourable status, in Europe and at the international level, Frenchmen like Schuman[31] and Monnet shared the dream of building unity and solidarity between European countries in a European federal union, together with the West German Chancellor Adenauer and the Italian Prime minister De Gasperi. One of their key objectives was to prevent a new war between European countries, especially between France and Germany, and secure a lasting peace and stability in continental Europe. The strong commitment of these men to a European joint organisation was partly the result of their personal experience of the war. They had courageously and actively fought totalitarian regimes, Nazism in Germany and fascism in Italy. Robert Schuman, born a German in Luxembourg, who had become French after the annexation of Moselle to France, and the German Konrad Adenauer were imprisoned for their opposition to Nazism during the war, while the Italian De Gasperi was jailed for his opposition to Mussolini.[32] They all were particularly aware of the devastating effects of nationalist passions on people and countries. As a reaction they were determined to prevent a new wave of destructive nationalism.

In the same way more than a decade later Edward Heath, the leader of the Conservative Party and British Prime Minister who successfully negotiated the UK's entry to the EEC on 1 January 1973, was very much influenced by his personal experience of war against Hitler's Third Reich. A native of Kent, close to the European continent, he was himself a staunch European. Like the fathers of Europe before him, he believed in reconciliation and reconstruction between European countries. It reflected the spirit of the founding document of the whole European project, which paved the way for the European community: the Declaration of 9 May 1950 also known as the Schuman Declaration. It was a call for unity and solidarity between European countries, especially France and Germany.

The Coal and Steel Community (ECSC) was established by the Treaty of Paris of 18 April 1951 pooling strategic resources like coal, iron and steel traditionally used as war materials, in order to bring reconciliation between former enemies like France and Germany for their mutual benefit. However, it was not an end in itself. The ultimate political objective of the

European community is too often confused with the economic and financial means used to facilitate the whole European building process. It was not to be followed by a smooth process towards European economic and political integration as the fathers of Europe had intended. One of its most notorious early failures was the collapse of the treaty on the Community of European Defence (CED), signed on 27 May 1952 and ratified by the German Bundestag and Bundesrat, which was rejected by the French National Assembly in 1954. This was due to the fierce opposition of both Gaullist and Communist members of the French parliament who voted against the text. Yet in spite of this setback, Schuman and Monnet proceeded with their vision of a united Europe with the Messina Conference in 1955 as a preliminary step to the signature of the Treaties of Rome[33] on 25 March 1957. Since then, European defence has become one of the areas where Europe has been particularly successful – partly owing to the effective bilateral cooperation between the French and (since 1973) the British military.

The principle of political integration was present from the start, as explicitly mentioned in the preamble of the Treaty of Rome of 1957, which set up the European Economic Community (EEC), stating that the six countries[34] which had freely agreed to sign such a treaty were 'determined to lay the foundations of an ever closer union among the peoples of Europe'. Indeed, the founding fathers of Europe intended not only to pool resources and establish a customs union where goods could circulate freely, but were also ready to pool sovereignty. They shared a federal vision of Europe and believed in supranational institutions transcending national ones. Yet, even if they were pioneers and also at the same time idealists, it was impossible for them to foresee how political integration would evolve. Like the French members of the Constituent Assembly who wrote the 1791 constitution, the drafters of the 1957 Treaty of Rome were so confident in the project of uniting European nation-states in a common European community that the very idea of withdrawing from such a treaty was simply inconceivable to them. Thus the Treaty of Rome, unlike the Treaty of Lisbon signed in 2007, did not include opt-out provisions or any exit clause.

France was one of the six signatory countries to the Treaty of Rome. For countries like France and Germany, the setting up of a European community was to help them on the road to reconstruction. Men like Adenauer and Schuman were deeply conscious of what the European project meant for their respective countries in terms of peace, reconciliation and also economic prosperity. At the end of the Second World War, Germany had to be totally reconstructed from a constitutional as well as from a political and social standpoint. The Federal Republic of Germany (FRG) came into being in 1949. The urge to break with the past, to avoid a new war and any possible revival of any regime comparable to the Third Reich, as well as the prolonged occupation by the troops of the victorious Allies, on the one hand, Britain and the United States later joined by France, on the other hand the USSR, underlay the new German constitution. The four occupying countries held a Four-Power Conference in London as early as 1947, where it had been accepted that the eastern part of Germany occupied by the USSR, could not be included in the constitution-building exercise of post-war Germany. This recognised the stark facts of the Cold War. A new constitution was to be drafted following the guidelines dictated by the Allies. The Basic Law for the Federal Republic of Germany of 23 May 1949 starts with a preamble, where the influence of the Allies' instructions can be felt as it puts forward the notion of responsibility and goes on to refer to the resolve to serve world peace, insisting on the pacific character of the German nation.

Although France was on the victorious side from 1942, its full territory had been occupied by German troops. The Vichy Laws of 18 July 1940 which had established an authoritarian regime under Marshal Pétain were abolished. A Fourth Republic set up, as has been described above, with the constitution of 27 October 1946 to launch a new and fully restored French democracy. The United Kingdom, by contrast, although heavily bombed during the blitz, and experiencing serious economic and financial hardship, had maintained the integrity of its institutions and democracy. The mystique of Britain 'standing alone' in the world against the menace of the Axis powers, the legends of Dunkirk and the Battle of Britain powerfully influenced the national psyche thereafter and reinforced the sense of insularity and isolationism dictated by history and geography. It had much influence on British debates on constitutional change. In 1975, sceptics like Michael Foot or Peter Shore could even compare the EU with the threat from the Spanish Armada, though Foot later changed his view, partly through his connection with Mitterrand, with whom he shared strong sympathy for the Revolution of 1789.

Thus France and Germany progressively became the driving force of the European building process while the United Kingdom made its own way outside the European community. The Treaty of Rome was at first treated casually, almost derisively, by most members of the British Foreign Office. It spoke of 'minor eruptions in Sicily'. It tried to compete with the EEC by setting up a rival looser intergovernmental organisation and free trade area known as the European Free Trade Association (EFTA) in 1960 together with six other countries – based on the Stockholm Convention – closer to its views in terms of economic cooperation. Unlike France and Germany, which shared a more political and cultural approach to the European Community, the UK chose to emphasise economic integration and the promotion of free trade to achieve growth and prosperity. By contrast, for countries like France and Germany,[35] the European Economic Community (EEC) which set up a customs union based on the free circulation of goods commonly referred to as the Common Market (although the latter was only formally achieved in 1987 with the Single European Act) has always meant more than just an economic form of integration. From the start they thought that 'an ever closer union' would lead in the future to full political integration. Whereas France and Germany were progressively moving closer to each other, the Common Agricultural Policy (CAP), provided for by the Treaty of Rome, was based on generous subsidies for farmers in continental Europe on which countries like France[36] with a significant rural sector were highly dependent. This controversial scheme divided France and the United Kingdom. In 1973 many in Britain felt the CAP challenged almost 150 years of cheap food dating back to the era of tariff-free food. It still is a cause of disputes between the two countries, together with the question of fisheries, and it contributed to the United Kingdom's delayed entry into the EEC. So, too, did the right of entry into European markets of meat and dairy produce from the British Commonwealth, whose strong links with the mother country, economically and psychologically, had been underlined during the war.

The UK officially joined the EEC on 1 January 1973 at a time of acute economic difficulties. It has been an essential feature of British constitutional arrangements ever since. The British government feared being permanently excluded from a successful enterprise after two failed attempts resulting from the fierce opposition of de Gaulle. He disliked Anglo-Saxon views on economic liberalism for Europe and close relations on defence issues such as Skybolt missiles, and went so far as speaking of the UK as 'the Trojan Horse of the United States' because of the special relationship between the two countries. Labour's James Callaghan, expressing the insular English view on the question explained what this relationship meant for the UK and the United States: 'we spoke the same language. The Common Law was known to us both. In 1945, America and Britain together formed the most powerful and influential combination in the world.'[37]

The French perspective by contrast was that the United Kingdom could not be trusted and de Gaulle doubted its will to commit itself to the European project.[38]

Two years after the UK joined the EEC under the premiership of Edward Heath, who had developed a good personal relationship with President Georges Pompidou, Britain's terms of membership were marginally renegotiated by the Labour leader Harold Wilson and Callaghan, now his Foreign Secretary. Many critics felt the new terms meant only cosmetic and superficial changes and they were enough to convince the electors when they were submitted to British voters in a nation-wide referendum, the first in the history of the country, in 1975. The discussions and negotiations focused on access to European markets for New Zealand and other Commonwealth meat and dairy products, as well as on reforming the British contribution to the budget. Cabinet solidarity was loosened during the campaign to allow Cabinet ministers to campaign freely for or against staying in the European community, as was also decided by David Cameron for the 2016 referendum on Europe.[39] Not only did the UK partly, and freely, surrender some of its national sovereignty in 1973 but, two years afterwards, British people themselves strongly confirmed the country's commitment to Europe in the referendum of June 1975. Unlike 2016, the British media were almost unanimous in backing entry. So the UK's will to remain within the European Community was confirmed, backed in fact by Margaret Thatcher who that very year had won her party's leadership election. The EEC membership referendum generated much interest as turnout reached 64 per cent. In all 67 per cent of British voters supported EEC membership. Every part of the country voted 'Yes' except the remote islands of the Shetlands and Western Isles. This time British people themselves confirmed their wish to be part of the European building process.

The European Union is neither a state nor an international organisation as such, but a union composed of sovereign nation states. It has integrated different sovereignties, so in that sense it is a supranational body, even though there is no collective European sovereignty as such. It is based on limited transfers of sovereignty and on mutual rights and obligations between Member States. So in order to join the European communities and benefit from the common – now internal market – the UK agreed to share part of its national sovereignty. As Lord Bridge argued in the famous case *R. v Secretary of State for Transport* (1991), 'whatever limitations of its sovereignty Parliament accepted when it enacted the European Communities

Act 1972, that was entirely voluntary.'[40] Indeed, the EU being composed of sovereign states, they cannot be bound unless they agree to be. In order to join what was at that time the EEC in January 1973 and give legal effect to the Treaty of Rome, the Westminster Parliament passed what became the European Communities Act 1972. So the UK's original relationship to the EU has been governed by this national statute, and effectively given European Community law precedence over UK domestic law, thus enacting the principle of the primacy of European law[41] over incompatible national law. So the Westminster Parliament itself is no longer free from any form of control. Its sovereignty can no longer be interpreted as an absolute type of sovereignty in the way Dicey defined it in the nineteenth century.

The European Community experienced a period of expansion and economic prosperity in the 1980s under the leadership of Jacques Delors, a former French Minister of Finance and Economy,[42] who presided over the European Commission for nearly a decade from 1985 to 1994. A pioneer in French politics, Delors also wanted to revive the original European flame of men like Schuman and Monnet by creating a new type of Europe, a far more social one. He was also bent on improving the status of workers and better protecting their rights within the European framework in the spirit of the French social model – thus adding to the French contribution to the European construction, in spite of the growing opposition he faced from the United Kingdom and its Conservative Prime Minister, Margaret Thatcher. Delors delivered a speech to the British Trades Union Congress (TUC) in Bournemouth on 8 September 1988 which was to have a decisive impact on the evolution of the Labour party's attitude to Europe. The British unions, hitherto Eurosceptic, greeted him as 'frère Jacques'. Under its new leader, Michael Foot (who had voted No in the 1975 referendum),[43] the Labour party had campaigned in 1983 on a left-wing platform which included the withdrawal of the UK from the EEC. In the 1992 general election it had totally reversed this view. Neil Kinnock, who succeeded Foot as leader, was later to become an EU Commissioner. Delors's aim was to promote the creation of an internal market by 1992 abolishing barriers to the free movement of goods, services, investment and people and also to guarantee European workers better protection thanks to the establishment of a platform of guaranteed social rights with a whole series of social measures including a minimum wage, the right to lifelong education and special provisions for women workers. It is under Delors's leadership, with the active collaboration of the pragmatic Margaret Thatcher, more ambivalent in her position towards Europe than her Eurosceptic speech delivered in Bruges on 20 September 1988 suggested, that the Single European Act 1986 amending the original Treaty of Rome as a prerequisite to the 1992 European single market was adopted.

On 1 November 1993, the treaty establishing the European Union (TEU) – more commonly known as the Maastricht Treaty – modifying the three original European Communities set up by the Treaty of Rome 1957, was implemented 'to continue the process of creating an ever closer union among the peoples of Europe'.[44] For the first time, a European treaty expressly acknowledged that all the nationals of the Member States are citizens of that Union, dissociating citizenship from nationality. More precisely, under article 9 of the EU Treaty, 'every national of a member state shall be a citizen of the Union,' adding that 'citizenship of the Union shall be additional to and not replace national citizenship.' Thus, with the principle of European citizenship, it created a different kind of union, much more political in nature, making French and British people – in addition to their status as subjects of a constitutional monarch – for the first time European citizens, giving them access to additional rights and responsibilities. This was not easy to reconcile with British statutory statements on nationality since the 1960s. It was confirmed in 2005 by the French referendum on the European Constitution that a significant number of citizens of EU member states had no real aspiration for a greater direct involvement in the European integration process.

The 2005 French referendum on the European constitution and the 2016 referendum on the UK's EU membership

The non-ratification of the European constitution was a critical moment, not only for France, but for the European Union as a whole. A former President of the French Republic, Giscard d'Estaing, a staunch supporter of Europe and much more favourable to the United Kingdom than de Gaulle had ever been, had been appointed chairman of the Constitutional Convention[45] in December 2001 by the European Council in charge of drafting the new European Constitution. When French electors turned it down, they not only discarded the work of the European Convention, inflicting a personal humiliation on Giscard d'Estaing, but also broke with a long French tradition of constitution-writing. Far from being simply another episode in the never-ending French quest for the perfect constitution, it was a manifestation of a growing French unease towards what the European Union had become and more generally towards Europe.

The original controversy around the draft European constitution emerged with the proposal from Catholic countries like Italy to introduce an explicit reference to a common Judaeo-Christian heritage in its preamble. This potentially excluded aspiring Member States like Turkey. Such a proposal was dropped for lack of consensus. Against all expectations and opinion polls, which predicted a comfortable majority of well over 60 per cent in favour of the European constitution,[46] the referendum held in France on 29 May 2005 – with a high turnout of 69 per cent[47] – ended with a 55 per cent majority of No votes. Apart from the traditional element of uncertainty inherent to all referendums, the domestic frustrations of the French people and their preoccupation with high unemployment (resolutely stuck at 10 per cent) and social welfare prevailed, together with an anti-politics mood fuelled by a chaotic referendum campaign[48] led by highly divided parties[49] with no clear message to convey to the population. French people were worried by a European integration process progressively undermining, in their view, the long-established French social welfare model. They also disapproved of the latest enlargement process to ten eastern and central European countries in 2004, and opposed the potential membership of Turkey, fearing the competition of a cheap labour force in an already struggling labour market as well as being swayed by religious prejudices against more Muslim immigrants. Beyond these various complex reasons Europe, no longer inspired them. It is not so much that French people opposed the idea of European integration as such, but they rejected a certain kind of Europe that, they felt, was imposed on them – a bureaucratic Europe which alienated them with its democratic deficit, and which no longer corresponded to their expectations. The French have in fact always been attached to a more cultural and political type of Europe and European ideal.

The negative result of the 2005 referendum should not necessarily be interpreted as the rise of Euroscepticism in France but it had powerful consequences. However, the French far right – the National Front – now emerged clearly as a Eurosceptic party advocating the withdrawal of France from the euro and from Schengen. The negative result of the 2005 referendum further weakened France's position within the European Union to the benefit of Germany. But, in spite of French opposition to the ratification of the European constitution,[50] which aimed at simplifying the numerous European treaties by merging them into a single European constitution and at being a strong symbol, both France and the United Kingdom nevertheless signed, then ratified via a parliamentary process, the Treaty of Lisbon[51] on 13 December 2007. The latter in fact reinstated many provisions of the original EU Constitutional Treaty, including the exit clause.

There are now common forces at work in both countries. Although Nigel Farage, the then leader of the United Kingdom Independence Party (UKIP), officially declared that he has nothing in common with the French National Front and refused to form a new political group with the latter in the European Parliament in the 2014 European elections, they share the same opposition to Europe. They use fear of immigrants to enlist supporters to their cause. The 2016 referendum on UK membership of the EU thus gave UKIP a unique opportunity to promote their anti-European views, and in the end win their case for a withdrawal of the UK from the EU. It was founded as a single-issue party – the independence of the UK from the EU – and this proved to be their chance to succeed. Marine Le Pen in France could indirectly benefit from the victory of 'Brexit' and has already suggested that France could hold its own 'Frexit'.

It would therefore be far too simplistic to think of France and the French as a fundamentally pro-Europe country in contrast to the United Kingdom as a Eurosceptic country rooted in its geography and history. Yet, as already seen in previous chapters, the three Celtic nations or regions have been more favourable to Europe and European integration than is England, even though UKIP made headway in the 2016 Welsh Assembly elections and Leave gained 52 per cent of the Welsh vote in the June 2016 referendum, polling strongly in the economically deprived south Wales Valleys. Although the relationship between the EU and the UK is a reserved matter, the 2016 referendum on Europe could have serious consequences on the devolved nations and administrations following the victory of the leave option. Hitherto the devolved nations had very much been left out of the process aiming at renegotiating the UK's terms of membership in the EU. They had the feeling that the 2016 referendum had been imposed on them against their will, a view felt as strongly in Labour-led pro-Union Wales – at least in Cardiff and places like Cardiganshire – as in SNP-dominated Scotland.

Both France and the United Kingdom thus have had ambivalent feelings about the European project. This has impinged on their respective debates on constitutional reform. If the United Kingdom is often described by the other EU member states as an awkward partner always asking for new concessions, France itself has been a difficult partner for the United Kingdom, especially under the presidency of de Gaulle. The French

Communists on the one hand, and de Gaulle and his supporters on the other, were at best suspicious – not to say hostile – towards Europe and European institutions from the start, although for different reasons. Thus France significantly delayed the incorporation of any clear reference to Europe and the European Community stemming from the Treaty of Rome (1957) into its constitution until the Treaty of Maastricht (1992). Title XV of the constitution, devoted to the European Union, and composed only of one long single article – article 88, divided into seven different paragraphs, is the last but one article of the constitution. Article 88, paragraph 1, which explicitly mentions that 'the Republic shall participate in the European Union constituted by states which have freely chosen to exercise some of their powers in common', denies the European Union a sovereignty of its own and therefore any status as a state. Yet like the British European Communities Act (1972), it acknowledges the supremacy of EU law over French domestic law.

When President Sarkozy asked the Veil Committee to revise the preamble of the constitution in 2008, its experts proposed to examine the case for including in the preamble itself a provision about Europe, an explicit reference to the European Union, to further strengthen the position of the French Republic in Europe. In its report, it concluded that any new reference to Europe in the constitution would be unnecessary and inappropriate as it would undermine France's constitutional identity and sovereignty. Members of the committee feared further references to the EU in the constitution would mean an implicit approval of new transfers of sovereignty by future European treaties without the need for a constitutional change, and would thus give a blank cheque to the European Union. As they explained in their 2008 report, 'the progressive integration of France into Europe has never been imposed on the French constituent power but it has always been debated and based on its consent.'[52] It is reminiscent of the provisions of the European Union Act passed by the Westminster Parliament in 2011 which provides for a referendum before any ratification of the UK of a new European Treaty conferring on the EU new, exclusive or shared competences or extending them, or imposing new requirements or obligations on the UK. Any further transfer of national sovereignty must therefore be approved by both an Act of the UK Parliament and by a national referendum.

Although, for the first time, the Lisbon Treaty does provide an exit door, it has never been used. The only two countries that have left the European Community – and in a way are two exceptions in the history of the European construction – are Greenland[53] and Algeria, as a consequence of their gaining their independence from Denmark and France respectively. The idea is to use the new secession power introduced by the Lisbon Treaty. Indeed, the right of withdrawal has been expressly enshrined in article 50 (1) of the EU Treaty and reads: 'Any member state may decide to withdraw from the Union in accordance with its own constitutional requirements.' For the first time, a European treaty grants Member States the possibility of 'repatriating' competences from the EU. But there are many uncertainties regarding the whole exit process and how long it would take for the UK, not only to leave the EU, but also to renegotiate a form of financial and trade relationship with it, especially with the internal single market, this time as a non-member state.

The 2016 referendum on the UK's EU membership could hardly have been held at a worse time for the European Union. It had still not recovered from the 2008 financial and economic crisis. The common currency, the euro, and the Eurozone more generally speaking, were struggling to survive, and there had been a horrendous crisis in Greece. Immigrants from eastern Europe, notably Poland, came in, in large numbers, from 2003 onwards. Besides, the European Union is now facing a colossal refugee crisis as one of the many consequences of the war in Syria, which seriously challenges the future of its Schengen borderless area and makes it even more urgent to strengthen the EU external borders. It is perhaps even more of an issue for France, a member of both the Eurozone and Schengen, than for the United Kingdom, which opted out from both to protect its national sovereignty. French people are very attached to the principle of free circulation of people, one of the pillars of the European integration process, whereas the UK feared that the abolition of internal borders under the Schengen Agreement (1985) would facilitate all kinds of trafficking – of drugs and also human beings – and would also encourage terrorist activities. Yet if one of the main objectives of the 1985 Schengen Agreement[54] (then its 1990 implementation Convention) was to facilitate the free circulation of EU citizens by easing internal common border controls between member states, progressively replacing systematic by random controls, the objective was also to strengthen external border controls with non-EU states.[55]

Even if the UK had already decided to opt out of the euro, Schengen and also Justice and Home Affairs and thus partly excluded itself from the EU, David Cameron was determined to obtain further concessions for the UK. In his 2013 Bloomberg speech he had promised this, bearing in mind British voters' desire for reduced immigration. So in February 2016, in a European Summit convened in Brussels to examine the UK case, he tried to renegotiate Britain's EU membership as a prerequisite to the UK referendum on the EU by 2017. Towards the end of the summit, in the evening of 19 February 2016 after intense negotiations, a deal was finally reached between Cameron and the other twenty-seven EU Member States. The British Prime Minister described the Brussels 2016 deal as 'a new renegotiated relationship between the UK and the EU', having negotiated successfully 'an opt-out on ever closer Union' – requiring EU treaties to be amended to explicitly state that references to ever closer Union do not apply to the UK. He had thus obtained a special status for the UK within the EU. A Council declaration was issued stating that Britain was not committed to further political integration into the EU, and exempting the UK from the treaty commitment to 'ever closer Union among the peoples of Europe'. In fact, this aspect was kept in the background during the 1975 referendum. It meant that the UK would not take part in any further political integration. In addition, the twenty-seven EU members unanimously agreed that the UK would never join the euro and would not take part in further fiscal integration. In addition, if any single non-Eurozone country considered that a decision regarding the monetary Union went against its interest, it would be able to compel the Council to discuss it, although this would not be a veto as such.

The UK had also been granted 'the emergency brake' that it claimed over migrant benefits[56] – including child benefits for EU migrants.[57] In the face of press agitation, Cameron wanted to restrict in-work benefits such as tax credits and child benefits for EU migrant workers for the first four years. It meant that EU migrants would not be able to claim benefits on their arrival in the UK but would have to wait. However, this was a minor issue, unlikely to deter people moving to the UK, which is still a very attractive country, with its low unemployment rate – at least that was the case before the Brexit vote – compared with other EU countries, and a flexible labour market. Besides, the UK and EU states would be able to use emergency brakes for up to seven years under exceptional circumstances instead of the thirteen years initially claimed by the British Prime Minister.

The least controversial part of the deal that was reached in Brussels in February 2016 was constitutional. It aimed at giving national parliaments more say over EU legislation and strengthened their power to control such legislation. If sixteen out of the twenty-eight national parliaments of EU Member States agreed to oppose EU legislation that they thought did not comply with the subsidiarity principle, they would be able to compel the Council to discuss the issue and think again. In a somewhat similar way, the 2008 Balladur Committee[58] on modernising and rebalancing the institutions of the Fifth Republic, criticised the lack of involvement of the French national parliament in European matters, and insufficient parliamentary control over the French government's decisions and policies regarding Europe. They thought that the French parliament could only play an unduly limited role, and only at a very late stage, in European matters. They advocated the setting up of a parliamentary committee in charge of overseeing EU legislation in each House of the French parliament, voting motions on European issues, facilitating the incorporation of European directives and ratifying texts on the enlargement process of the EU. Today, article 88-4 of the French constitution specifies in its very first paragraph that 'the government shall lay before the National Assembly and the Senate drafts of European legislative acts as well as other drafts of or proposals for acts of the European Union as soon as they have been transmitted to the Council of the European Union.'

Also the amendment to the constitution introduced by the constitutional Law of 23 July 2008 in the wake of the Balladur Report, replaced what was only a delegation of the National Assembly to the European Union[59] with a parliamentary committee, the Committee for European Affairs, which informs the government on European matters and the activities of the European Union while holding the government to account on Europe. Together with the Committee for European Affairs of the Senate, they scrutinize draft texts on European matters before their adoption by EU institutions. They play an active role in securing respect for the principles of subsidiarity and proportionality together with the European Commission, with which they collaborate. In the same way, in the UK, the European Scrutiny Committee of the House of Commons and the House of Lords EU Select Committee examine the importance and legal impact of draft EU legislation and are in charge of scrutinising the government's actions and policies regarding the European Union. It also means that in France, as in the United Kingdom, government ministers can no longer accept a measure in the European Council of Ministers without the latter having been approved beforehand by national parliaments. The House of Lords EU Committee for its part went even further by introducing pre-European Council evidence sessions with the British Minister for Europe in 2014.[60] This is a way of trying to improve the much-needed transparency and accountability of European institutions.

No sooner had David Cameron won a deal than Michael Gove, the Lord Chancellor and Secretary of State for Justice, announced that he would campaign to leave the EU. It was a surprising move on the part of a Justice Minister, since European cooperation between national authorities in terms of security and justice is vital in the fight against organised crime and terrorism. In 1998 the European Judicial Network (EJN) was set up[61] to facilitate judicial cooperation in criminal matters, followed by the creation of Eurojust in 2002, responsible for judicial cooperation between EU member states and for the administration of the EJN. French judges for their part consider cooperation between national judicial authorities of EU member states essential and the European Arrest Warrant[62] as of strategic importance in facilitating extradition, as it allows suspected criminals and alleged terrorists to be deported rapidly from other EU countries. The British Justice Secretary's decision followed the suspension of collective Cabinet responsibility on 5 January 2016. It was a major blow for the Prime minister. Gove was soon joined by Boris Johnson, another prominent Conservative and then Mayor of London, even though the great majority of its citizens are in fact pro-EU.[63] Of course, since a (small) majority of British people voted for their country to leave the EU in June 2016, the Brussels 2016 deal has become null and void.

The EU Referendum Act 2015 under section 1 – as a legal requirement – provided the question approved by the National Electoral Commission and put to the British people on 23 June 2016: 'Should the United Kingdom remain a member of the European Union or leave the European Union?' This followed a defeat for the government in the House of Lords on a motion moved by Lord Armstrong, formerly Mrs Thatcher's Cabinet Secretary, on the wording of the question asked. A perfectly neutral referendum question was essential. But what was striking throughout the referendum campaign, which was supervised by the National Electoral Commission, was that there was no strong case made for Europe. The 'remain' campaign was a colourless one, headed by an uncharismatic businessman, the head of Marks and Spencer. The Labour leader, Jeremy Corbyn, was a marginal, unenthusiastic figure throughout, and attacked for it within his party. Nobody in the Remain side clearly explained why the United Kingdom was better off in the European Union rather than out. Theresa May, nominally a Remainer, stayed inscrutable. Many economic statistics and figures were provided by both sides[64] to promote their cause. Both focused on immigration and also on the economic and financial risks that the United Kingdom faced in either remaining in or leaving the European Union. Thus the same kind of negative rhetoric that dominated the run-up to the 2014 referendum in Scotland – playing on people's economic fears – was used in the referendum on Europe.

Few positive arguments were put forward to explain what the European Union brought to British people and their children, not only in economic terms but in terms of human rights including social rights – employment, health, and most certainly education. European exchanges between students and universities, in the ERASMUS and Da Vinci programmes,[65] offered cross-border cooperation in the field of education. A whole network of European universities and other institutions of higher education was introduced in 1987 by a distinguished Welshman, Hywel Ceri Jones, who had worked closely in Brussels with the French President of the European Commission, Jacques Delors. As Jones explained, the idea was to engage universities themselves by giving them direct responsibility[66] and by developing relations based on trust between student and academic communities across Europe. Students from EU countries thus benefit from the same access to higher education as EU citizens and the mutual recognition of diplomas. Thus they can validate their own studies and degrees abroad – acknowledged by potential employers – as part of their curriculum and work in other European countries if they wish. Developing links between young Europeans is essential not only for them as individuals but also for a better understanding of other European nations' history, culture and ways of thinking. Abolishing mental barriers and fears due to the ignorance of people's differences and diversity could contribute to fighting extremism as well as to the civic education of young people. The 2016 referendum led to these hopes being extinguished, at least for the moment. The Conservative Prime Minister, Theresa May, urged that the government could act, through prerogative power, without consulting Parliament, but a historic judgment in the High Court on 3 November 2016 overthrew this view. Remainers could therefore take heart once again.

Conclusion

The United Kingdom and France are two highly divided countries today. The former is divided over Europe with the result of the 2016 EU referendum tearing the Conservative party and the British government apart. It led to the immediate resignation of David Cameron as Prime Minister. France is split over how to improve employment, fight terrorism and tackle the issue of immigration in the run-up to the 2017 presidential election. The stability and future of the European Union is challenged from within since one of its key members, the United Kingdom, has voted to leave it, which could trigger in the process a chain reaction.[67] It contributes to making the European Union vulnerable at a time when terrorism is on the rise, having hit in rapid succession France in November 2015, then Brussels in March 2016. It would be an illusion to think that leaving the EU would make any country safer, as terrorism knows no boundaries and strikes both inside and outside the EU. The causes of the refugee crisis are global and lie far beyond Europe. Non-members of the EU such as Norway and Switzerland have equally high rates of immigration. The 2016 referendum on Britain's membership of Europe will not solve the question of the relationship between the United Kingdom and the European Union once and for all, just as the 2014 referendum on the independence of Scotland did not settle the issue. Maybe a better option would be to try to reform the European Union from within, developing social justice and making it more accountable to European citizens while enabling them to play a more active role in the European construction. The 2016 British referendum on the EU, had the result been positive, could have offered an opportunity for securing such reform and thus played a constructive role within a world in turmoil.

People who have not experienced the Second World War, like the great majority of British and French people today, too often take peace[68] and stability in Europe for granted. They forget the role played by the European Community in securing it.[69] It brought and/or restored democracy in countries like Greece, which joined the EEC in 1981, Spain and Portugal, which became members in 1986 – or more recently eastern and central European countries. Any member or aspiring member of the European Union must fulfil the Copenhagen criteria as part of the *acquis communautaire* which include the rule of law, a pluralist democracy and the protection of human rights, as well as the rights of minorities. As article 6 (1) of the consolidated version of the Treaty on European Union states: 'The Union is founded on the principles of liberty, democracy, respect for human rights and fundamental freedoms, and the rule of law, principles which are common to the member states.' It is more than ever important to secure those values as many EU member states including France, and to a lesser extent the United Kingdom, are faced with the rise of aggressive nationalist extremist parties. Although a minority, they are nonetheless dangerous for the stability of Europe and for its democratic values.

Important deadlines were looming for both countries – the referendum of 23 June 2016 on the UK's EU membership followed by the prospect of long-running Brexit negotiations; the 2017 presidential election in France.[70] The immediate crisis came from the British referendum, the third UK-wide referendum in the history of the country. In spite of the agreement reached, David Cameron and the leaders of the other twenty-seven European member states in February 2016, the outcome of the 2016 referendum on Europe was a huge political and personal defeat. Key issues like sovereignty, the EU's democratic deficit and especially immigrants were central to the debate – and the defeat. It was the most serious constitutional moment both for the United Kingdom and for the future of the European Union. The stunning victory of Brexit set up a maelstrom of conflicting and divisive forces from which the United Kingdom would take decades, if ever, to recover. A process of progressive constitutional reform ended with the bleak prospect of national introspection and long-term decline.

Notes

1. Victor Hugo, Opening Speech of the Peace Conference, 21 August 1849 (Brussels: The European House for Culture, 27 September 2009). In his concluding remarks Victor Hugo declared: 'In our ancient Europe, England took the first step, and by her example declared to the people "You are free." France took the second step, and announced to the people "You are sovereign." Let us now take the third step, and all simultaneously, France, England, Belgium, Germany, Italy, Europe, America – let us proclaim to all nations "You are brethren."'
2. The United Kingdom is one of the main (net) contributors to the European budget in spite of the special rebate negotiated by Margaret Thatcher in 1984.
3. Haiti was freed from French slavery in 1804 and became the first Black Republic.
4. The Cabinet Manual, 'A guide to laws, conventions and rules on the operation of government', October 2011.
5. The Report of the Fabian Commission, 'The Future of the Monarchy' (London: The Fabian Society, July 2003), p. 46.
6. Report of the Fabian Commission, 'The Future of the Monarchy', p. 53.
7. The proposal of the 2008 Balladur Report to make such parliamentary authorisation compulsory for every military engagement of French troops lasting more than three months was not turned down.
8. The most emblematic battles being Trafalgar and Waterloo.
9. For example, the French carrier *Charles de Gaulle* operates side by side with the British carrier HMS *Queen Elizabeth*.
10. 'Treaty between the United Kingdom of Great Britain and Northern Ireland and the French Republic for Defence and Security Co-operation', signed in London on 2 November 2010, Cm8174 (London: The Stationery Office, 2011).

11. There are still only five permanent members: the United States, Russia, China, the United Kingdom and France.
12. Wales hosted the NATO summit of 4–5 September 2014.
13. France first tested a nuclear weapon in 1960, eight years after the United Kingdom.
14. He famously opposed the UK's entry to the EEC fearing it would mean letting in the United States of America.
15. It also highlighted the role and potential influence of the Opposition leader in the United Kingdom. From that point of view, this could be very instructive for France, a country where there is no culture of the Opposition though there is undeniably a culture of protest.
16. House of Commons Political and Constitutional Reform Committee, 'A New Magna Carta?', p. 348.
17. However the Napoleonic Constitutions of Years VIII, X and XII as well as the Additional Act of 1815 did not include a formal Declaration of Rights.
18. It states that 'no one shall be arbitrarily detained', and therefore enshrined in the French constitution the principle of *habeas corpus* that can be traced back to the English Magna Carta and the Habeas Corpus Act 1679.
19. Yet, article 66 of the constitution also states that 'the judicial authority is the guarantor of individual freedom.'
20. Unlike what is often believed on the French side of the Channel, no legal void in the United Kingdom in terms of human rights preceded the Human Rights Act 1998, which incorporated the European Convention on Human Rights into English common law and came into force in October 2000. The country had already developed a substantial legal corpus of human rights, though not gathered in a single written document which became a source of inspiration for other common law countries and also countries like France.
21. 'Redécouvrir le préambule de la Constitution', Report of the Committee presided over by Simone Veil (Paris: La Documentation française, 2008), p. 11.
22. 'Redécouvrir le préambule de la Constitution', Veil Report, p. 98.
23. The preamble of the 1946 constitution is based on social collective rights, such as the right to go on strike, and the so-called 'principles particularly necessary to our time', such as defence rights, academic freedom of higher education and independence of university professors
24. It is even more the case as the decisions of the French Constitutional Council are binding on all public, administrative and jurisdictional authorities under article 62 of the constitution.
25. 'Redécouvrir le préambule de la Constitution', Veil Report, p. 75.
26. Winston Churchill and Ernest Bevin represented the United Kingdom, Robert Schuman France.
27. The European Convention on Human Rights – most of the time referred to as the ECHR in the legal community – was signed in Rome on 4 November 1950 and came into force on 3 September 1953.

28. He chaired the Committee on Legal and Administrative Questions of the Consultative Assembly of the Council of Europe.
29. The major improvements introduced in the United Kingdom by the Police and Criminal Evidence Act 1984 regarding the way suspects were treated during police custody – including the right to free legal counsel from the very beginning of custody – inspired the French reform of police custody of 2011.
30. James Callaghan. *Time and Change* (London: Collins, 1987), p. 84. This retrospective view was not one that Callaghan pursued with great vigour during his political career, at least down to 1976. In the early 1970s he went through a distinctly Eurosceptic phase, though he did complete a successful 'renegotiation' of terms for the UK's relationship with the Common Market in 1974–5, and became far more sympathetic to Europe as Prime Minister, striking up a warm friendship with the German Chancellor, Helmut Schmidt; cf. Kenneth O. Morgan, *Callaghan: A Life* (Oxford: Oxford University Press, 1997).
31. The then French Foreign Secretary Robert Schuman – influenced by Jean Monnet – had himself actively fought oppression and totalitarian regimes like Nazism in Germany and fascism in Italy as a member of the French resistance.
32. For more information see Sylvain Schirmann (ed.), *Robert Schuman et les Pères de l'Europe: cultures politiques et années de formation* (Brussels: Robert Schuman Foundation and Peter Lang, 2008).
33. The two treaties signed on 25 March 1957 between six European countries were the European Economic Community (EEC) and the European Atomic Energy Community (EAEC or Euratom).
34. France, Germany, Italy, Belgium, Luxembourg and the Netherlands.
35. As European integration developed, the Franco-German relationship within the European Community tilted in favour of Germany, the latter becoming a kind of role model in institutional and economic terms for both France and later on the United Kingdom. Germany which had sacrificed its national currency, the Deutschmark, a strong symbol of its post-war economic and financial recovery, pressed for the European Central Bank to be modelled upon its own highly independent central bank and imposed a stability pact based on low levels of debt and deficit that France always struggled to comply with. See Kenneth O. Morgan, *The People's Peace* (Oxford: Oxford University Press, 1990), p. 136.
36. But also nations like Wales within the United Kingdom once the latter became a member of the EEC.
37. Callaghan, *Time and Change*, p. 89.
38. From de Gaulle's perspective the then British Prime Minister Harold Macmillan had given priority to the UK's transatlantic relationship by reaching a separate agreement with the US President John Kennedy at Nassau on 22 December 1962 over the supply of American Polaris submarine-based nuclear missiles, essential for the UK to build its capacity as a nuclear power.

39. To this day, there have only been three national or UK-wide referendums. The first, in 1975, was on Europe; the second, which led to a negative result, was the referendum on the Alternative Vote for the election of MPs, held in 2011, where British voters expressed their wish to keep the first-past-the-post voting system for electing members of the House of Commons; the third, on Europe again, was held on 23 June 2016 following the promise made by David Cameron in January 2013 in his Bloomberg speech and later in the 2015 Conservative manifesto. For many reasons, including the 2017 presidential election in France, but also important elections in Germany in 2017, the British government decided to hold the EU referendum as early as possible in 2016.
40. *R. v Secretary of State for Transport, ex parte Factortame* (N2) [1991] 1 AC 603.
41. *Van Gend and Loos v Netherlands Inland Revenue Administration* [1963] ECR1.
42. He had served in 1969–72 under the premiership of Jacques Chaban-Delmas, who was also Mayor of Bordeaux from 1947 to 1995.
43. Yet, in 2016 he actively supported the Remain campaign in the run-up to the June referendum on Britain's EU membership.
44. Under articles 1 and 2 of the EU Treaty.
45. As part of its remit the experts of the Constitutional Convention had to examine fundamental issues such as the clarification and simplification of the EU's often overlapping treaties, the relationship between national parliaments and the EU, and had also to find an agreement on the status to be granted to the EU Charter of Fundamental Rights and Freedoms.
46. A few months before the referendum, the French Socialist party had organised its own consultation process on the European constitution including a mock referendum, which resulted in a positive result for the supporters of the EU constitution.
47. Opinion polls held in the UK at that time showed that the UK, which was expected to hold a referendum after its May 2005 General Election, would also have rejected the EU constitution. Up to ten countries had indicated that they would hold referendums to enable their citizens to express their views on the new treaty, and unanimity was required before the final approval of the EU constitution. One country failing to ratify the Treaty on the EU constitution was enough to put an end to the whole process.
48. The No campaign was a cross-party campaign composed of members of the Socialist party, of the moderate right and of the far right, who were opposed to the EU constitution for different reasons.
49. What added to voters' confusion was a leadership contest opposing two main rivals within the Socialist party more concerned with the then forthcoming presidential election: François Hollande, who became President of the Republic in 2012, and Laurent Fabius, the new chairman of the Constitutional Council, who campaigned against the European constitution.

50. The European Constitution Treaty of 2004 was rejected both by the French referendum held on 29 May 2005 and a Dutch referendum held on 1 June 2005.
51. It amended both the Treaty on the EU (TEU) and the Treaty establishing the European Community (TEC) which became the Treaty on the Functioning of the EU (TFEU).
52. 'Redécouvrir le préambule de la Constitution', Veil Report, p. 42.
53. It took Greenland, a tiny nation, three years to finally leave the European Community in 1985.
54. The Schengen Agreement originated from the Saarbrücken Agreement between France and Germany in July 1984 which sought to abolish border controls between the two countries.
55. It provided for the temporary re-establishment of internal border controls under exceptional circumstances, including serious and immediate threats to the integrity of the territory of signatory countries to the Schengen Agreement.
56. Yet there is no evidence proving that EU migrants move to the UK to benefit from in-work benefits.
57. The UK has also been granted the possibility to index child benefits to the living standards of countries where the children of EU migrants live.
58. Balladur Report, 'Une Vème République plus démocratique', pp. 58–63.
59. It was originally set up in 1979.
60. 'The EU Referendum and EU Reform', House of Lords EU Committee, 9th Report of Session 2015–2016 (London: The Stationery Office, 30 March 2016), HL Paper 122.
61. The same year (1998) the European Police Cooperation Agency based in The Hague, more commonly known as EUROPOL, was also set up and soon became very active in cross-border joint investigations police forces sharing sensitive high-security information such as previous convictions of EU nationals.
62. The European Arrest Warrant which was introduced in 2004 is a warrant for search, arrest, detention and surrender to the judicial authority of the issuing country.
63. Later another significant member of David Cameron's Cabinet, the Work and Pensions Secretary and former leader of the Conservative party, Iain Duncan-Smith, resigned. Even if he officially left office on 18 March 2016 on different grounds, his opposition to the government's cuts to benefits for the disabled, he is a staunch supporter of Brexit and was a leading Eurosceptic rebel against John Major at the time of the Maastricht revolt in 1993–4. He was succeeded at the Department of Work and Pensions by the former Welsh Secretary, Stephen Crabb, who is married to a French woman and in favour of the UK remaining in the EU, arguing that the Welsh economy itself significantly benefits from the single market.
64. It was all very confusing for British voters as both sides were divided into different subgroups which tended to promote different views and had many

difficulties trying to coordinate their strategies. Thus, to give but a few examples, the Brexit side was divided between Vote Leave chaired by Lord Lawson, who while campaigning actively against the EU lived in a remote part of French Gascony, and Leave.eu, the UKIP-based group. As for those campaigning in favour of the UK remaining in the EU, there was a cross-party group, Stronger-In chaired by Will Straw, while the leading Labour Yes Campaign for the EU was presided over by Alan Johnson.

65. The ERASMUS+ Scheme is an EU programme for education, training, youth and sport which allocated around one billion euros to the United Kingdom for the period 2016–23.
66. In the same way many efforts have been made in the last few years to develop the autonomy of French universities.
67. The findings of a survey launched by the University of Edinburgh together with the German think-tank D/Part at the beginning of February 2016 show that 53 per cent of French people would like a British type of referendum on Europe. The same survey also found that, of all the European citizens interviewed, the French were the most favourable to Brexit (44 per cent of French people would favour leaving). Yet surveys like opinion polls have not proved to be very reliable; most polls before the UK referendum in 2016 forecasting victory for Remain. Even the most extremist groups like the French National Front do not advocate full independence from the European Union but only a withdrawal from the Eurozone and from Schengen. The Greek former Finance Minister, Syriza's Yanis Varoufakis, though sharply critical of the Eurozone's harsh and undemocratic treatment of his nation, still urged Britain and Greece to remain in the EU.
68. One of the main aims of the current European Union is still to promote peace as it is now enshrined in the consolidated version of the Treaty on European Union, Title I, article 3 (1): 'The Union's aim is to promote peace, its values and the well-being of its peoples.'
69. The project of European integration was awarded the Nobel Peace Prize in 2012.
70. The revision of the constitution preamble was largely the work of Simone Veil, Minister of Social Affairs in the Edouard Balladur government (1993–5). On 30 June 2017, aged 89, Simone Veil died after a long and distinguished career as a high-ranking judge, a member of the French Constitutional Council, and as a senior politician both at the national and European levels. Having survived the Nazi concentration camps, she then won another battle within the French National Assembly, a Bill decriminalising abortion in 1975 while Health Minister under Giscard D'Estaing. She constantly fought for the reconciliation between France and Germany and an 'ever-closer' European Union. The newly elected French President, Emmanuel Macron, announced in 2017 that she would rest with the *grands hommes* ('*et femmes*') in the Pantheon in Paris as the very incarnation of France and French humanist values.

Conclusion: Towards a New *Entente Cordiale*[1]

No constitutional revolution has taken place in either France or the United Kingdom in the recent past. But significant constitutional change following a fairly similar pattern has happened in both countries with potentially long-lasting effects. In those two parliamentary regimes, parliament has undeniably been strengthened, most notably through the growing influence of its committees and a better control of its own agenda – even if the French parliament has not reached the level of emancipation the 2008 Balladur Committee had hoped for. There is still, nonetheless, a need to reinforce parliamentary control and the pre-legislative scrutiny of draft bills as well as the ability of parliament to challenge the executive in a more effective way. The House of Lords remains a half-reformed, though still effective, chamber as the long-awaited stage two of the reform launched in 1999 has not yet been reached, while the French Senate has not undergone dramatic change. This is even more the case of the British monarchy and the French presidency, though in the latter case, the 2017 presidential election and the resurgence of the far-right Front National may produce new challenges. There is also still a need in both countries for better defining the powers of the Prime Minister and for clarifying his status.

While human rights are now institutionally better protected in France with the strengthening of the position of the Constitutional Council and the opening of its referral system to citizens involved in legal proceedings, France was still officially in a state of emergency after the terrorist atrocities of November 2015. In May 2016 the latter was prolonged for another two months to protect French nationals and foreigners during the European Football Championship. On 20 July 2016, following the Nice terror attack on the Promenade des Anglais, the National Assembly voted overwhelmingly for further extending the state of emergency. As terrorist threats are unlikely to peter out in the near future, France could end up being in a long-term, even permanent state of emergency, which would be damaging for civil liberties and fundamental freedoms. In the same way, the legislative programme put forward in the 2016 Queen's Speech has given priority to national security in the United Kingdom and new legislation to 'prevent radicalisation and tackle extremism in all its forms'. Moreover, the Conservative government appears determined to go ahead with its proposal to repeal the Human Rights Act 1998 and replace it with a British Bill of Rights and Responsibilities.

The 2016 Queen's Speech stated that 'proposals will be brought forward for a British Bill of Rights' though no timetable was suggested. Even if it does not seem to have made much headway up to now, the serious implications that such a text could have for the level of human rights protection in the United Kingdom cannot be brushed aside since it is still on the political agenda. Such a proposal is very alarming for all those who believe in the rule of law, since the necessity and usefulness of a new British Bill of Rights is doubtful. There is still much uncertainty on what it would include. Even if the idea of trying to extend the protection of rights to new areas not yet covered by existing texts is far from being objectionable – quite the contrary – merely listing new rights and freedoms is not enough. Pierre-Henri Teitgen, building on his own experience in the elaboration of the European Convention on European Rights, recommended careful thought on the mechanisms needed to protect them effectively. At the moment there are not enough such guarantees. The French-style approach to human rights, consisting in building on existing rights and texts protecting them rather than abrogating them, has many merits, whereas nothing except perhaps political considerations seems to justify the repeal of the British Human Rights Act 1998 instead of building on it. Rights have never been more strongly protected in both the United Kingdom and France than since the incorporation of the European Convention on Human Rights into their own national law, and this should at all costs be underlined and treasured for generations to come.

Devolution in the United Kingdom, and to a lesser extent decentralisation in France, is most certainly the area where constitutional change has made the most significant and rapid progress. Devolution deals in England created combined urban authorities alongside directly elected Mayors to play their part to the development of local democracy. With the new English mayoralty,[2] a French type of political career and political culture seems to be emerging where a local mandate is both a prerequisite and testing ground – as well as a springboard – for anyone who wishes one day to join Parliament. The election of Labour's Sadiq Khan as Mayor of London in May 2016 at once propelled him to a higher level of authority. In the French parliament, holding a local and a national mandate is commonplace, especially among French senators. Displaying a record of local administrative or executive competence in a lower tier of government might become a new career path in British politics too as an alternative to reaching front-bench Opposition status. On the other hand, the Lords Constitution Committee criticised central government for imposing a fixed model on localities and for the absence of local democratic input.[3] Besides, referendums have been used extensively in the devolution process to secure the approval of the people themselves in Scotland, Wales and Northern Ireland – in 1997, in 2011 in Wales on the Assembly's primary legislative power, and more recently in 2014 on the independence of Scotland. In one way or another they have all led to more devolution. By contrast, at the national level, earlier referendums in the United Kingdom have sustained the *status quo* rather than constitutional change, as over AV in 2011 and membership of the European Union in 1975. The 2016 referendum told an ominously different story.

The use of national referendums in both France and the United Kingdom has proved inconclusive in the two countries, however, in the sense that they have not provided clear answers to major constitutional issues. Although they are in essence instruments of direct democracy, they have shown democracy in France and the United Kingdom at its worst, with a few exceptions. The French constitution in its article 3 states that the people can exercise their sovereignty not only via their representatives in Parliament but also through referendums. The result has been variable. Unlike the 1962 referendum, which undeniably strengthened French democracy by replacing the indirect election of the Head of State with direct universal suffrage, the 1969 referendum, to which de Gaulle had deliberately linked his personal future, put an end to an attempt at reforming the French senate, delayed French regionalisation and accelerated de Gaulle's political departure. The 2005 referendum had perhaps an even more damaging impact as it killed off the European constitution. The three UK-wide referendums held to this day in a country at the origin of parliamentary representative democracy have not served the cause of participatory democracy. Not only have they undermined the authority and sovereignty of Parliament but they have been seen as damaging for the values and principles at the basis of British democracy. The latest national referendum on Europe, held on 23 June 2016 and revolving around the themes of sovereignty, immigration and economics against the backdrop of a leadership crisis within the Conservative party, exacerbated divisions within and between political parties and also between the various communities forming the United Kingdom. It generated dangerous fears over the influx of immigrants, created a backdrop of fear and hate, and debased the entire political process as a serious moral exercise.

A climax was reached, in a campaign fuelled with anti-immigrant,[4] anti-politics, anti-Establishment feelings, with the assassination on 16 June 2016 of Jo Cox, a young, highly successful woman Labour MP, devoted to the cause of refugees and human rights, and passionately pro-Europe. On that very day, UKIP's leader Nigel Farage released a new campaign poster showing refugees crossing the Croatian–Slovenian borders, thus using the refugee crisis in Europe as an emotive (and undeniably effective) argument for the Vote Leave camp. It was inspired by English nationalism. Jo Cox was the first serving MP to be killed since Irish republicans murdered Ian Gow in 1990, and the first ever to be murdered by a constituent. It led the campaign to grind to a halt, and both Houses of Parliament were recalled to pay tribute to Jo Cox's life and work as an MP. French society is generally thought to be more prone to far-right ideas than the United Kingdom, with the continuing rise of Marine Le Pen's National Front, whereas the BNP in the United Kingdom is very much a party on the fringe. Yet the 2016 referendum brought to light a darker side of British society, generally praised for its tolerance. The recall of Parliament was a time to reflect on British democracy, the role of Parliament and of parliamentarians and on how to restore dignity, tolerance and respect in political life and beyond in British society. It was also a call for action to try to reconnect and reconcile British 'citizens' (technically 'subjects') with their national institutions and representatives. The referendum result suggested that this had failed.

However, in a fairly grim context in both the United Kingdom, and also in France, struggling with fierce opposition to its labour law reform from the CGT trade union, two strong symbols of 'hope over fear and unity over diversity'[5] emerged. One was the victory of the Labour MP for Tooting, Sadiq Khan, a former human rights lawyer of Pakistani origin, who with 57 per cent of the votes succeeded Boris Johnson. He thus became the first ethnic-minority Muslim Mayor of London, and perhaps the most powerful Muslim in Europe. The other was the election of Labour Marvin Rees as Mayor of Bristol, the first person of Afro-Caribbean descent to become a directly elected Mayor, who, like Sadiq Khan had grown up on a working-class housing estate in London. Beyond the cases of individuals[6] who actively contribute to bringing communities closer, the United Kingdom and France benefit from strong, stable institutions already improved by constitutional change but still needing to be further democratised. The progress of English devolution, following the Celtic nations, will take this process further.

Despite the referendum victory for Leave, there is more than ever a need for a new entente not only between the various communities and individuals who make up British society but also between the United Kingdom and its European allies, including France. The French and British constitutional journey goes on with France and the United Kingdom as partners in Europe. In his speech at Verdun in the autumn of 1916, David Lloyd George pleaded for a new *entente cordiale,* in an accent not always easy for his audience to understand owing to his Welsh pronunciation. He argued passionately that France was the right ally for the United Kingdom on moral grounds, as France was far more democratic than other countries and enjoyed a unique tradition of revolutionary reform. He and Georges Clemenceau formed an effective wartime partnership thereafter, unlike Churchill and de Gaulle after 1940. France and the United Kingdom are close in their historical and democratic experience, and have developed numerous points of contact over the years. The last serious dispute – although not a war – was the Fashoda incident in 1898, yet no actual shots were fired. The two countries were on the same side in the Middle East in the 1840s and then in the Crimean War. Both supported the unification of Italy. The Napoleonic wars were the last time that they were in military conflict against each other. They were staunch allies in the two world wars. Churchill even suggested in 1940 that the two countries should unite, which Reynaud and others supported. Nowadays they sometimes take different positions but no longer engage in conflict. Some isolated voices were heard during the EU referendum campaign pleading for a new *entente cordiale*, but they were soon silenced by more hostile divisive nationalist messages. After the referendum, it may be profoundly hoped that those voices be listened to anew and their aspirations turned into action. For the only secure way forward is for the United Kingdom and France to remain allied together in a more democratic, stronger and more tolerant Europe.

Notes

1. The term *entente cordiale* comes from a letter written to his brother in 1843 by Lord Aberdeen, the British Foreign Secretary. It was used by King Louis Philippe in the French Chamber that year. But more recently it has almost always been used to speak of the *seconde entente* of 1904.
2. There are now seventeen directly elected Mayors in England, including those of London and Bristol.

3. 'The Union and Devolution', House of Lords Select Committee on the Constitution, 10th Report of Session 2015–2016, HL Paper 149 (London: The Stationery Office, 2016), pp. 96–105.
4. On 9 May 2016, the Defender of Rights, Jacques Toubon, issued a report entitled 'Les droits fondamentaux des étrangers en France' denouncing discriminatory practices against foreigners in France which clearly violated human rights.
5. This was the slogan used by Sadiq Khan in the campaign to the London 2016 mayoral elections.
6. With the thumping victory (66 per cent of the popular vote in the second round) of the young pro-European centrist Emmanuel Macron in the 2017 French presidential election followed by a clear parliamentary majority (308 seats in the National Assembly), hope was rekindled in France, and beyond, in Europe.

Bibliography

Books and Articles

Avril, Pierre and Jean Gicquel, *Droit parlementaire* (Paris: Lextenso, 2010).

Avril, Pierre and Jean Gicquel, *Lexique de Droit Constitutionnel* (Paris: PUF, 2003).

Badinter, Robert, *Les Epines et les Roses* (Paris: Fayard, 2011).

Bagehot, Walter, *The English Constitution*, introduction by Richard Crossman (London: Fontana Press, 1963).

Baston, Lewis and Stuart Wilks-Heeg, 'How strong is the case for having fewer MPs?', *Democratic Audit* (November 2010).

Bates, Stephen R., Peter Kerr, Christopher Byrne and Liam Stanley, 'Questions to the Prime Minister: A Comparative Study of Prime Minister's Questions from Thatcher to Cameron', *Parliamentary Affairs*, 67/2 (2014), 253–80.

Bel, Jean-Pierre, *Le Sénat à l'heure du changement: plaidoyer pour un bicamérisme rénové* (Paris: Fondation Jean-Jaurès, 2011).

Bingham, Thomas, *Lives of the Law: Selected Essays and Speeches 2000–2010* (Oxford: Oxford University Press, 2011).

Bingham, Thomas, *The Rule of Law* (London: Allen Lane, 2010).

Blackburn, Robert, *Engineering Constitutional Change: A Comparative Perspective* (London: Routledge, 2012).

Bogdanor, Vernon, *The Coalition and the Constitution* (Oxford: Hart Publishing, 2011).

Boyron, Sophie, *The Constitution of France. A Contextual Analysis* (Oxford: Hart Publishing, 2013).

Brazier, Rodney, *Constitutional Reform: Reshaping the British Political System*, third edn (Oxford: Oxford University Press, 2008).

Brown, Gordon, *My Scotland, Our Britain: A Future Worth Sharing* (London: Simon and Schuster, 2014).

Camby, Jean-Pierre, Patrick Fraisseix and Jean Gicquel, *La révision de 2008: une nouvelle Constitution?* (Paris: L.G.D.J., 2011).

Carcassonne, Guy, *La Constitution* (Paris: Seuil, 2013).

Carré de Malberg, Raymond, *Contribution à la théorie générale de l'Etat* (Paris: Sirey, 1920; new edn Dalloz, 2004).

Chagnollaud, Dominique, *Les 50 ans de la Constitution* (Paris: LexisNexis, 2008).
De Gaulle, Charles and Philippe de Gaulle, *L'Esprit de la Cinquième République. Mémoires d'espoir* (Paris: Plon, 1970).
Denquin, Jean-Marie, *La monarchie aléatoire* (Paris: PUF, 2001).
Dicey, Albert Venn, *An Introduction to the Law of the Constitution*, eighth edn (London: Macmillan, 1915).
Dickson, Brice, *Introduction to French Law* (London: Pitman Publishing, 1994).
Dobner, Peter and Martin Loughlin, *The Twilight of Constitutionalism* (Oxford: Oxford University Press, 2010).
Duverger, Maurice, 'A New Political System Model: Semi-presidential Government', *European Journal of Political Research*, 8/2 (1980), 165–87.
Errera, Roger, *Et ce sera justice … Le juge dans la Cité* (Paris: Gallimard, 2013).
Errera, Roger, *Les libertés à l'abandon* (Paris: Seuil, 1968).
Esmein, Adhémar, *Eléments de droit constitutionnel français et comparé* (Paris: Panthéon- Assas, 2010).
Erskine May's *Treatise on the Law, Privileges, Proceedings and Usage of Parliament*, twenty-fourth edn (London: LexisNexis, 2011).
Favoreu, Louis, *La révision de la Constitution* (Aix–Marseille: Presses Universitaires d'Aix- Marseille, Economica, 1992).
Feldman, David, *Oxford Principles of English Law: English Public Law*, second edn (Oxford: Oxford University Press, 2009).
Finer, Samuel Edward and Vernon Bogdanor, *Comparing Constitutions* (Oxford: Clarendon Press, 1995).
François, Bastien, *La Cinquième République: Pourquoi, Comment?* (Paris: Les Petits Matins, 2015).
Gibson, Elizabeth and Alexis Chommeloux (eds), *The Rights and Aspirations of the Magna Carta* (London: Palgrave Macmillan, 2016).
Hazareesingh, Sudhir, *How the French Think* (London: Allen Lane, 2015).
Heuschling, Luc, *Etat de droit, Rechtsstaat, Rule of Law* (Paris: Dalloz, 2002).
Jennings, Jeremy, *Revolution and the Republic: A History of Political Thought in France in the XVIIIth Century* (Oxford: Oxford University Press, 2011).
Jan, Pascal, *Les assemblées parlementaires françaises* (Paris: La Documentation française, 2010).

John, Jacob and Gary Jeffrey, 'Theorizing the Constitutional Revolution', *Journal of Law and Courts*, 12/1 (2014), 1–32.

Juppé, Alain, *Montesquieu: le moderne*, second edn (Paris: Perrin/Mollat, 2015).

Kennedy, Helena, 'The Glory and the Myths of Magna Carta: French Kissing', *New Statesman* (11 June 2015), 24.

King, Anthony, *The British Constitution* (Oxford: Oxford University Press, 2007).

Lauvaux, Philippe, *Parlementarisme rationalisé et stabilité du pouvoir exécutif* (Brussels: Bruylant, 1988).

Loughlin, Martin, *The British Constitution: A Very Short Introduction* (Oxford: Oxford University Press, 2013).

McLean, Iain, *What's Wrong with the British Constitution?* (Oxford: Oxford University Press, 2010).

Maitland, F. W., *The Constitutional History of England* (Cambridge: Cambridge University Press, 1919).

Massot, Jean, *Le chef de l'Etat, chef des armées* (Paris: L.G.D.J., 2011).

Mastias, Jean and Jean Grangé, *Les secondes chambres du Parlement en Europe occidentale* (Paris: Economica, 1987).

Mathieu, Bertrand, *Constitution: Rien ne bouge et tout change* (Paris: Lextenso, 2013).

Maus, Didier, *Les grands textes de la pratique constitutionnelle de la Ve République* (Paris: La Documentation française, 1998).

Mény, Yves and Olivier Duhamel, *Dictionnaire constitutionnel* (Paris: PUF, 1992).

Mitchell, L. G. (ed.), *Edmund Burke: Reflections on the Revolution in France*, Oxford World's Classics (Oxford: Oxford University Press, 1993).

Montesquieu, *De l'Esprit des Lois*, introduction by Victor Goldschmidt (Paris: Flammarion, 1979).

Morgan, Kenneth O. and Jane Morgan, *Portrait of a Progressive: The Political Career of Christopher, Viscount Addison* (Oxford: Clarendon Press, 1980).

Norman, Jesse, 'The glory and the myths of Magna Carta: Not so radical', *New Statesman* (11 June 2015), 25.

Norton, Philip, *Does Parliament Matter?* (University of Hull: Harvester Wheatsheaf, 1993).

Norton, Philip, *The Constitution in Flux* (Oxford: Blackwell, 1982).

Pactet, Pierre and Ferdinand Mélin-Soucramanien, *Droit Constitutionnel* (Paris: Dalloz, 2012).

Pierre, Eugène, *Traité de droit politique, électoral et parlementaire* (Paris: Loysel, 1989).

Pinon, Stéphane and Pierre-Henri Prélot, *Le droit constitutionnel d'Adhémar Esmein* (Paris: Montchrestien, 2009).

Poncelet, Christian, 'Le bicamérisme, une idée toujours neuve', *Revue politique et parlementaire*, 1007 (July–August 2000), 218–20.

Radice, Giles, *Odd Couples: The Great Political Pairings of Modern Britain* (London: I. B. Tauris, 2015).

Rogoff, Martin A., *French Constitutional Law* (Durham, NC: Carolina Academic Press, 2011).

Rousseau, Jean-Jacques, *The Social Contract and Discourses*, trans. G. D. H. Cole (Markham, Ontario: Fitzhenry and Whiteside, 1973).

Russell, Meg, *Reforming the House of Lords: Lessons from Overseas* (Oxford: Oxford University Press, 2000).

Shennan, Joe, *The Parlement of Paris* (Ithaca, NY: Cornell University Press, 1968).

Starkey, David, *Magna Carta: The True Story behind the Charter* (London: Hodder & Stoughton, 2015).

Starkey, David, 'The Magna Carta of 1215 was designed to create a revolutionary regime', *BBC History Magazine* (May 2015), 63–5.

Stroud, Daphne, *Magna Carta* (Southampton: Paul Cave Publications, 1987).

Twivy, Paul, *Be Your Own Politician: Why it is Time for a New Kind of Politics* (London: Biteback, 2015).

Venter, François, *Constitutional Comparison* (Cambridge, MA: Kluwer Law International, 2000).

Verdier, Marie-France, 'Le Sénat dans les institutions de la Cinquième République 1958– 1992' (unpublished Ph.D. thesis, University of Bordeaux, 1991).

Vine, Barbara, *The Blood Doctor* (London: Viking; Penguin edn, 2002).

Wales, Peter, *Elements of Comparative Government* (London: Butterworths, 1967).

Weil, Patrick, *Qu'est-ce qu'un Français?* (Paris: Gallimard, 2009).

Official Documents

Bingham Centre for the Rule of Law, *A Constitutional Crossroads: Ways Forward for the United Kingdom* (London: Bingham Centre for the Rule of Law, May 2015).

Cabinet Manual: *A Guide to Laws, Conventions and Rules on the Operation of Government* (Cabinet Office, October 2011).

Comité Balladur, Comité de réflexion et de proposition sur la modernisation et le rééquilibrage des institutions de la Ve République, Rapport, *Une Ve République plus démocratique* (Paris: La Documentation française, 2008).

Comité Balladur, Comité pour la réforme des collectivités locales, Rapport, *Il est temps de décider* (Paris: La Documentation française, 2009).

Comité Veil, Rapport, *Redécouvrir le Préambule de la Constitution* (Paris: La Documentation française, 2008).

Commission Jospin, Commission de rénovation et de déontologie de la vie publique, Rapport, *Pour un renouveau démocratique* (Paris: La Documentation française, 2012).

Commission to Strengthen Parliament, *Strengthening Parliament* (London: The Stationary Office, 2000).

Commission Truche, Commission de réflexion sur la justice (Paris: La Documentation française, 1997).

Conservative party manifesto, *Strong Leadership, a Clear Economic Plan, a Brighter, More Secure Future* (2015).

Constitution de la Ve République, Texte intégral et officiel, édition 2014/2015 (Issy-les- Moulineaux: Gualino, 2015).

Constitution Unit, *House Full: Time to Get a Grip on Lords Appointments* (London: UCL, 2011).

Electoral Commission, Report on the May 2011 Referendum, *Referendum on the Voting System for UK Parliamentary Elections* (London: Electoral Commission, 2011).

Fabian Society, *The Future of the Monarchy*, Report of the Fabian Commission (London: Fabian Society, 2003).

House of Commons Reform Committee, First Report of Session 2008–2009, *Rebuilding the House*, HC 1117 (London: The Stationery Office, 2009).

House of Lords, *Companion to the Standing Orders and Guide to the Proceedings of the House of Lords* (London: The Stationery Office, 2010).

House of Lords, Constitution Committee, First Report of Session 2000–2001, *Reviewing the Constitution: Terms of Reference and Method of Working*, HL 11 (London: The Stationery Office, 2001).

House of Lords, European Union Committee, 12th Report of Session 2015–2016, *The UK, the EU and a British Bill of Rights*, HL 139 (London: The Stationery Office, 2016).

Labour party manifesto, *New Labour because Britain Deserves Better* (1997).

Legatum Institute, *Roads to Freedom: The Future of the Union* (London: Legatum Institute, 2014).

Ministerial Code: *A Code of Conduct and Guidance on Procedures for Ministers* (Cabinet Office, 1997).

Political and Constitutional Reform Committee, Second Report of Session 2014–2015, *A New Magna Carta?*, HC 463 (London: The Stationery Office, 2014).

Index

Q

R

T